FORTUNATE ACCIDENTS

MATT SOLOMON

18-11-23

The stories shared in this book are the author's memories, from his perspective. Events are represented as faithfully as possible. Some names were changed by request.

Permission for cited pieces granted by DailyOM – Inspirational thoughts for a happy, healthy, and fulfilling day. Register for free at DailyOM.com.

ISBN 978-1-7378289-0-7 (pb)
ISBN 978-1-7378289-1-4 (Kindle)
ISBN 978-1-7378289-2-1 (ePub)
ISBN 978-1-7378289-3-8 (hc)

Library of Congress Control Number: 2021918689

First edition November 2021

Cover design by Dylan Saunders/Tier 1 Creative
Proofreading by Proof Corrections by Callie

Published by Fortunate Accidents, LLC, PO Box 5341, Eagle, CO 81631

For information or to contact the author, please visit:
www.FortunateAccidents.com.

For my mother.
Now she knows.

CONTENTS

FOREWORD

I am so damn proud of Matt Solomon.

If we're lucky, we get to have a handful of good friends in our passage from the womb to the tomb. I'm lucky: Matt is one of mine.

I met Matt over the Wild West version of the gossip fence, leaning on a horse fence with a bunch of guys and plinking ground squirrels, part of what we lovingly dubbed The Horse Pasture Sportsmen's Society. We orbited around each other's lives for a time before finally sticking together as good friends do.

Matt has been everywhere and has tried everything at least twice. I've known him for decades, and over those years, I've been bemused, informed, entertained, and inspired.

Our lives are comprised of time, and stories about how we spent our time. Matt spends most of his life doing things that create more stories . . . like the time a dead body fell on him. Or the time he opened a firearms shop as the economy seemed to be spiraling down to some special level of hell that even Dante's *Inferno* had not considered. Or the time he worked in the Utah desert, teaching military special forces personnel how to drive off-road. Like so many of us, they thought they knew how. And like so many of us who think we know stuff, but don't, neither did they. Now they do because of Matt's unique training methods.

Matt owns some seriously cool gear—kayaks, motorcycles, and mountaineering gear. Most of it exists to carry him to his next adventure and new stories. He doesn't have much actual house stuff in his house, probably because no good story has ever opened with, "So I was shopping for an ottoman when . . ." Sitting on his porch sipping good bourbon and swapping tales is usually the launchpad for a flight on the ethereal plane. Philosophy ensues; so does foolishness. That's balance, and we need balance. As we consider balance, we begin to marvel at lives in progress and how they're a wonder to behold. Not only are we alive, we are living, or ought to be.

Matt lives, and has the physical and emotional scars, and laugh lines, to prove it. Shakespeare called it "the slings and arrows of outrageous fortune."[1] The great Texas author Dan Jenkins called it *Life Its Ownself.*

Some of the stories in this book are hilarious; some are heartbreaking. All are woven around the interlocking themes of mindfulness and resilience. In other words, pay attention and keep trying. There are life lessons to be learned.

Matt is one of those people we sometimes love to hate, but mostly we envy: a good-looking, successful multi-sport athlete who turned pro as a kayaker, a factory-sponsored snowboarder, and even a paid evangelist spreading the good news of the then fledgling sport of stand-up paddleboarding. His firearms shop was thriving. Then that dead body fell on him, and he needed about a half million dollars worth of surgeries. The cycle repeated itself every four months: surgery, rehab, surgery, rehab—a cycle requiring mindfulness and resilience.

His friends often said he should put those stories and lessons in a book. He has, and now you're holding it. That speaks well of you. Enjoy.

Randy Wyrick is too old to slam dunk and too young to have made the Nixon's Enemies List. In almost four decades as a journalist, with a couple stints as a minister thrown in, he has observed and chronicled almost every function and malfunction known to the human condition.

---

[1] Shakespeare W. *Hamlet, Act III, Scene I [To be, or not to be].* Poets.org. https://poets.org/poem/hamlet-act-iii-scene-i-be-or-not-be

PREFACE

The unorthodox assortment of experiences and lessons that life's buffet has offered me tends to leave people highly entertained and somewhat mystified. When discussing leadership philosophies and when teaching students in various courses, I have been able to pull from said experiences to offer insights with a different perspective than students receive from other instructors or leaders.

Countless times, I have been told, "You should write a book."

I finally stopped resisting the suggestions.

I embarked on the journey of writing a book about mindfulness and resilience, highlighting how they work together to build leadership qualities through personal growth. I gathered input and feedback in an attempt to formulate my thoughts before putting them on paper. The topic of growth and leadership through mindfulness and resilience were well received, garnering initial enthusiastic and positive feedback.

The most chilling response came from a friend who worked on a search and rescue team. He said, "Interesting time to ask these questions. We had an avalanche death this morning. I had to advise a friend on scene to stop CPR on his best friend so he could escape before being caught in another slide. The body is still out there since it is too dangerous to recover right now. Mindfulness . . . I will think about that."

It truly was an interesting time to write a book on mindfulness. So often, I found myself getting into a routine, a cycle. During the stay-at-home order, the routine was even more pronounced. I would wake up, work out, eat breakfast, study and read, take a break to clean the house, eat a snack, exercise, prepare dinner, watch a movie or read a book, then sleep. Repeat.

Whether navigating a pandemic or living "normal" daily life, routine does not need to be mindless. I—we—must remember to be mindful, acting and speaking with precision and intentionality, during our daily routines. Living in the moment, thinking and preparing ahead. As part of my daily routine, I continued to make time for fishing and paddling, maintaining my connection to nature, and absorbing the spiritual energy from the river. Balance was key.

Through introspection, accepting my own reflection, and sustaining a will to improve, I began to discern a pattern, a method to the madness. Discussions, observations, and mentorship from professional athletes, outdoor industry icons, and leaders in various industries allowed me to test the hypothesis of an idea. I built a foundational platform for developing strong interpersonal relationships and leadership skills, which I share with you in the pages to follow.

The word "accident" is something of a misnomer in the title because the events that took place were not coincidental. There was intention, collaborative effort, and the cultivation of a very specific formula behind my growth and good fortune.

Though the lessons in this book are not original, I believe their context, viewed against the backdrop of my personal life stories, lends a unique perspective. These are stories of personal growth, finding hope when circumstances seemed far from hopeful, discovering the silver lining behind the clouds, and, through it all, staying true to myself. In short, I learned what it meant to be *me*. By sharing this journey, I hope you will learn just a little more about what it means to be *you*.

Against the seemingly random and disorganized backdrop of my life, I share a philosophical thought about leadership and growth. My personal experiences, work, and travels provide a framework for discussing how awareness, mindfulness, and resilience blend together in an engaging series of fortunate accidents.

I chased experiences over material goods, so long as my needs were met. I looked deep within myself and sought guidance from others, exploring life's greatest questions with those around me. My inquisitive nature led me down a path full of mistakes and apologies. It also provided a lot of great stories along the way.

I remain a work in progress. The cornerstone of my foundation is still being polished. I lived a life of curiosity, filled with a desire to find meaning. If awareness plus mindfulness led to intentionality, then I could couple that with some perspective and good communication to build resilience. It was with intentionality that I could evolve and grow into a better version of myself, helping to facilitate *Fortunate Accidents*.

Despite the comprehensive collection of stories included, it still feels like so many important people and stories were left out. Selecting the material that best matched the message was a daunting task. There were great stories with high entertainment value lost in editing because they did not fit the message. Applying mindful precision to the art of writing became a newly learned application of the very lessons shared. I can only hope I found the right balance.

As my friend Luke offered, "If each word costs twenty-five dollars, and you only have one thousand dollars to spend, how can you manage your budget for maximum return?"

In the management of the writing budget, I invested energy into words that coupled together to form entertaining, enriching, and encouraging written images.

I hope you find yourself entertained and inspired to choose a new path at each crossroads you encounter. More importantly, I hope you acquire strategies to help you play the hand you were dealt, preparing you to receive the next fortunate accident that comes your way.

FORTUNATE ACCIDENTS

CHANCE

Eight months before I turned forty, my marriage ended. Three months later, while working for the coroner's office, a (dead) body fell on me. I had a premonition twenty years earlier that led me to believe I was going to die in my fortieth year. At the time of the premonition, it was not just a hunch or a guess—it was something I intuitively *knew* in the very core of my being.

As it turned out, my death was allegorical, not physical. Shortly before my fortieth birthday, the crushing weight of the dead body caused a debilitating injury, undermining my identity as an athlete. Coupled with the open wounds of a recent divorce, my ego was battered and I was lost.

Why did those things happen to me?

Were they accidental? Were they avoidable?

The debilitating events of my fortieth year caused me to contemplate all the accidents leading up to those, and other, events throughout my life.

Some events were a surprise. After all, who would have guessed a dead body would fall on me? Others were predictable. The circumstances leading up to my divorce bore signs left unheeded. During times of trial and tribulation, I was inexorably sucked into downward emotional spirals. Other, seemingly random, events in my life led to upward emotional spirals. No matter the cause or outcome, there seemed to be a lesson for me to learn in each.

Many daily life events felt accidental, but inconsequential. Then, there were those accidents that struck fear into my heart when contemplated: the accidents that shook every branch of my being, threatening to topple the trunk, leaving roots bare and exposed. Why do accidents happen?

Accidents. Some involved culpability; others seemingly came out of the blue. Some worked in my favor; others wasted valuable time and money. Accidents may have been a surprise to me at times, but in retrospect, my seemingly chaotic life had been following a surprisingly orderly path. There was a rhyme to the reason. I was not satisfied writing it all off as chance, nor would I chalk it up to fate. The truth seemed to lie somewhere in between.

Were there seeds of truth in the premonition of death in my fortieth year, or was it just a dream coupled with bad luck twenty years later?

The Nature of Accidents

I was raised in a Catholic family. My elementary school years were spent in an Episcopalian school. After a three-year stint at a public junior high school, I attended high school at a Catholic school.

I read countless books on religions of the world. I found both the similarities and the differences of those belief systems fascinating. I certainly did not claim to be an expert on religion; however, I gained enough theological and philosophical understanding to feel comfortable formulating my own beliefs and values from a well-educated perspective.

Religion offered a feeling of security. For me, the most compelling aspect of religious belief emerged when focusing a lens on the center of the Venn diagram created by the overlapping philosophies of the major world religions. There, in the center, was where I felt the truth could be found.

Behind every religion were the questions asking, "Why are we here?" and "What is my role in all of this?" Throughout history, it seemed that man was trying to make sense of the seemingly random events in life, attempting to provide context: a safe, orderly framework to keep chaos at bay.

I was not a fan of institutional religion. Nor was I a fan of the belief in a higher power that showered us with blessings (good accidents) when we followed the rules and punished us (bad accidents) when we broke the rules. In that regard, I considered myself a "recovering Catholic."

I was inclined to believe that I learned the lessons I needed to learn from parents and other teachers who influenced significant life events. I also believed in the supporting energy all around us, in nature, and in each other. Rather than subscribe to a doctrine that viewed accidents as punitive in nature, I viewed accidents as fortuitous, contributing to my growth and development. An accident was not something that happened to me, it happened for me.

It was like standing on a spiral staircase. Each accident that elicited a negative emotion drew me into a downward spiral. Those were the accidents that provided clarity on what I did not want. Each accident that elicited a positive emotion inspired me to continue the upward climb. Those were the accidents that provided clarity on what I did want. Both types of accidents were fortuitous and beneficial because both yielded potential personal growth.

Downward Spirals

My divorce was not an accident; it was one part of a series of events that culminated in one negative, unplanned outcome: an outcome that really did a number on my ego. There had been alarm bells that I chose to ignore.

I met my ex-wife four years earlier at a local restaurant when a group of us went out for dinner and drinks. At the time, I was working as a paramedic on the ambulance in the beautiful mountains of Colorado and was in the second year of operating a successful local gun business.

She and I continually texted and called each other throughout the weeks leading up to and during the time I was in Lyon, France, training European freestyle kayak judges for the upcoming kayak season. When I returned to Colorado, it was all fireworks between us. Fireworks can be both beautiful and dangerous. Either way, they burn out, as did she and I.

There was no prescience, no telltale signs leading up to my accident with the coroner's office. The ensuing surgeries, each requiring four months of rehabilitation, prevented me from participating in the athletic pursuits that played a foundational role in my self-image. The surgeries, physical therapy, and medical care also wreaked havoc financially. I nearly lost my home and my business.

Prior to the accident, the firearms business had been thriving and growing. Plans for further expansion were underway. When I discovered I would need two surgeries, I put expansion plans on hold and tried to come up with a plan to mitigate $400,000 of business debt. My livelihood was in jeopardy.

Prior to these injuries, I had been an athlete. In high school, I was a three-sport letterman, second in the state for weight lifting, and an all-conference football player. I played football in college. After college, I was a locally sponsored snowboarder, Team Dagger sponsored kayaker, and an inland pioneer and team ambassador for stand-up paddleboarding (SUP) companies C4 Waterman and Boardworks.

After the accident, I was a different person. My body was not responding the way it used to. Something was broken.

Until that point in my life, I had not given much thought to accidents. Previous accidents had not required introspection to re-establish a shaken identity. I guess I just thought that accidents happened without any rhyme or reason: no point to them, no greater purpose. With the emotional impact of my divorce, coupled with the physical injury and financial strain after the accident in the coroner's office, I worried there might be a pattern I was missing. By missing the pattern, I was doomed to repeat a cycle until I learned the lesson life was trying to teach me.

In my observation, the cycle went something like this: I was rolling along, living a good life. Then, I experienced a setback, a departure from the path. It was as if I had rolled right off the edge of a cliff. Those events predicated a downward spiral. At some point, I would make the decision to start over, trekking up the hill until I got to solid pavement again. Just when I was humming along, the cycle repeated itself. Events felt unplanned, random. It felt like life was something that happened to me, not for me.

Eighteen months after my injury with the coroner's office, the downward emotional spiral was making me sick to my stomach. I wanted to get off the emotional roller coaster.

Upward Spirals

As I pondered the meaning of accidents, I realized that many of the positive events in my life arrived as mysteriously as the negative ones.

Just as downward spirals were caused by unplanned events that hit life's pause button, upward spirals hit the play button, setting fortuitous events into motion. These positive upward spirals seemed as random as the downward spirals, except the positive accidents made me feel like a hero, not a zero. Positive accidents left me feeling connected, inspired, alive. The right people seemed to show up at the perfect time with exactly the information I needed to make my next move. These fortuitous circumstances materialized virtually out of thin air in a process that can only be described as accidental.

The birth of my firearms business was one example of the way positive accidents could create an upward spiral. I drove two hours to a gun show in Denver, Colorado, with a friend. I needed a firearm for some upcoming work.

"You should get your FFL[2] and do transfers," my friend Hobie suggested. At the time, I laughed it off and gave him a dozen reasons why it was a bad idea. However, as soon as he said it, we both knew it would

---

[2] Federal Firearms License, which is required to legally engage in the firearms business.

happen. The seed was planted, and I could not get the thought out of my head. His casual suggestion sparked my imagination.

Within a week, I filled a legal pad with potential business names and checked domain availability. I researched information on gun laws through the Bureau of Alcohol, Tobacco, Firearms, and Explosives (ATF) and online websites. A month later, I was ready to submit my application to become a firearms dealer. My work rotation as a paramedic for the ambulance district allowed me to start this new venture as a very small side hustle with minimal overhead.

Our high country corridor in the Central Rockies of Colorado did not have a full-service gun store before my business opened, and there had never been a Class 3[3] firearms dealer in our area. My clients were happy to have local access to firearms and ammunition without having to drive one to two hours east or west. The business steadily grew, and I became known as "the gun guy" in addition to "the medic" and "the paddler."

After the injury at the coroner's office, I called my suppliers to let them know what was going on. I told them the store would be closing for a few months while I dealt with my medical issues. I asked them to give me four months to pay everything due.

Much to my surprise, my suppliers were not upset. I learned that most people hide from debt. When I communicated with my suppliers ahead of time, they not only agreed to my payment plan, but they thanked me. They appreciated that I took the time to be proactive and wished me good luck with the recovery.

Then, I did something I had not done before. I wrote a newsletter to my clients, informing them as to what was going on in my personal life. I brought my customers into the fold and opened up to them on a personal level. I shared the fact that my health and financial challenges were impacting the business. My clients responded with love and support. Through that experience, many of my clients became friends. Transparency

---

[3] A classification of license granted by the ATF allowing approved FFL dealers to sell items regulated by the National Firearms Act.

was critical on both a business and personal level. With the support I received from my clients and friends, coupled with the proceeds from a huge sale, I was able to liquidate enough inventory to pay all of my vendors—in full and on time.

I tried to piece together the puzzle of circumstances that drove me to move from Florida to South Carolina to Colorado to West Virginia to California and everywhere else I lived and played: the string of events that led to that open communication with my vendors and clients.

How did mentors surface in my life at exactly the time I needed them? How did all those random connections yield opportunities that enriched my life, making it fuller and more complete? I knew a lot of people stronger, smarter, and faster than I. No amount of strength, intelligence, or insight could have allowed me to foresee the bricks that created my path.

With the benefit of hindsight, I noticed patterns taking shape: seemingly random events connected in a linked chain of circumstances, one event predictably and inexorably leading to another. I found that the patchwork quilt of my professional life was not as chaotic. Unlike other lives that followed a straighter road, at first glance, mine was more like a series of unrelated circles. Only in retrospect could I see that the circles were connected in a daisy chain of decisions.

Introducing the Formula

For most of my life, I thought there were two kinds of accidents: the good kind and the bad kind. The older I grew, the more I realized there might be just one kind of accident: the fortunate kind. "Fortune" is the root of "fortunate." My fortune, or fate, was neither good nor bad. It just was.

It seemed that accidents gently or not-so-gently shifted the trajectory of my path. Course changes were neither good nor bad. Like a sailboat on the open sea, my life's boat encountered conditions that required navigational intervention to avoid inclement weather or maximize speed when the wind died. The weather that caused the course corrections was neither good nor bad; it just happened. Accidents became waypoints along the trail. It was up to me to make the adjustments required to get where I wanted to go rather than allowing the accidents to take me off course.

My response to accidents, my attitude, disposition, and demeanor, was what put me at the helm of the ship. Though the accidents themselves may have been out of my control, seemingly an incident of chance, my response to them was 100% in my hands. When it came to life satisfaction, steering the ship to an intended destination, attitude counted more than circumstances.

A few years after recovering from the surgeries and reopening in a new location, I sold the firearms business. Prior to the sale, I began planning the next steps and started a new company. This new project began with the same ease I regularly experienced when inspired to begin a new business venture; however, the outcome was far from expected.

I wanted to use survival skills training to teach people how to apply leadership and communication techniques in everyday life. I wanted to apply what I had learned and taught over the previous twenty years to a program teaching life skills. I wanted to teach resilience.

While brainstorming with a friend, Ken,[4] about the goals of this business venture, a new plan emerged. Ken's company taught overland travel and recovery skills to top-tier military groups. He also helped private individuals and groups plan and execute overland trips all over the world.

Overland driving is a self-reliant form of adventure travel. Off-road vehicles are used to navigate remote regions for weeks or even months at a time. While an expedition is a journey with a purpose, overland drivers see the journey as part of the destination and must be adept at handling any circumstance that may surface.

As Ken and I were talking, our brains were spinning. We decided to join forces in creating a week-long "man-camp" that included firearms

---

[4] In the 1996 Camel Trophy Ken Cameron was 2nd place overall, and accomplished the 1st in the East-West 4WD Crossing of Borneo. Ken was also the NORRA rally master for the Mexican 1000 race. His company is www.cammobility.com

training, basic medical skills, off-road driving, and remote wilderness camping/survival. That vision was not limited to men—it was also for women, children, business leaders, couples, and mixed groups.

As I developed a website and started working on logistics and curriculums, the concept continued to snowball. I met with another friend, Jeff,[5] mapping out a concept to grow the man-camp into a greater-reaching franchise for personal development and growth by teaching life skills.

While I was meeting with Jeff, Ken was meeting with his contacts, and they converted the idea into REAL—Resilience for Executives and Leaders®. The program taught executives and business leaders how to be resilient through stressful situations.

The REAL curriculum combined off-road driving with problem-solving exercises and daily meetings with a psychologist, who coached participants on personality strengths and weaknesses. By recognizing behavioral patterns in themselves and others in stressful situations, they learned how to communicate more effectively.

The man-camp concept became reality through open communication, partnerships, and a willingness to pursue an idea. While the final product did not belong to me, I played a key role in its conception and execution.

As I looked back at the chain of events—the fortunate accidents—that eventually became REAL, I was awed by the number of coincidences that had to occur for a program of that magnitude to come together in a very short period of time. Each of us had a piece of the puzzle. We had to work together for the picture to take shape. Each piece appeared at exactly the right time, like a perfectly orchestrated play on the football field.

Like so many things in life, the difference between a negative accident and a positive accident was perspective. An event occurred. There was no denying the fact that it occurred. At first blush, it may have been perceived as negative; however, looking at the same event with a different lens yielded an entirely different perspective, and, ultimately, a different response.

---

[5] Jeff Brausch, 1968–2021, helped found a company that ran some of the largest culinary, music, and sporting events in Vail, Colorado, and across the USA.

The original concept of man-camp came as a flash of intuition, a spark shared with Ken, which grew into a blaze as Ken and I piled mental fuel on the fire. The blaze continued to grow as more players added their ideas to the fire. Somewhere along the way, it wasn't my fire anymore. My spark was engulfed in a blazing inferno as new energy and new ideas were added. I was no longer directly benefiting from its warmth. I could view this series of events as unfortunate, resenting the fact that I wasn't a long-term stakeholder, or I could choose to step back and appreciate the bigger picture.

Man-camp was an idea I had planned to launch through my new company. The more I shared this idea with like-minded entrepreneurs, the more traction the idea gained. If I had held my cards close, insisting on doing it alone, man-camp would not have evolved into the program that it became, changing the lives of many business leaders. Rather than being resentful, I remained mindful of the contribution my ideas made in the lives of business executives, their employees, and their companies.

As I put the pieces together, looking at my life's circumstances through both a positive and negative lens, I felt a need to identify the underlying themes that predicated my life experiences. I wanted to remain open to possibilities, grooming more positive energy in my life. I wanted to develop a formula that would help me grasp a better understanding of the conditions that led to upward and downward spirals.

How could I receive maximum benefit from accidents: the big ones, the little ones, the ones I could have prevented, the ones I could not have foreseen? Upward spirals and the joy associated with them seemed to be temporary. I began to dread the next cliff. Was there a way to maximize my joy and minimize the depth of an impending fall?

More importantly, how could I adjust my trajectory, arresting the momentum of the fall so I did not spiral so far down? How could I maintain faith in myself, my path, and the destination of my journey? When life's lawnmower ran over the garden, how could I send out new shoots and come out smelling like roses?

When an exciting opportunity presented itself, seemingly out of the blue, how could I tune into my intuition to maximize the upward spiral? How could I grab a hold of the brass ring on the merry-go-round and claim the next prize?

In the words of General Mattis, "Leaders define the problem, then find solutions."[6] By looking down the rabbit hole and asking the questions, I had taken the first step. In order to identify a solution, I needed to dig deep to truly define the problem.

I noticed my use of specific verbiage to articulate the experiences related to upward and downward spirals. I began to dig into the etymological roots of these words. For me, mindfulness required introspection. Mindfulness, containing the word "mind," conveyed an internal action. Awareness was external. Awareness was the recognition of the role played by external forces, like the people and events around me.

Self-awareness became the point where mindfulness and awareness met: my sense of self in the context of my external environment. Self-awareness yielded intentionality.

If awareness plus mindfulness yielded intentionality, then I could couple that with some perspective and good communication to build resilience. Becoming more emotionally mature allowed me to evolve, growing into a better version of myself with each fortunate accident.

All accidents were fortunate accidents. They contained the seeds of fortune. When an accident took me on a downward spiral, I watered the seeds with resilience. When I was on an upward spiral, I watered the seeds with awareness and mindfulness. In either case, my perspective and attitude provided the water that helped my fortunes grow. By remaining mindful of myself and aware of the confluence of factors that governed the course of my life's river, I continually learned, expanded, and grew.

---

[6] "General Jim Mattis on 'Call Sign Chaos.'" The Ford Foundation. April 21, 2021. Webinar available at https://fordschool.umich.edu/event/2021/general-jim-mattis-call-sign-chaos?theme=cflp

Application: Chance in Your Life

This opening chapter introduced chance, accidents, and beliefs. The following are questions to help relate my stories to your experiences.

1. How do your beliefs shape your outlook on life?
2. How would you define "chance" and "accidents"?
3. Think of a time when you experienced a downward spiral. Describe how it made you feel.
4. Based on that experience, what actions did you take to create an upward spiral, or are you still living with the results of the downward spiral today?

Books are meant to be read, used, written in, and referenced. Please take a moment to think about your answer for each of these questions. Whether you use this page or a page somewhere else, write down your answers and maximize the exercise of reflection.

AWARENESS

I f life were a game of cards, my family of origin would be the first hand played. Just like accidents, there would be no such thing as a good hand or a bad hand. It would all be in the way I played the cards I was dealt.

My family of origin included a pair of kings. No matter the game of choice, I certainly was not dealt a junk hand; it was no royal flush either.

There are those whose story began with a childhood fraught with challenges. Trials and tribulations beset them from the moment they first drew breath. Then, there are others who lived with a shiny, lucky penny in their pocket. No matter how many times the coin was flipped, they always turned up heads.

In my opinion, perception of one's life circumstance carries greater weight than the circumstance itself. If a person feels rich, he is rich. If he feels poor, he is poor. Wealth has little to do with the money in his pocket.

It seems to me that many people perceive themselves as optimists, but behave like pessimists. Pessimists seek and find fault in themselves and others. Optimists seek and find good in themselves and others. Perception shapes perspective; perspective shapes behavior.

At first glance, my path from childhood to adulthood was not much different than that of any other kid growing up in a middle-class family. Upon closer inspection, my formative years were as unique as a fingerprint. Childhood left an impression on my soul. Family, friends, foes, and experiences were the arches, loops, and whorls embedded in the print, leaving an indelible impression that aided or inhibited future growth.

The most powerful lessons and values I learned from my family were centered around respect and hard work. The expectation of honor roll grades and the family's love of sports (especially football) played key roles in reinforcing these lessons. Other lessons were learned by experiencing something unwanted. I was taught to suppress my feelings; in time, I learned it was healthier to express myself. Throughout my childhood and early adult years, I became increasingly aware of these values, integrating them into daily decisions and actions.

Learning Respect

I was taught to respect my elders and to respect my country. My grandfathers and my father served in the US Navy. Both Grandma and Grandpa, grandparents on my father's side of the family, were very proud Americans, children of parents who had immigrated from the Middle East.

Grandpa's parents were from Lebanon, and Grandma's parents were from Syria. They instilled pride in our family heritage. The phrase "He who denies his heritage has no heritage.—Kahlil Gibran" hangs on my wall, cross-stitched in Arabic letters. My mother stitched that picture for me, just as my grandmother did for her when she married into the family.

Growing up in a household rooted in Arabic culture and tradition meant full capitulation to authority. The message was clear: "You can be anything you want to be . . . as long as it is what your father wants and approves."

My mother could best be described as intense. She was fiercely loyal and protective. I never once questioned her love for me. Unlike mothers who coddle their kids, my mother allowed me the latitude to explore and learn from my own mistakes, helping me rise when I fell and correcting me when I suffered an error in judgment.

She began training me to respect women early in life; however, when I was old enough to drive, my training began in earnest. As a teenager, I would drag my feet, allowing the distance between us to grow, when I was forced to go shopping with my mother. Without fail, I would arrive at the store's exit to find my mother standing outside, patiently waiting for me to open the door for her. Every Southern gentleman was taught that women were to be respected. Opening the door was one sign of that respect.

After getting my driver's permit, I wanted to drive every time I got the chance. My mother was usually happy to oblige. At first, I would jump in the driver's seat, eager to leave. My mother would patiently stand outside the passenger-side door, waiting for me to get out and open the door for her. Then she would say, "Thank you," and seat herself in the vehicle.

The act of opening the door for my mother underscored the message of respect. Respect for women was ingrained in my consciousness with every door I opened. My mother defined, reinforced, and established respect, emotional boundaries, and perspective throughout my life.

The vast majority of my youth was spent outdoors. I was only allowed thirty minutes a day for television or playing video games. On Saturday mornings, my brother, sister, and I were expected to be out of the house by nine. We were not allowed back inside until dinnertime.

My mother was the oldest of three children who were separated in age by a span of sixteen years. Nine years my elder, Uncle Cord was closer in age to me than my mom. He was just starting high school when I was in elementary school. I did not just respect Uncle Cord, I idolized him.

Though I treated my father respectfully, and I learned a tremendous amount from him, I had no desire to spend the rest of my life working in the family business the way my father had. Uncle Cord and I were more closely aligned. We both loved the water. We both loved adventure. To a greater degree, neither of us had the slightest interest in taking over a family business.

Cord taught me to water-ski when I was six. He introduced me to hydrosliding years before wakeboarding became popular. When that grew old, we would pop up on his surfboard behind the boat, something I practiced on sunny afternoons in his backyard swimming pool. My lifelong liquid addiction was inspired by those early adventures with Uncle Cord, and I became very comfortable in the water at an early age. From water-skiing, fishing, and canoeing during my childhood to white-water kayaking, rafting, and stand-up paddleboarding as an adult, water provided the perfect metaphor for many life lessons. I learned to respect water in its many forms.

In Jacksonville, Florida, there were alligators along the banks of the river where we skied. I was afraid of them, but Cord exuded a confidence that set my mind at ease. He was not afraid of anything. I wanted to be brave so he would be proud of me. Cord taught me to respect the alligators, but not fear them. Fear is a red light: full stop. Respect is a yellow light: proceed with awareness and caution. Cord inspired me to be mindful of the difference between fear and respect as well as the conditions that warranted each. This became a central theme in my life.

In addition to introducing me to a variety of water-related activities, Cord taught me to drive a manual transmission with his baby, a Nissan 280Z. This experience tested the boundaries of our patience with each other and his patience with me. Learning to drive a stick was yet another example of respect versus fear. I learned to respect the power of a vehicle, but not fear it. This approach of respect versus fear provided me an expanded comfort zone, creating a foundational platform for future off-road driving adventures and employment, in the process.

Emotional Cliffs

Not every part of my family legacy was healthy. Not every lesson yielded tools that facilitated future growth. The process of awareness was one of discernment, where positive messages were differentiated from negative ones.

One night when I was eight years old, tucked into bed fast asleep, the phone rang. Our old-school landline telephone hung on the wall in the kitchen. It had a piercing ring that reverberated through the entire house and rarely rang at night. Most people knew not to call after dark unless it was an emergency. I lay in bed, straining to hear the conversation.

My heart filled with dread as I heard footsteps coming down the hall toward my room. The bedroom door creaked open, and Mom's head peeked around the corner. "Matthew, are you awake?"

"Yes, ma'am . . ." I replied cautiously.

"Do you want to go to work with Granddaddy tomorrow?"

This was entirely unexpected and unprecedented. My mother might as well have asked if I wanted to explore an alien spaceship that had landed in the backyard. Though I was often called upon to lend a helping hand at the family salvage business my father's side of the family owned and operated, I had never been invited to visit Grandaddy's law office.

My mother's father was a real estate attorney in downtown Jacksonville. He and Grandmommy lived in a nice neighborhood, just across the river from downtown and only a few miles from our house.

The shock of this outlandish proposal banished foggy remnants of slumber from my eight-year-old head as I eagerly nodded my assent. Grandaddy had to leave for work early, so he insisted that I spend the night with them.

As we pulled up in front of the house off Atlantic Boulevard, Grandmommy was there to greet us. Cord was away at college, so the house was quiet. The anticipation of going to work with Grandaddy left me too excited to sleep.

The next morning, I chattered through breakfast as Grandmommy piled my plate with steaming scrambled eggs, sausage, and toast. Then, Grandaddy drove me to his office in his gold Mercedes convertible.

For an eight-year-old, work at a law office was pretty boring. There was not much to remember about that day except for the hour my Grandaddy and I spent playing darts on the "secret" dartboard hidden behind his office door. I do remember every detail from the ride in that gold Mercedes convertible: the smell of cigarette smoke in the car, the Certs Grandaddy kept in the armrest next to the quarters used to pay the

Hart Bridge toll, and the way I felt grown-up when he offered me one of his Certs.

The following year, Grandaddy went into the hospital with a brain tumor. I begged to be allowed to visit him, but I was told children were not allowed to go to the hospital. Three days later, my mom announced that we were going over to Grandmommy's house for drumsticks. I was perplexed. Drumsticks? Did Grandaddy get a drum set when he came home from the hospital?

There were several cars parked in front of Grandmommy's house. Opening the door, I was surprised to find the kitchen full of family. My mother's middle brother, Uncle Fred, was there, along with Uncle Cord. There was no drum set or drumsticks to go with it, but a delicious plate of fried chicken sat in the middle of the kitchen table. Looking around the room, I noticed Grandaddy was not there, so I asked where he was. Everyone got quiet. Someone said, "He's not coming home. Grandaddy died."

Time stopped. I felt the air being sucked out of the room. There was silence. My Grandaddy had died, and I had not gotten the chance to say goodbye. Worse yet, nobody had even bothered to tell me! I lost it. I started bawling.

Uncle Cord looked at me and said, "Matthew, men don't cry."

It was like he had slapped me across the face. Uncle Cord was cool. He was my childhood hero. I stifled a rising sob, choked back the tears, and stuffed down the pain as the muffled conversation in the room resumed. It took years for me to grow up enough to realize that he had just lost his father and was hurting worse than me. It was decades before I allowed myself to cry again.

This was my first experience falling off a cliff. In mere months, my first greatest memory was created, only to be followed by my first worst memory. Some accidents did not look fortunate in the moment. With awareness, I would grow to see how formative lessons (even negative ones) contributed to future gains. To put it another way, identifying what I did not want helped me gain clarity for what I did want.

As a young person, I was taught to suppress my feelings. It impacted many of my early relationships, inhibiting my ability to develop authentic connections. I later recognized the value of being true to myself. I became more mindful. I practiced introspection and tried to tune into my feelings without shying away from vulnerability. I remained far from perfect, but I aimed to get better every day. With awareness, each accident, lesson, and experience provided the potential for future good fortune.

The Gift of Hard Work

In our family, work hard, play hard was more than a catchy motto. It was a way of life. On my mother's side, her uncle Price wrote a sentiment that applied to both sides of my family, saying, "When a hog is hungry, he will root a whole field finding buried food, roots, or anything to eat. That describes how the Butler family survived those trying times."[7] That description of a hog rooting through an entire field resonated with me. My career was a series of side hustles. I did whatever needed to be done to survive and thrive.

My grandfather on my father's side owned a salvage business. While my carefree peers enjoyed their summer days at the beach or boating on the river and lake, I was a card-carrying member of the pool . . . the labor pool.

Grandpa, along with his three sons, ran the store six to seven days a week, fifty-two weeks a year, for forty years. According to our family's history book, my grandparents took only one vacation: "Sara and George closed the store for one week in 1959 to take a family vacation. The seven

---

[7] Butler PJ. *Root Hog or Die: Memories of the Life and Times of the Butler Family.* Authorhouse; 2004.

family members traveled the state of Florida by car. Other than this one vacation, they always worked six to seven days a week."[8]

The family business provided a platform for education as well as income. I learned math at an early age, working in the store alongside my grandfather and uncles in the family business. Grandpa taught me to count cash, sorting bills into stacks by denomination, each bill facing the same way. I had to count the bills in each stack, make a note of each stack's total, then add the totals together. He also taught me to play gin rummy, never letting me use my fingers to count. I had to learn how to quickly count in my head.

Grandpa instructed me to carry four things in my pocket at all times: a Sharpie, a quarter, a knife, and a magnet. At first, I was not sure why each of these items was important. The value of the Sharpie, quarter, and knife became apparent. Why the magnet? In time, the magnet's value was revealed.

One truly formative experience, and a shining example of the work ethic my family instilled, arrived in the summer before my senior year of high school by way of forty-five Gator Freightways semitrailers.

I was on summer break, training for my upcoming senior year football season and working for the family business. Gator Freightways went bankrupt, presenting an opportunity for our family-owned salvage business. Grandpa and his sons joined forces with another salvage company, agreeing to an even split on the unknown contents of the forty-five trailers.

We had thirty days to unload them all, split the freight into two equal shares, and reload the inventory into box trucks that would deliver the goods to their respective warehouses. How many people did we have to do the job? Technically . . . two. I provided muscle alongside Reece, a long-time employee of the business. Grandpa, in his seventies, claimed the role of supervisor. Uncle Douglas did the real supervision and

---

[8] Solomon C. *The Family of Sara and George Solomon.* Self-published for the family to memorialize her parents and their history; 2018.

administrative work, taking counts, making phone calls, and ensuring we did our jobs correctly.

Thirty days to unload forty-five trucks. Easy, right? Compared to climbing Mount Everest with no oxygen, this project was easy. Compared to swimming the English Channel, this project was easy. Compared to spending each day moving an average-sized five-bedroom house complete with mattresses, sofas, furniture, and appliances, this project was hard. However, muscles that screamed in protest early in the month became accustomed to the routine of lift, haul, deposit, and repeat.

I spent thirty days listening to my grandfather telling me to "get the lead out of your ass," and reminding me, "there aren't any girls watching. Get to work!" It was grueling. We spent thirty days carrying load after load in the sweltering Florida summer heat and humidity. Our shirts were off by ten, useless and dripping with sweat. However, I would not trade those thirty days with my grandfather for anything in the world.

After losing my mother's father when I was eight, I knew how tenuous and precious those ties could be. I made the most of my time with my father's father.

On the days Grandpa drove me home or took me to the gym for preseason football workouts in his navy-blue Cadillac El Dorado with white leather interior, we savored the time alone with just the two of us. I was sticky and salty with sweat and physically exhausted. He asked me about girls. He talked to me about life. We would talk about money. Sometimes, we would drive, just listening to talk radio, not saying a word.

After unloading forty-four trailers, we were down to the last trailer. The last trailer on the last of the thirty days. Reese and I were long past the point of being sore on a daily basis. Our arms and backs were truly beach-worthy. We opened that last trailer, eager to discover its contents.

Knowing I always carried the Sharpie, quarter, knife, and magnet, as Grandpa instructed, Uncle Douglas said, "Matthew, let me see your magnet." The magnet's purpose suddenly became clear.[9] The trailer was filled with steel. We hit the jackpot! The contents of that trailer alone contained enough value to pay for the entire lot.

It was another lesson in awareness. Life's payload is not evenly distributed. Sometimes, the work is disproportionately hard for meager gains. Other times, a single bet pays off in spades. It all washes out in the end. I just needed to stay steady and accept the gift of hard work.

Waking Up

My father was an all-American nose guard at Newberry College. Raised in a home with Arabic values, my father was expected to respect his parents' wishes, which meant working for the family business after college. My father later discovered that he had been drafted to play for the Miami Dolphins. Grandma hid the letter because she did not want him to get hurt.

I attended Wofford College in Spartanburg, South Carolina. I had been recruited by many of the colleges in the Southeast, offering me several opportunities to play college football. I narrowed down my choices to Wofford College, The Citadel, and Duke University.

My family wanted me to go to Duke because my mother's parents were both Duke graduates. My grandparents' close friend was an art professor at Duke, whose ashes were spread in the rose garden on campus when he died. We were huge fans of Duke basketball. Our family spent the night of my Uncle Fred's wedding watching Duke beat Kentucky for the national collegiate basketball championship. My decision not to attend Duke was a hard decision to make because I did not want to disappoint my family.

I chose to attend Wofford College because I connected with the head football coach, Coach Ayers. He and I clicked. There was also something about my campus visit that just felt right. I became a Wofford Terrier,

---

[9] The quarter was for a pay phone if I needed to make an emergency call (no cell phones back then), the knife was for cutting open boxes and for self-defense, the Sharpie was for writing notes on anything at hand, and the magnet was for testing metals.

lettering all three years I played football. After my first semester, I earned a football scholarship, which went toward my sociology degree.

Playing college football required discipline. Double or triple practices in August, early morning weight lifting sessions, and late-night study sessions. I also worked as the only paid trainer at the Gold's Gym in Spartanburg.

Though I was disciplined, college was not an "all work, no play" proposition. I lost any hope of nomination for sainthood while savoring the truly hedonistic pleasures of college life with my fraternity brothers. I took both work and play 100% seriously.

Halfway through my junior season, I was starting at tackle and was on track for a great season. A senior defensive starter on the team suffered a concussion. He was frustrated and angry to have an injury that caused him to miss game time during his final year of college. As the saying goes, "The nail that sticks up gets hammered."[10] I was that nail and I got hammered. As someone who was enjoying success on the field, I became the target of his frustration.

Coach Ayers instituted a strict ten o'clock curfew the night before a game. The night before Wofford's homecoming football game, I was dutifully on my way back to the dorm at nine-thirty when I stopped by the fraternity house to drop off a six-pack of beer for the band that was playing.

I nodded to my injured teammate, who was standing outside the fraternity house. Then, I walked into the house, beer in hand. My radar pinged. I felt a little churn in my gut, and the hair on my neck stood on end. I dismissed the feeling because I was not technically doing anything wrong. I was just bringing beer to the band. I was not drinking it.

The next morning, after pregame warm-ups, I was in my game mindset, fired up and ready to go. Coach Ayers pulled me aside and told me to take off my gear. When I asked him why, he said he heard that I had

---

[10] This is a variation of the Japanese proverb 出る釘は打たれる (deru kugi wa utareru) or "the nail that sticks out gets hammered down." Wiktionary, The Free Dictionary. Updated September 21, 2021. https://en.wiktionary.org/w/index.php?title=the_nail_that_sticks_out_gets_hammered_down&oldid=63992762

been drinking the previous night and I must be a "special kind of stupid." I looked at him dumbfounded and told him I had not been drinking the previous night.

I knew Coach Ayers did not change his mind once a decision had been made. This situation was no exception. I took off my gear in a tornado of rage. My dorm room furniture took the brunt of my anger and frustration over the next two hours. I suspected it was Concussion Boy who had ratted me out, so it was good our paths did not cross.

On Monday morning, I went to meet with Coach Ayers. Coach confirmed my suspicion that it was my injured teammate who reported I had been drinking at a party. I explained that it was an outright lie. Yes, I was at the fraternity house. Yes, I was delivering beer to the band. I was not drinking. Furthermore, I told Coach, I was in my room before ten, as per our curfew requirement.

Coach Ayers listened intently, then informed me that I had made some questionable decisions and associations, so I was to be suspended for four games, which was the remainder of the season. He wanted to crack down on this kind of behavior and meant to make an example of me. Coach said I had enough playing time to letter for the year and I could have my position back in January. In the meantime, I was not to go to practice or games for the last four weeks of the season.

I was at a major crossroads. Should I accept a punishment that felt unfair and resume my college football career in January? Or should I close this chapter of the book, walking away from the sport? I chose to pivot, ending my life as a college football player.

From one perspective, an accident ended my football career. It was not a physical injury, but it hurt like hell emotionally. My pride was badly bruised. From another perspective, an accident opened the door to a whole new set of college adventures that never would have happened if I had been on the team.

The decision I made at that particular crossroads changed the trajectory of my life. I dropped thirty pounds of football weight, eschewed my regularly scheduled haircuts, got a job at UPS, worked security, bartended, and started selling drugs on the side. I dove headfirst into life away from football for the first time since seventh grade.

Prior to my four-game suspension in college, football played a central role in my identity. I loved the game. It conferred many attributes I respected: mental toughness, hard work, and discipline. It also came with a set of rules and expectations I found confining. Entering my senior year of college, I chose not to play football. Without training and practices as a daily undercurrent for the first time in my life, I was forced to define who "I" was without football as a contextual reference. The experience was both frightening and exhilarating.

In a cinematic version of my life story, the movie script would paint the picture that my post-football experience was a fall from glory. The choice not to play after the four-game suspension created an identity crisis. Bartending and hustling party favors to fellow students would be characterized as a fall from grace. Life was not a movie. The advantages of getting suspended from the team outweighed the disadvantages. I was waking up.

Instead of spending the following January interim[11] semester doing spring training workouts for football, I dove into writing and photography. I took a photography class, went snowboarding on weekends, and spent more time reading and writing. I became aware that I wanted to play a role different from the one my family expected. In a quest to understand what that new role might be, I embarked on a path of personal development and growth that might not have happened if I had continued to play football.

---

[11] "During the month of January, faculty and students are permitted to concentrate on a single study project. These projects are designed to move beyond traditional classroom courses and teaching methods and to encourage innovative, experiential learning. Projects are graded on an honors/pass/fail basis which allows students to explore projects in which they have interest but not necessarily a full background, without risking their GPA. Students annually enroll in on-campus projects, internships, service learning, and travel/study projects. Students are also able to propose independent study projects." "Frequently Asked Questions." Wofford College website. Accessed October 13, 2021. https://www.wofford.edu/academics/interim/faq

I spent much-needed time in reflection and introspection. Choosing to give up my identity as a member of the Wofford football team was unsettling. Some friends from high school were starting a new company and asked me to join their team. Being part of a team again was very tempting, especially when combined with the prospect of making money. I had to make a choice: leave Wofford and participate in an exciting new business venture or stay and finish my degree.

It was a tough call. I was not happy at Wofford, yet leaving college felt like running away. If I did not finish my degree at that time, I most likely would never go back. I was one year away from graduation and could see the light at the end of the tunnel.

Up to this point in my life, most decisions had been based on what my parents wanted me to do. For the first time, I was exercising my right to make choices free of their influence. I realized that if I could not be happy where I was at any given moment, I would not be happy anywhere. I realized that my problems were internal and my perspective was limiting my ability to be happy. Free from my identity as a college football player, I needed to dig deep to find a way to thrive at Wofford in this new norm. I needed to re-examine my values and see what the world looked like from this new perspective.

I believed that my family of origin was both chosen and accidental. Before birth, I chose my parents to teach me the lessons I needed to learn. Upon birth, I forgot what those lessons were, so I experienced the events in my early life as a series of accidents. Like developing photos from an old-fashioned film camera, the pictures from some lessons were clear, with bright colors and sharp lines. Examples of these lessons in my life were respect, discipline, and hard work.

Other lessons were learned from the film's negative. Early experiences taught me to repress my feelings and adopt my father's values, whether I shared those values or not. In time, I became aware of the fact that these lessons yielded behaviors that had to be unlearned.

As I became more self-aware, I learned to sift through the mental photo album, determining which photos were worth keeping and which still needed to be developed from the negative.

Awareness introduced the process of becoming cognizant of my environment and the external forces at work in my life. As much as my formative experiences and relationships may have been accidental, awareness was the process of identifying patterns and integrating those experiences into my sense of self.

Early childhood interactions with my mother taught me to respect others and savor the beauty in life. My father imbued a strong work ethic and inspired me to develop grit when times were hard. Sorting through my varied childhood experiences, I chose to integrate those values.

Cord's admonition taught me to suppress my feelings. Processing that experience required a departure from established family values.

The good, the bad, and the ugly in my formative experiences and relationships were all part of the process of waking up to the awareness that I had a choice. I could not choose my circumstances; however, I could choose my response to those circumstances. Accidents could be perceived as good or bad, depending on how I looked at them. Each accident shaped future events. In this way, being suspended from the football team was a wake-up call. I was still blinded by immaturity and fear of unknown paths; however, something stirred inside me, and this was the beginning of learning to be aware of my role in my own life. Learning an awareness of the fact that accidents—unplanned events—could become fortunate would come later.

Premonitions

Premonition to me is the ability to catch a glimpse of the future, to perceive incidents as something more than mere coincidence. I started becoming aware of premonitions that filled me with a sense of foreboding leading up to a negative accident. That same sense of precognition was accompanied by tingles of excitement when I was caught up in the serendipitous events leading up to a positive accident. As I wrapped my mind around this concept, I remembered a time when I felt a sense of foreboding and chose not to pay attention to the warning bells.

When I was in high school, I lived in San Marco, a neighborhood on the St. Johns River, just across the bridge from downtown Jacksonville. My friend Joe lived on the west side of town, near 108th Street. Most Saturdays, I worked for our family's salvage business. This particular Saturday, I had been granted a rare reprieve to spend the day at the beach with Joe. Our plan was straightforward: play volleyball and meet girls at Jacksonville Beach.

Joe pulled up in front of my house. Gas prices being what they were and our meager teenage income being what it was, I figured we could split the drive and the fuel cost.

Magnanimously, I said, "Hey, let's take my car."

Just as the words were out of my mouth, I had this overwhelming urge to take them back. A sense of foreboding came over me, like a dark cloud blocking the hot Florida sun. I shook the feeling off when Joe cheerfully replied, "OK!"

We arrived to find that Jacksonville Beach was packed. Joe and I headed across the sand to play some volleyball, enjoy the female scenery, and kill the day.

After many games of volleyball and a fun day at the beach, Joe and I climbed into my car and cranked up AC/DC's "Thunderstruck" on the radio. We were heading south on Third Street, toward J. Turner Butler Boulevard when—WHAM! The front end of my Honda Accord collided with the rear end of a car that had stopped suddenly in front of me. I was shaky, weak in the knees, scared out of my mind. A cocktail of emotions swirled through my body: fear that the woman driving the other car would yell at me (or, even worse, cry!); devastation that my first car was damaged; and, worst of all, an unmitigated terror at the prospect of getting an ass-whupping from my dad.

I pulled into a gas station parking lot to exchange information with the driver of the other car. When we got back in my car, I looked at Joe and said, "I had a feeling something like this was going to happen. I should've listened."

I wish that was the last time I ignored a sense of foreboding. There were many times I failed to heed the gentle voice of intuition. Street smarts are not groomed living on easy street; pain can be a better teacher than pleasure. That little fender bender should have taught me to give my intuition the respect it deserved.

That accident intrigued me over the following years as I explored my own belief systems and became more aware. Where did premonitions come from? Sometimes, intuition felt like a gentle nudge. At other times, the voice of premonition was as loud and clear as a person sitting next to me.

As my sphere of awareness increased, learning to differentiate my own beliefs from my family's beliefs, I was drawn to the teachings of philosophers, religious writers, shamans, astrologists, auraologists, palm readers, and all manner of spiritual advisors. I also explored the work of Dr. Timothy Leary, a highly regarded Harvard psychology professor. Dr. Leary was part of a team of psychologists who reasoned that psychology is the study of the mind, including its relationship to the brain, body, and environment. Therefore, to them, research into the effects of mind-altering substances on cognition, perception, and emotion were legitimate pursuits in the field of psychology.

What I found most fascinating were not the differences between the various psychological and philosophical explanations, but the similarities of their insights. Each followed a unique path to a similar destination. It was like asking for directions in a big city. I could ask ten people how to get somewhere, and I was likely to get ten different answers. Each answer would be correct and would ultimately get me where I wanted to go.

In my junior year of college, I had a profound premonition that influenced the next twenty years of my life. On a gorgeous spring day, I was in the midst of one such experiment, sitting in the outdoor area of

Fraternity Row at Wofford College, savoring the delicious taste of sunshine.

A guy I knew well from one of the other fraternities came up to me, asking for help carrying a keg from his car for a party at their fraternity house that evening. Normally, I was willing to lend a hand to help. There was no such thing as a circumstance that prevented me from saying yes when someone was in need. As a result, I often felt used, like people took advantage of me. More importantly, I was often an enabler, preventing people from doing things for themselves. On this day, I said no to my friend, instantly feeling a wave of guilt and self-reproach. It killed my buzz.

Back in my room, I lay on a couch, staring up at the walls and ceiling of a room I had painted black. "The Big Picture" was spray painted on one wall in huge cartoon-like dayglow letters. My mom often referenced the big picture as a reminder to maintain a broader perspective. Staring at those words on the wall, fuzzy concepts loomed at the edge of my mind. Was I really just a yes-man? Why did I always do what people wanted me to do? Was it a genuine desire to help people, or was I just seeking approval? Why was the approval of others so important?

Time stopped as I dove deeper into meditation. Seconds, minutes, or hours later, I snapped awake. A very real, very clear premonition took form, and I knew with absolute certainty that I would die when I turned forty. It was not just a hunch or a feeling. It was an all-encompassing shift in my belief system that influenced the way I thought and behaved over the next two decades.

Mark Twain wrote that he had the most remarkable dream: "In the morning, when I awoke, and the dream was so vivid, so like reality, that it deceived me, and I thought it was real."[12] He wrote it off as a dream, until, several weeks later, the events of his dream played out almost exactly as he had dreamed them. Twenty years later, he published his observations and

---

[12] Kripal JJ. *The Flip: Epiphanies of Mind and the Future of Knowledge*. Bellevue Literary Press; 2019.

theories about incidents like his dream, . . . referring to them as "mental telegraphy."

As Jeffrey J. Kripal points out in his book *The Flip*, Twain's term "mental telegraphy" was a reference that encompassed both "cutting-edge technology of the day" and "Twain's conviction that such precognitive dreams and instant communications were connected to the acts of reading and writing."[13]

Sometimes, it's the lucid dream, the out-of-body, existential come-to-Jesus moment, that feels more "real" than reality itself. The knowledge that I would die at age forty permeated the core of my being, a centripetal force that shaped my identity and anchored my sense of self.

I found that I enjoyed life after football. I loved the intellectual stimulation and the deep dives into fascinating subjects like expanded consciousness and precognition. I hustled, worked multiple jobs, and spent time experimenting with a variety of pleasures while exploring new ideologies. I had to learn balance, as I was no longer living under the watchful eye of the coaching staff. My premonition created an expanded awareness allowing me to approach each day with less fear and more confidence. "I know I'm not going to die today, so I might as well take a few risks."

Cultural Expansion

The January interim semester at Wofford provided a unique opportunity for students to participate in internships, explore fields of study outside of their major, or travel. My senior year, unencumbered with spring training or football obligations, I decided to join my creative writing class on a trip to Indonesia. What began as an excuse to go rafting in Malaysia turned into a month-long journey across Java, Bali, and Lombok.

The culture shock of international travel was a fantastic perspective-

---

[13] Kripal JJ. *The Flip: Epiphanies of Mind and the Future of Knowledge*. Bellevue Literary Press; 2019.

shifter. Confronted with the sheer magnitude of people living lives different from my own was an eye-opening experience.

People who travel internationally on a regular basis extol the virtues of immediately assimilating to a new time zone upon arrival. In Japan, while my American classmates slept, I embraced my new time zone by partying the night away with a boisterous group of New Zealanders. I was amused to discover that they referred to Americans as "Colonials," and I soon began referring to them as "Kiwis." Though I paid the price of that all-nighter for the next two days, from that point forward, I felt great while the rest of my class dragged on with their adjustment to the new time zone.

In Indonesia, the multitude of colors, the lush vegetation, the enticing scents, the exotic foods, and the foreign culture were as intoxicating as the air was humid. Early in the trip we were having dinner at a restaurant in Java. I was speaking with the waitress, and she said, "You speak good English—in America. Now you are in Indonesia." It was a gentle reminder that as a visitor in a foreign country, I needed to make an effort to learn the basics of the local language. It reminded me of an experience I had as a child.

When I was about six or seven, Grandma tried to teach me to speak Arabic. Grandpa entered the room and heard what was being taught, then yelled at her in Arabic. Knowing I could not understand, he said to me in English, "We are Americans now. We are in America. We speak English." In other words, assimilate and respect the local culture.

On a high school trip to Italy with my mother, I observed an American couple at a deli in Rome trying to order lunch. They spoke loud, slow English to the Italian couple behind the counter. The Italians shrugged their shoulders, replying, in Italian, that they did not speak English. Watching this go down, as I was next in line, I pulled out my Italian-English translation book. I began the process of butchering the Italian language in an attempt to place an order in their native tongue. Stopping me mid-struggle, the wife interrupted. In perfect English, she said, "Thank you for respecting our country. We speak English. You can relax. What would you like?"

Making the commitment to learn a few words in a foreign language did not take a lot of effort. It did require an important shift in perspective. It meant acknowledging the fact that I was a guest and my host deserved respect. I learned that even though English was widely spoken in foreign countries, it was easy for Americans to come to expect everyone to speak English. Additionally, ethnocentrism made it nearly impossible to experience a foreign culture authentically.

In Indonesia, as in Italy, I learned that taking time to familiarize myself with the lingua franca went a long way when establishing relationships with the locals.

After my death-at-forty premonition and experimentation with expanded consciousness, I wanted to meet an indigenous shaman. The concept of exploring the spiritual roots of an ancient culture was intriguing, to contrast what I had studied about Native American beliefs with beliefs held by indigenous Indonesians. I was introduced to an Indonesian shaman who told me about specific crossroads and choices that would emerge during my life's journey. Much of what he said did not make sense until twenty years later when it all came full circle. The shaman told me I would marry and divorce and that I would come to a crossroads in my life shortly after.

The shaman's perspective expanded my awareness, and I decided to use that information for the essay I was required to write in order to receive credit for the interim semester class.

My challenges were presented in the precise manner that would yield the greatest growth. It was as if those challenges were designed to meet me in exactly the right place at exactly the right time, facilitating my expanding awareness.

I spent much of the summer after my college graduation ceremony couch surfing while completing a sociology class, my last requirement for official graduation. I was doing what had become my normal hustle, trying to balance work and play with studies.

After four years wading through countless hours of books, lectures, and exams, I had no clue what I was going to do. Up to this point in my life, I did as I was told: staying on the honor roll and playing sports in high school, attending college on a football scholarship, and hustling to pay bills with income from an assortment of jobs.

My family expected me to graduate college and return to Jacksonville to work in the family business. When I did not play football my senior year of college, my flight path was interrupted. The trajectory shifted. I was no longer confined to the flight path my parents had planned for me. This provided a gateway to a world of possibilities I had not ever considered.

Football faded in the rearview mirror, taking any thoughts of working in the family business along with it. My trip to Indonesia created a perfectly timed shift in my broader perspective. I did not know what post-college life would look like. I did know that I wanted to travel and that I was not afraid to hustle.

Spontaneity

I gave myself permission to live life for myself. I began walking and thinking on my own. I became inquisitive, approaching each crossroads with curiosity. I became more spontaneous, saying yes to new adventures.

My friend Tino asked if I wanted to go on a road trip to Canada to fish for walleye.

Sometimes, a simple, well-timed "Hell, yeah!" can set off a series of positive events. Passing my final sociology exam, I graduated from Wofford College and drove west with Tino two days later.

Our first stop was Macomb, Illinois, home of Western Illinois University. It was summer, so the town was quiet. We ran into one of Tino's high school friends, who invited us to a house party. At the party, I saw a guy on the back patio yelling at a girl while holding her up against the wall by her neck, her feet dangling inches off the ground.

I was not one to start fights; I certainly finished them. Having been in my fair share, on my own and when working security, I knew how to handle myself in a physical altercation. My mother had taught me to respect women. Her values overruled the fact that I did not know anyone at the party. I did not want to jump into someone else's business; however, I could not sit back and watch this girl get whupped, so I walked across the back patio, reached under his left arm, and grabbed the guy by his neck. Pulling him off her, I said, "Hey, man, let's cool off and take it easy."

Yeah. That did not fly.

Redness around the girl's neck gave a hint of a future bruise. To my shock, this girl went from swinging at the guy, trying to get free, to yelling at me for messing with her boyfriend. While the girl assailed me with a barrage of verbal abuse, her boyfriend went inside and came out with six of his friends. They were clearly in a beer-addled fog, angry, and looking for a fight. Smelling trouble, I kept my back to the yard, looking for an opportunity to make my exit.

One by one, the guys peeled off, nonchalantly trying to circle around behind me. One beefy dude grabbed a scrap piece of two-by-four, another was gripping an empty beer bottle. I spied an empty Jack Daniel's bottle on the table and casually grabbed it as I walked past.

Luckily, Tino's friend saw what was happening and ran to get the truck. He backed the truck into the yard, just off the patio.

"Get in," he hissed, swinging the passenger door open.

As I took the last few steps backward, easing myself into the passenger seat, the drunken mob broke into a run. One guy lunged and grabbed my arm in an attempt to pull me out of the truck. I kicked him in the face and slammed the door. Grass flew into the air with force from the spinning tires as we exited the scene. We hid my truck in an old barn for two days, then left for Iowa.

We were delighted to learn that Britt, Iowa, was home to the annual National Hobo Convention. Train-hoppers from all over the country gathered to select their king and queen and partake in a good ole Midwestern celebration. We were just in time to join the festivities!

The Hobo Convention was a great metaphor for my newfound sense of freedom. The image of speeding along to the sound of the wheels on the track, nothing but an expanse of open prairie outside the open door of the train car, a star-studded velvet curtain of night, and that boundless sense of openness and freedom, was intoxicating.

Tino and I stumbled across a dunking booth, where some of Britt's most prominent citizens were raising money for local charities. Joining the camaraderie, we volunteered to be dunked. Soon, we were celebrities, known by half the town. A group of locals even took us cliff jumping at the rock quarry.

Later that evening, we joined a hobo campfire and listened as the group discussed routes and shared adventures from traveling the rails. Some of the travelers were eloquent storytellers. They were proud of their nomadic lifestyle, eschewing social convention and conformity. Listening to their stories, I started to recognize a pattern. Hobos were spontaneous. They gave greater weight to intuition as opposed to intellect in their decision-making process. Intuition provided more fertile ground for spontaneity and the fortunate accidents spontaneity begot. I felt a sense of kinship with this ragtag collection of itinerants, unfettered by rules of social convention. The week went by too fast. Just as we settled in for the fun, we were off to Canada.

Within what felt like minutes of crossing the border, we were engulfed in remote Canadian wilderness. Three hours later, we parked the truck in the precise middle of nowhere. We would be staying at cabins only accessible by seaplane.

Soaring just above wild glades sprinkled with birch and surrounded by endless stretches of towering ponderosa pines, we glided into a landing on a remote mountain lake. I was immediately taken by the beauty and wildness of the isolated camp, the only sign of human habitation for hundreds of miles.

Our daily agenda consisted of a long day of fishing, cooking our catch of walleye for dinner over the fire, drinking whiskey, and telling stories late into the night. It was a great week! Spontaneity and my newfound sense of freedom were taking root.

Making Connections

Working our way back to South Carolina, Tino and I discussed future plans. I had my college degree from Wofford; however, I still did not know where to go next. The 1996 Summer Olympics were taking place in Atlanta. The Olympic events were due to begin in mid-July. A few of our friends were heading to Atlanta to fill temporary positions associated with the Games. I made the decision to join them.

I called my friend Greg, who had graduated from Wofford the year before me. He lived a few miles from downtown Atlanta in an area known as Five Points. Greg let me rent space in his apartment, providing a place to stay and good company in a new city.

I was disappointed to discover that the Olympic Games felt highly commercialized and sterile when viewed from behind the scenes. Visiting the venue left a bad taste in my mouth. Since working for the Olympic Committee was not what I envisioned, I decided it would be more fun to work for a local sports bar in Five Points. I found a gig where security staff was paid cash plus a share of the tips and a bonus for each fake ID collected. I still needed to generate a little more cash flow.

Someone told me that the House of Blues was hiring. During the interview, the manager confirmed that he wanted me to work security, just not at the door as a bouncer. He was looking for someone reliable to watch the cash. That job was a gift from heaven. I spent a few nights a week listening to some of the best music in the world, enjoying free drinks, hobnobbing with celebrities, and watching the money. I caught several bartenders pocketing money and saved the business more than enough to cover my fee.

Sometimes, a disaster was the catalyst for change and opportunity. A pipe bomb went off at the Summer Olympics in Atlanta. One person was killed, and one hundred and eleven people were injured. Thousands of spectators, athletes, press, and security personnel flooded Five Points to share stories, swap pictures, and receive comfort in the company of strangers. Many languages were spoken as patrons called their families to let them know their loved one was safe. It was a melee of celebration and grief. An average busy night quickly snowballed into a jam-packed street party, filling the bar and spilling into the hot summer night of Atlanta's downtown streets.

Spirits were high as glasses were filled with spirits. I met several Olympic athletes, a couple of whom hung out with me at the door to the bar, sharing stories of travel and competition. One European athlete described his second-place Olympic finish. I listened intently and asked if an Olympic medal was heavy. He checked over his shoulder to make sure nobody was watching. My jaw dropped as he pulled a ribbon from under his shirt with a giant silver medal attached.

A few days later, I was talking with the owner of The Bar, a bar down the block from the sports bar I was working. We were sharing stories from the night of the bombing. Through the conversation, I discovered that The Bar's owner owned a bar in Vail, Colorado, as well. The more we talked, the more I was intrigued by the idea of living in the mountains. "If you ever find yourself in Vail, Matt, you'll have a job at The Club," the Atlanta businessman promised.

The wheels were spinning and my intuition was ringing. I loved living in Atlanta and even considered moving there. The movement, activity, laser light shows at Stone Mountain, beautiful women, easy money, and overall good time made a compelling case for settling in Atlanta long term.

Then there was the Swedish girl with whom I shared deep philosophical and political conversations. I fell in love, then I never saw her again. The depth of our conversations lasted, and my mind remained open to the variety of viewpoints and systems in the greater world outside the Southern charm I grew up with.

However, the job offer in Vail felt right. Seemingly coincidental connections, people who mysteriously surfaced on my path, were often collaborators in fortunate accidents. This discovery would serve me well in the months and years to come.

As the Olympics drew to a close and life in Atlanta started returning to normal, I missed the high energy and buzz around the events. Even among friends, favors expired. Greg and I had been friends for four years at Wofford; after seven weeks of sleeping on his couch, he hinted by asking, "What's next for you, Matt?"

On a whim, I said, "Colorado." I told him about a ski trip to Keystone, Colorado, junior year of high school. I had fallen in love with Colorado and felt like the mountains were luring me back with their Siren call. Since I had not been training for football during the past winter, I had the chance to go snowboarding on weekends. The ski slopes in North Carolina were nothing compared to the Colorado Rockies.

Greg said, "What are you going to do there?"

"I don't know. I'm gonna snowboard. I guess I'll go to Florida for a couple of months and figure out a plan, save some money, and then head out before winter. I have a job lined up if I go to Vail."

I told him about the conversation I had with the owner of The Bar. Being somewhat conservative, Greg gave me a smile tinged with a shadow of concern and said, "Well, I hope it all works out for you, Matt." Little did I know how a casual conversation in Atlanta would act as a beacon, inspiring me to follow my dream to go west. I was beginning to trust my intuition, attuning my awareness to these little gifts of fate, people, and connections that paved the way for new, exciting adventures.

Liquid Lessons

I moved back to my parents' house in Jacksonville a week after the Olympics came to a close, spending two months working to save money for the move to Colorado. My parents had mixed feelings about my plan to move west. Mom's brother Cord was living in Denver, granting my mother some relief. My father's excitement was limited, as he expected me to follow his path: returning to Jacksonville after college to help run the family's salvage business. There was unspoken tension between us because of his will not being heeded, so I opted for employment outside the family business.

Working as a waiter from ten to three in a cafe, I quickly learned that bartending fit my aptitudes better than waiting tables. After a month, the cafe owner came to the same conclusion, allowing me to tend the bar rather than wait tables. I did not make as much in tips, so I started a side hustle, bartending for private parties.

Once again, chance encounters led to fortunate accidents. Soon after returning to Jacksonville, I went to a Pantera and White Zombie concert with my younger brother. Standing on the edge of the mosh pit, I was keeping an eye on my brother and his friends when I noticed a massive guy standing next to me. He must have been 6'4" and 280 pounds. Even though I was shorter, at 5'10" and 180, after years of weight training and playing college football, my shoulders and chest were just as stacked. He and I shared a few laughs as we stood shoulder to shoulder on the edge of a mosh pit swelling with energy, pushing idiots away from our zone, while I kept an eye on my younger brother and his friends

The week after the concert, I applied for a second job at a local nightclub. When I showed up for my shift at Club Five, another new guy had just started and would be working the door with me. His collarbone-length goatee and resting grimace looked extremely familiar. I could tell he recognized me as well. We both tried to figure out where we had met. A couple hours later, his head snapped up. "White Zombie last week!"

"YES!" I exclaimed. "You were standing next to me in the pit."

He and I became fast friends. Casual banter made the shifts go faster and made it easier to deal with drunk people.

The security director, Mike, played ski and kayak movies on the big screen for visual stimulation while the DJs mixed music. My attention was often drawn to the kayaking clips. One of my favorite professors at Wofford, John Lane, was an avid kayaker and outdoorsman. For years, I had asked him to teach me to kayak. For years, I had allowed football, work, and school to thwart our efforts to get out on the water together.

I was standing overwatch on the balcony of the club one night with the director. We were watching paddlers run waterfalls, navigate steep creeks, and show off aerial tricks on the big screen while keeping an eye on the crowd of fifteen hundred people below. I told him that I had always wanted to kayak. To my surprise, he said, "You're in luck. I'm a kayak instructor. Do you have access to a boat?"

No way! Perfect. Of all the places in Jacksonville I could have worked, I ended up working security with a kayak instructor for a boss!

I told him that our family had a sit-on-top kayak that we used to surf when the waves were bad. He said that would work, and we spent the next month traveling to various creeks in Northeast Florida so he could teach me the basics of reading water and paddling. I was immediately hooked and was eager to make a trip to the mountains to apply my skills on bigger water. A couple weeks after our lessons began, he asked me if I wanted to go on one last paddling trip with him and some friends, as the season was drawing to an end. I was definitely in. We planned a weekend trip to the Nantahala River in North Carolina with two of Mike's kayaking friends.

He and I got off work at five on Sunday morning. White coffee on board, the four of us embarked on the eight-hour drive from Jacksonville to the Nantahala River. Monday morning arrived and I was fired up. We had three paddlers and one beautiful lady to drive the shuttle.[14] I was introduced to the idea of a shuttle bunny, learning that we paid her way and she drove the vehicle from the put-in to the take-out.

We paddled down the Class I–II[15] section without incident. The final S-turn rapid was the biggest white water this Florida boy had ever seen. I crushed it, gliding to the bottom with ease. I was feeling pretty proud.

I was an absolute neophyte and was having a blast, along with the others. We decided to extend our trip by a day to paddle the Chattooga, which forms the boundary between South Carolina and Georgia. We camped close to the put-in, drinking beer and enjoying the party favors, tired from the day and eager for the next.

I was really nervous. Everyone else had traditional white-water kayaks. My sit-on-top kayak, waterski PFD (personal flotation device/life jacket), and shorty wetsuit, while good enough for the rivers we were paddling, gave away my rookie status. The brisk October air pushed the limits of a shorty. I was tough, though, and was not about to complain. Mike told me our run that day would primarily consist of Class II and III[16] white water. The last rapid, Bull Sluice, was normally a Class IV[17] rapid. Late-season low water levels downgraded the rapid to Class III.

"You'll be OK," he said reassuringly. "If you fall off, just remember to keep your feet up and downstream until you can jump back on your boat."

---

[14] A shuttle requires at least two cars—one to sit at the bottom and the other to drive the paddlers and their gear to the put-in. An alternative option is to have a shuttle driver drop off the paddlers at the put-in and drive to the take-out to pick them up.

[15] The scale of difficulty for white water is a classification system that goes from I to VI, each step up becomes exponentially more difficult. There are also variations that can be rated + or − rapids for each level. Class I is considered moving water: flat and easy. Class II is still a beginner rapid but has a few rocks and obstacles that are easy to avoid: easy to maneuver with minimal consequence.

[16] Class III white water has obstacles that the paddler should avoid: moderate consequences.

[17] Class IV white water has must-make moves. There is still some margin for error; however, there is a risk of injury if the move is not made.

The next morning, cold river water dispelled any lingering grogginess from the previous night's imbibing. Was I feeling great? No. I was a nervous wreck. My ego and excitement helped me to fake it till I made it.

We took our time going down the river, diligently stopping to scout the trickier rapids. Through each section, I was getting better at reading the water and quicker at identifying my line.[18] I was also getting a false sense of security, fueled by magical confidence and youth.

About halfway through the run, I melted down[19] into a hole at the bottom of one of the rapids. The entire sit-on-top was completely submerged. When it surfaced, the boat's buoyancy popped me two feet into the air. My thigh took the hit when I landed on a rock. I tried to shake off the pain, telling everyone I was fine. We successfully ran Bull Sluice and celebrated with beers at the take-out.

Driving back to Jacksonville, my thigh was killing me. The cold water and compression of the wetsuit kept the swelling down, and the seven-hour drive provided plenty of time for the bruise to form. It was my badge of honor, a token to remind me of my first kayaking trip.

Breaking Free

My relationship with my father deteriorated while I was living in Florida. He resented the fact that I was living at home and not working in our family's store. I was finally breaking free of my family's expectations. Once and for all, I was making it clear that running the family business was not part of my personal destiny.

Over the two months in Jacksonville, I spent my downtime with a girl who had recently returned home after spending a year in Breckenridge, Colorado. One afternoon, she called her old roommate in Breckenridge.

---

[18] Chosen path through a rapid.
[19] When the kayak enters the water vertically and completely submerges.

Hanging up the phone, she announced, "OK. You've got my old room, and my roommate there is getting you set up with my old job as a lift op." It was nice to know I had another option!

The time for my departure finally arrived. I would be driving west in the morning. High school friends were planning to take me out for drinks that night, so I spent the day packing and getting the truck loaded.

A call from Uncle Cord fueled my excitement. "Matt, have you left yet? You need to leave now. It's dumping!"

"I'm leaving first thing tomorrow morning."

"Are you going to Vail or Breckenridge?" he asked.

"Not sure yet. I'll get there and decide."

"You should go to Beaver Creek," Cord said. "I have a friend in Avon. You can crash at his place while you get settled. The mountain is better, and you'll like it there."

"OK. Well, let's go snowboarding there, and I'll figure out the rest from there. I'll call you from the road tomorrow," I replied.

The next morning, my mom got up to exchange goodbye hugs and kisses. I had enough cash, a snowboard, and clothes. Upon arriving in Colorado, Cord and I spent four days skiing chest-deep powder in Vail and Beaver Creek.

If college was the place where my independence and sense of self was incubated, Colorado was the place where my self-awareness grew and flourished.

I spent my first month in Colorado sleeping on someone's couch while working at a ski and apparel retailer in Beaver Creek. Three co-workers and I found a three-bedroom town house and signed a six-month lease. With my name on that lease, I had checked all the boxes. Job? Check. Ski pass? Check. Housing? Check. Somehow, I managed to avoid running out of money.

Spring arrived, melting my income along with the snow. The ski shop closed for the season, and tourist traffic slowed to a trickle.

Rafting companies were hiring new guides, so I signed up for a training program with Lakota Guides. I was also working for a temporary staffing company and was assigned a job working at a construction site. The foreman, impressed with my work ethic, offered me a full-time job with a six-figure income. Working construction was temporary, not what I wanted to do and not nearly as interesting as being a white-water rafting guide. I respectfully declined his generous offer.

Raft guide training was fun and intense. I was thankful for the mental and physical toughness developed through years of two-a-day football practices. For two weeks, we spent eight to ten hours on the frigid water, taking two or three runs a day. At the end of our two-week training period, our instructors took us to Glenwood Canyon to show us what the Colorado River looked like when running at over fourteen thousand CFS.[20] It was HUGE! Shoshone was the segment most often used by commercial rafting outfitters running Glenwood Canyon. Rafting companies normally ran Shoshone when the river was below five thousand CFS. At fourteen thousand CFS, the Colorado River was a changed being.

The trainers took us to the Hanging Lake Dam to scout the upper sections, Upper Death and Barrel Springs, before we rafted the standard run. Scouting Upper Death, I felt an intuitive, visceral connection to the river. Within seconds, I saw the line and pointed it out.

Jeff, one of our instructors, laughed. "Matt, nobody runs this. It's called Upper Death for a reason. It's a Class VI[21] rapid!"

"I will run it. The line is right there," I proclaimed.[22]

---

[20] Cubic feet per second. Measurement of water flow by counting the number of cubic feet of water passing a single point every second. Picture that many basketballs passing your finger every second.

[21] Class VI rapids are considered un-runnable by commercial rafting standards. Some expert-level kayakers run previously rated Class VI rapids; however, they risk severe injury or death. These rapids are for top-level experts only.

[22] A few years later, I did run Upper Death. Not only did I run Upper Death, I proceeded to run it daily, for years, by myself. (This was unsafe, and I do not recommend for others to mimic my actions.) I created a workout routine where I would park at Hanging Lake, kayak through the dam, then navigate Upper Death, Barrel Springs, and Shoshone to the Grizzly Creek take-out where I left my bicycle. I would ride my bike the six miles back up to the put-in, load it in my truck, pick up my kayak at Grizzly, then drive home having completed a dual-sport day.

Lakota hired me, and summer flew by in a blur of rafting, kayaking, hiking, and photography. The guys from the construction job booked a white-water rafting trip and requested me as their guide. They were all supportive that I was choosing to chase experiences instead of paychecks.

I signed up for kayak lessons as soon as the summer started. That first lesson, I possibly set a record for the number of swims in a single day on the Upper C, a Class I–II section of the Colorado River used for teaching. I swam out of the borrowed kayak at every eddy line[23] and small rapid we came across.

Mike, the instructor and owner of the local shop, looked at me with humor and pity. I did not care. I was on a mission. I took another lesson and then met with some guys with whom I raft guided, who took me paddling every day after our trips. I learned to brace, then I learned to roll. I threw myself into every hole (hydraulic) on the river so that I could practice recovery and get better. The same drive I had when I played football was now applied to kayaking. By the end of the summer, I was keeping up with guys who had been paddling for years.

I learned that there are two mud seasons when you live in the mountains. The stretch of time between Labor Day and opening day of ski season is spectacularly beautiful. Like the spring, it is financially dry. Many raft guides traveled to West Virginia for Gauley Season. Others took vacations, traveled, or hustled to do whatever work they could find. I was not experienced enough for the Gauley River, yet, so I combined the other three options.

---

[23] Eddies form wherever there are areas where current is impeded. They can form behind an obstruction like a boulder or on bends in the river and along the shore, away from the main channel. Eddies are typically calmer water that can be used to set safety or catch one's breath. Eddy lines are basically the edges of the eddy, where the two opposing currents meet. This is often a lot rougher than the eddy itself, as it is the point where the water is moving in two different directions. This is what can cause whirlpools.

Taking Detours

I met Alison during that first winter when replying to a help wanted ad for her new photography business. She was looking for a photographer to capture digital photos of people enjoying après-ski revelries, which could then be instantly emailed or printed. Digital photography was a brand-new field, and Alison's business was sponsored by Olympus and Toshiba. It was a fun gig. More importantly, it provided much-needed cash.

Alison moved to California for the summer, offering me the use of her condo in exchange for utilities and continuing to keep her photography business going. It was perfect timing, as my lease had just expired.

At the end of the summer, Alison called. "Hey, Matt. I connected with the owner of the Giggling Marlin in Cabo San Lucas, Mexico. He said we can take digital photos of his guests, like we do in Vail. Come down to Cabo!"

My answer was a resounding "OK!"

End of conversation. Flight booked.

I arrived in Mexico a week later, Spanish-English dictionary in hand. Standing outside of baggage claim, fifteen minutes passed, then thirty minutes, then an hour. Where was Alison? I fervently wished I had a clearer plan before getting on a flight to a foreign country. I had given her my flight info. Maybe she had gotten the day wrong?

Another hour passed. Where was Alison? We did not have cell phones. Even if we did, I did not have a number to call. I passed the time chatting with a local Mexican girl, practicing my Spanglish while passing the translation book back and forth. Her mother invited me to their house for dinner that night. Touched by the offer, I declined. The girl and her mother left.

Finally, I found a taxi to downtown Cabo. Fortunately, I remembered the name of the bar we were supposed to be working with, so that's where I went.

Stepping out of the cab in front of the Giggling Marlin, I was a twenty-two-year-old in a foreign country, alone, trying to communicate with locals who did not speak my native tongue of English, in a bar, filled with drunk tourists and music too loud to hear myself think.

Oh, joy.

Attempting to explain the situation to one of the bouncers at the door, my words were met with a blank stare. He took me to the bartender who spoke a little English.

"I'm here to take pictures," I said loudly, pantomiming taking a picture with a camera. "For Alison. Al-i-son," I enunciated.

At the mention of Alison's name, both the bouncer and the bartender got very animated. "Al-ee-son!" they exclaimed with big smiles. Encouraged and greatly relieved by their enthusiasm, I exchanged high fives with them. Their smiles went from nonexistent to huge. They were expecting me and were very happy to see me.

Alison was in the hospital. The bartender was foggy on the details, partially due to the language barrier and partially due to the fact that nobody knew exactly how to contact Alison. It most likely was not a life-threatening situation, he reassured me. The bartender invited me to hang out at the bar, and we would figure out how to get in touch with Alison in the morning.

That night turned into breakfast and kept going well into the next day. I learned that the bigger the buzz, the better I understood Spanish—and the better they understood English. By the late afternoon, all of the bar employees loved me and I loved them. Since we did not sleep, I did not have to worry about accommodations. I was worried about Alison. My second night in Mexico went the same as my first, and on my third day in Cabo, the manager of Pazzo's pizza restaurant came looking for me at the Giggling Marlin. Pazzo's had two locations in Colorado and one in Cabo. The manager knew Alison from his time in Vail. He told me that Alison had suffered a severe asthma attack and was still in the hospital. She would be fine. She needed to rest for a few more days.

"Grab your bag and come stay at the Pazzo's house with me. We will go surfing tomorrow and hook up with Alison when she gets out of the hospital," he announced enthusiastically.

I thanked my new friends for their hospitality, told them I would be back when we started working, and headed to Pazzo's for a slice and a drink. It was a relief to know that Alison was going to be OK. Now I could turn my attention to the true underlying purpose of this two-month adventure: surfing.

The next two months in Cabo, I woke up between four and five in the morning, surfed until lunch, went to Pazzo's for a slice of pizza and a beer midafternoon, took a nap, then took photos at the Giggling Marlin until late, typically after midnight. The highlight reel from those two months in Cabo included Día de los Muertos parties that got entirely out of hand; double overhead waves at San Cerritos; driving our Land Rover Discovery through thigh-deep flooded streets; full-moon surfing at Missions; discovering my favorite right-hand point break; hiding from the Federales on an immigration raid; meeting pro surf legend Gerry Lopez at Zippers; and the introduction to a lifelong friend, StevieG. These experiences, without my knowledge at the time, set me up for decades of future fortunate accidents.

Being aware of the opportunities life's detours offered, I became aligned with like-minded people who pursued rich, diverse experiences rather than stable, steady careers. Not once was I asked, "What are you going to do with your life?"

Instead, I was asked questions like "Do you want to ride today?" "Where are we paddling?" "What are you doing tonight?"

Sometimes, that lifestyle made it tough to pay the bills. Somehow, I managed to make ends meet. Locals supporting locals; we helped each other out. Life was good.

Unexpected Opportunities

Have you ever met someone and known from the start they would play an influential role in your life? Meeting Steve, affectionately known as StevieG, felt so natural it is hard for me to detail.

In his mid-forties at the time, StevieG had recently retired from his career as an architect and was in the process of developing a new line of technical gear for surfers. He and his wife were in Cabo for a surf vacation so Steve could test and evaluate his new product line, Mysterioso.

I met him in the parking lot at Zippers, a surf break north of Cabo. I had finished my morning surf session and was headed back to town to hang out at Pazzo's before working my shift at the Giggling Marlin. I was sunbaked and filled with that post-session euphoric buzz of satisfaction that comes from pushing yourself past the point of exhaustion.

A guy wearing something that looked like a Hawaiian shirt climbed out of the car next to me, grabbed his surfboard, and walked past me toward the beach. Though many people wear T-shirts to keep the sun off their shoulders, his shirt was a little over the top. I could tell this guy had a fun sense of style.

"Hey man, you forgot your shirt," I commented, joking.

He turned around with a chuckle and said, "Naw man, it's my rashie."

"What?! That's a rash guard? It looks like a Hawaiian shirt."

Apparently, I made his day; he told me to give him a call when I got home, and he would send one my way to check out. In StevieG's words, "You were a grom with an energy about you that was unique. You made my day with that conversation."

True to his word, StevieG sent me some gear when he got back to the States. Throughout spring paddle season, I received several compliments on my new rash guard and board shorts.

A spark of inspiration prompted me to call StevieG a few months later. "You know, river people need a taste of surf style. The cultures are similar," I commented.

I then explained the missing link: "Raft guides sit on a rubber boat every day with the high-altitude sun baking their skin. We wear whatever we can to keep from getting scorched. Your rashies are rated SPF 50 and they look great. They will sell. Will you work out a deal if I put an order together?"

"Matty, I'll tell you what," StevieG replied. "I'll give your rafting buddies whatever they want at cost. You'll get your stuff free as part of the company team. And I'll pay you a commission for every kayak or white-water shop you open."[24]

"Really? Yes! That sounds awesome. I'll call the shop down the street right now, and we will get an order in next week."

StevieG chuckled. "No worries, Matty. I had a really good time meeting you down in Cabo. You've got a good vibe."

When we got off the phone, I immediately went down to the local kayak shop and talked to Mike Duffy, the store owner. I was a shop rat when I was not on the river or at work. He let me hang out and use his tools to customize the fit of my kayaks. When I was there, I helped him sell boats if he got busy. He was only about ten years older than me, yet, to this long-haired grom, he was an old man, and I reminded him of that daily.

"Mike, will you bring in something new to the shop?" I asked.

"Sure. What is it?"

"It's a friend of mine's company out of California. I met him last year in Mexico, and I think it will sell like crazy to the paddlers. Paddling gear is boring: it has no style. This has style AND it's SPF rated, so you can sell on that. Try it out, and if it sells, buy more. If it doesn't, we tried."

---

[24] Meaning every new dealer that would stock and sell his product as a result of my efforts. He was offering for me to be his sales representative.

Mike agreed and sold through three orders of rash guards and board shorts the first season.

At the rafting company where I worked, I told the guides we could get one order at cost. A week later, I called Steve with a pretty big order. Less than two weeks later, our whole company was decked out in new gear. When we went to place our second order, StevieG offered to make custom board shorts as a uniform for the company guides.

With a solid team of guides as brand influencers and a full-service kayak shop selling his products, StevieG's company was officially in the rafting and kayak industry. Meeting him in Mexico was a fortunate accident that introduced me to the hustle of being a sales representative and sponsored athlete in the outdoor industry.

The following winter, I was working in the ski shop with Paul, one of the assistant managers who worked part-time on the weekends and during the busy season. Paul owned SporTube, a manufacturing company that made hard cases for skis, allowing people to travel without their gear getting damaged. He needed some help in the office filling orders and opening new dealers. "Matt, do you want to give me a hand one or two days a week?"

"Sure. What do you need?"

"Come by the house tomorrow and I'll fill you in. It's easy work."

I started out packing boxes and filling orders for FedEx to pick up. After a little while, he showed me how to use his software to print the packing lists and shipping labels while he was on the phone with distributors and dealers all over the world. I was learning what it meant to be in the back office for a growing company.

The components of Paul's product were manufactured in a variety of places. Those individual pieces were shipped to a fulfillment center where the products were assembled, packaged, and shipped. Half of his garage was filled with warranty parts like screws, nuts, and wheels. He also had a few fully assembled units so we could fulfill smaller orders on the fly.

I was in a solid flow. Working in the ski shop four or five days a week, I took a four-hour lunch break to go snowboarding. I also worked for Paul one or two days a week. On powder days, he and I started work after lunch to snag a few morning powder runs. I topped it off with one night a week working security at a bar. I was hitting my stride with 100% work and 100% play.

One day in early January, Paul asked, "Hey Matt, do you want to go to SIA with me in March?" The Snowsports Industries America (SIA) show was the largest trade show for winter sports in the USA. I was stoked. SIA was held in Las Vegas, Nevada, and I had never been to Vegas before.

"Yes! Absolutely. I want to go. What about work at the ski shop?" I replied.

"Don't worry about that. I can pull a few strings," he said as he winked at me. We both knew he regularly helped the manager with scheduling. Paul would make it work. The guys in the shop were jealous, so I promised to bring back lots of swag.

We spent the next month immersed in trade show preparations between shifts at work. Paul educated me on the finer points of blackjack, which inspired me to get books on how to beat the dealer. My grandfather had taught me simple math by playing gin rummy, resulting in an affinity for cards. Playing in Vegas held great allure for a twenty-three-year-old.

We planned nine days in Vegas: two days to set up, five days for the trade show, then two days to tear down and come home. Setting up a trade show booth involved a lot of work. That is the kind of education you do not learn in school. Paul taught me skills like bribing the union workers to get our pallets first, building the booth from a sketchy set of instructions, polishing all the product in order to give the best impression possible, then making sure everything was secured in a way that would prevent someone from taking product out of the booth at a five-finger discount.

After long days of work, our nights were just as long. We ate dinner at eight or nine, then attended ski film premieres and parties thrown by manufacturers. Of course, a trip to Vegas would not be complete without a couple hours at the blackjack table before going to bed. Each day, we rallied for a full schedule of meetings and product presentations followed by the same nightly routine.

In addition to teaching me the fine art of blackjack and craps, Paul introduced me to the world of manufacturing, distribution, sales reps, and dealers. In short, he showed me what it takes to build a brand. We also spent time brainstorming designs for a snowboard case and working up marketing plans together.

I began to recognize the incredible series of circumstances that put me in the right place at the right time to learn about building a brand. I was not actively seeking that knowledge. Neither Paul nor StevieG were actively looking for me. It seemed that fate brought us together in a manner that benefitted both parties. I hustled, helped Paul and StevieG, and absorbed as much knowledge and experience as I could along the way. I had the opportunity to look behind the scenes of two grassroots business ventures and see how the machine worked.

At the end of the day, it was the people I met and the relationships I developed that ultimately shaped each subsequent fortunate accident. As time went on, it got easier to spot the patterns and smell the opportunities.

Excellence

Oftentimes, seeds planted in my childhood bore fruit in my adulthood. For example, the seed of a strong work ethic grew into a broad-reaching quest for excellence. As a child, I learned to do a job and do it well. As an adult, I applied that principle to every area of my life. I did not participate in recreational activities like skiing and kayaking as a casual pastime. Whether it was a mountain or a river, I approached each run, stroke, turn, or maneuver with the intention of excellence.

At the start of my second summer in Colorado, I was enjoying a daily sunset kayak surf session with Billy and Matty, two people with whom I spent most hours on the river in those days. The wave we were surfing in

Eagle-Vail was only surfable during a short window created by spring runoff. A dozen kayakers were stacked in the eddy, waiting for their turn to surf the wave.

Billy and I were off to the side, and Billy said, "Matt, see how many strokes it took that guy to get up the eddy?"

"Yeah," came my reply.

"Good paddlers use the water and don't waste strokes. Watch."

Billy covered a distance that had taken the other paddler fifteen strokes in three graceful, powerful strokes. After we both cycled through the lineup and were at the bottom of the eddy, Billy said, "The best paddlers make it look easy, and you can't tell how much work they are doing." I was determined to be the best and made it a mission to use as few paddle strokes as possible on the water.

My focus shifted from making it to the bottom of a run in one piece to making it to the bottom of the run as gracefully and with as much intention as possible. I became aware of myself in the water and how I used the paddle, the position of my boat, and the power of the water. I would kayak a Class IV section backward—ferrying backward, catching eddies backward—just to see the run from a different perspective.

Some days I would float down a Class III or IV section without paddling to feel how the water's flow directed the boat and how shifting my body weight affected the journey. It became a game I would play alone to take the fewest strokes possible. If I dropped into a hole, I would brace and climb my way out of it. If I came to a rock, I would lean into it. If I got stuck in an eddy line, I would use the angle of my paddle blade to get back into the current as opposed to taking a full paddle stroke. All of these exercises enabled me to observe the river's dynamics, cultivating a newfound awareness of the river.

By the end of the summer, I was ready to kayak my first Class V[25] section of white water. Billy, Matty, and I, with a group of other raft guides

---

[25] Class V is for experts only. Highest level of commercially navigable difficulty: risk of injury or death.

on a training run, headed to Gore Canyon. Gore Canyon is widely regarded as one of the most iconic Class IV–V sections of white water in Colorado. It requires strength, stamina, and high-level boating skills to navigate the river's many obstacles. The Gore Canyon put-in is located at the confluence of the Blue River and the Colorado River, near Kremmling, Colorado. It is absolute flat water for the first three miles, before entering the main canyon.

As we floated down the flat-water section, taking in the scenery, Billy said, "Hey, Matt! Can you do this?" He stopped paddling and stuck his blade in the water just in front of his hip. His boat kept moving forward as he slipped sideways about five feet.

I was dumbfounded. "How'd you do that?!"

"It's called a duffek. You use the angle of your paddle blade to steer the boat."

A bend in the river created an eddy just above the mouth of the canyon. Billy said, "Watch this." With that, he stuck his paddle blade in the eddy line and effortlessly spun his boat 180° around his paddle into the eddy, smooth as silk. "Catch the current of the eddy with your power face, lean into the turn as you edge your boat, and let the water do the work for you."

I was in awe. Billy, master of grace on water, just taught me another fundamental skill of kayaking.

As we entered Gore Canyon, I practiced allowing the river's energy to ferry me across the river effortlessly. After the long flat-water section, the Colorado River has a short series of Class III rapids before hitting Fisherman's Nightmare, a quick Class IV rapid. Fisherman's is historically regarded as a dangerous section of Gore Canyon because fishing boats would accidentally drift into a gnarly pile of rocks on the left side of the river. The true line was on the right, which I blasted through with ease, calming my nerves and setting us up for a fun day.

We scouted our line through Gore Rapid. We also scouted Scissors and Pyrite Falls, two Class IV sections that come up quickly after Gore

Rapid. The line through Gore Rapid was clear, and I made a mental note to avoid a treacherous hole in the middle of Scissors, then work my way left to set up for Pyrite.

Pyrite Falls precedes a series of super fun Class III and IV rapids before Tunnel Falls. Billy and Matty took the opportunity to show me the nuances and knowledge required to be a safety kayaker for the canyon. I explored various boofs[26] and fun creek lines. We were having fun.

We ran Tunnel Falls in a Blue Angels succession, using the wave above the falls to set up our boof, landing one after another in the calm water below.

The next rapid, Toilet Bowl, was a low-head dam-style Class IV rapid. The river is wider, so not as pushy as some of the other rapids. It is, however, possibly the most treacherous drop of the canyon, as there is a twenty-foot boil line below the river-wide hydraulic. This meant that if I did not paddle hard, the hydraulic would suck me back into a recirculating hole.

Gore Canyon ends with Kirshbaum, a long, rewarding Class IV section that left me grinning from ear to ear.

Successfully running Gore Canyon was a benchmark in my paddling experience. Being conservative with my paddle strokes, using the river's energy rather than brute force to navigate, I accomplished more than "surviving" the run. I enjoyed it. I had fun. It was electrifying and exhilarating, not terrifying. Running Gore Canyon expanded my resume as a kayaker as well. This trip gave me the confidence and experience to go to West Virginia. The following fall, I traveled east with my friend Mather to video and safety boat on the Gauley River: a choice that yielded years of seasonal work on the rivers in West Virginia and built friendships that lasted a lifetime.

What's the point? Why does excellence matter? More importantly, what does excellence have to do with fortunate accidents? Answer:

---

[26] A powerful stroke and hip thrust off the lip of a waterfall, flake, or rock, projecting the boat forward and flat.

everything. Ninety-nine percent of my kayaking opportunities would not have happened without an unrelenting quest to improve my skills. I was able to hang with an elite group of kayakers who shared a skill level only a handful of kayakers possess. Excellence opened doors. Ultimately, it provided employment and invitations for adventure. Excellence paved the path for fortunate accidents, both on and off the water.

Sphere of Awareness

During my rookie season as a raft guide, I approached rafting with the same attitude and discipline required to play football. If I wanted to be the best, I needed to learn from the best. Every day, I polished my guiding skills by mirroring the actions of the top guides. I asked questions, striving to learn everything I could about the river and how it behaved at different flow levels.

When we were not training or working raft trips, Tom, Matty, Billy, Rob, and I were on the river kayaking. They were all senior rafting guides. Our shared passion for river life quickly blossomed into friendship. They helped me better understand the skill of reading water, letting the river's power work to my benefit rather than fighting to get where I wanted to be. Time spent on the river applying kayaking skills to rafting helped to fast-track my status from rookie to professional. One day, I was reminded what it meant to be a rookie and was taught the value of awareness.

Spring is the high season for rafting in Colorado. That winter's ski season yielded a deep snowpack, which meant the spring runoff was higher and lasted longer than most years. A typically easy Class II–III run, filled by rookie guides, was now a swollen, pushy river. That year, the challenging river conditions relegated most first-year guides to shuttle driving and equipment cleaning.

Every trip was sold out and all the senior guides were booked, so I was scheduled to work as a guide, with my fellow rookies stuck driving the shuttle. Being scheduled to guide the trip was a privilege, and my co-workers were eager to see me succeed. This would be my first official white-water trip with a boat full of clients.

My fellow guides clapped me on the back as I headed out the door. "You've got this, Matt!" "Don't worry. You'll do great!"

We got the rafts staged, and once the forty tourists were divided into groups, my group walked over to me, leaned against my raft.

"Hi. My name is Matt and I'll be your guide today." I could feel my heart throbbing in my neck as I went through my on-shore safety talk with the eager group of clients. Looking each of them in the eye, I felt the weight of responsibility resting heavily on my shoulders.

"This is my first time guiding a commercial trip, so I really need us to work together—as a team—so that we can get down to the take-out together, warm, smiling, and happy." The smile faded from a couple faces. Others looked at each other and then back at me nervously.

I could read the questions on their faces: He's joking, right? This isn't really his first trip . . .

I am a believer in exploding the bomb up front. It would be much worse if they discovered that this was my first trip and I was not the one to tell them.

To break the tension, I started my safety presentation with a popular joke among rafting guides: "This is your paddle. It's not an oar—that's a promiscuous woman in England or the name of a bar in Vail."

Gripping the paddle with both hands, I raised it over my head and continued, "When I hold it like this, notice my hands are placed shoulder width apart: one hand on the T-grip and the other on the shaft." I paused for effect, then continued.

"It is key that you never let go of the T-grip, even if you are swimming in the water. If you do," I let go and swung the T-grip end of the paddle in a semicircle in front of me, "it doesn't allow you to have a strong grip on the paddle. Additionally, if it slips and hits your neighbor in the face, you could give them summer teeth."

I stopped and looked at my eight-person crew. Within predictable seconds, someone asked, "What are summer teeth?"

I looked her in the eyes as I answered, straight-faced, "Summer in their mouth, and summer in the water."

I received the anticipated eye rolls and laughter. I began to relax. This was going to be easy. Yes, this was my first commercial raft trip. Yes, the water was high and it was going to be fun. I had been kayaking and rafting this section of the river almost every day. My crew was doing a good job of listening and taking instruction well. Today was going to be a good day.

Being a rafting guide was a balancing act. Clients needed a certain amount of safety information to be conveyed in a way that would not scare them off the water or make the experience unpleasant. I sprinkled lighthearted jokes into my pre-paddle instruction. Reviewing paddle commands and worst-case scenarios, I worked to learn the names of everyone in the group. When the lesson was complete, we lifted the raft as a team and walked it down to the river.

We slid the raft into the water and practiced forward, back, left, and right, until the crew was able to work together as a team to propel the raft quickly and efficiently. We also practiced jumping from one side of the raft to the other, in case we hit a rock sideways or were side-surfing in a hole. Our crew learned that jumping to the high side of the raft could help to prevent flipping.

We had five rafts, including mine, running that section of the river that day. The trip leader would lead the first boat, and the most medically experienced guide would run sweep at the end of the line. The lead boat would set the pace, and the sweep boat would make sure everyone in the middle was keeping up with the pace. Our trips ran smoothly and efficiently, as the less-experienced guides were supported by more experienced guides to the front and rear of the procession. On this particular trip, I was fourth in line.

I was late getting my boat headed downriver. A whistle blew while I was in the midst of practicing safety drills with my new crew, and I realized the sweep boat was already downstream. The other four guides were lifting paddles vertically in the air, signaling, "All ahead, let's get the show on the road, er, river."

We eddied out above the first major rapid. That run was normally categorized as Class II with four Class III rapids. On that day, the gauge was reading more than twelve inches higher than normal flows for a rookie to be guiding. Higher water levels meant the river was pushier, the waves were bigger, the hydraulics were more prevalent, and the consequence of an error was much steeper. The typical Class III rapids would be pushing Class III+ or IV.

Guides reviewed safety reminders, crew members got focused, and all eyes were on the lead boat as it peeled out of the eddy and headed downstream. We lost sight of the lead boat as it rounded a corner fifty yards downstream. The second boat took off, setting up early for a successful line. The third boat peeled out, and my crew was silent, picking up on my intensity and focus. Then it was my turn. I was up. Making eye contact with the sweep boat's guide, I was reassured by his smile as he gave me a nod and mouthed, "You got this."

I called commands to my crew while maneuvering the raft into the stream's current. Focusing on the wave right in front of me, I was intent on approaching the wave with a left-hand angle. By setting the raft at a ten o'clock angle, I could use the lateral waves to help set the proper angle for the next lateral.

I heard three whistle blasts in rapid succession echoing through the canyon—tweet-tweet-tweet—signaling an emergency. Swimmer in the water. My attention shifted from the wave in front of me to the chaos taking place downstream. The boat in front of me had flipped on a huge breaking wave. As a result, eight clients were swimming a Class III+ rapid with their guide kneeling on top of their overturned raft.

I sat upright, at full attention; my alert status went from yellow to red. I was choking back panic. My crew picked up on this sudden change in their guide's demeanor, doubt and fear displayed on their faces. The synchronicity and rhythm we had practiced at the put-in was lost.

Sensing my stress, some clients froze, unable to follow my directives. Others went into overdrive, paddling for their lives. We were quickly off balance. I tried to steer the boat into position to assist the flipped raft. As a result, my own raft ended up floating sideways above a fourteen-foot-wide hydraulic at the bottom of the rapid. This obstacle was considered the mandatory feature to avoid and was fairly easy to avoid at lower flow. Our training drills were completely forgotten: my crew was in a state of panic.

"JUMP LEFT! JUMP LEFT! HIGH SIDE!" I yelled at the top of my lungs. Two of the eight people in my raft jumped left. The rest fell to the floor in a huddle. I was in the stern of the raft, fighting against the river's pull with the biggest draw stroke of my life. Our raft catapulted into the air, and seven of the eight clients found themselves swimming in thirty-four-degree water.

With my raft's single remaining client, a sixteen-year-old girl, and me sitting on the high side, my draw stroke was strong enough to pull the raft free of the hole. Then it was time to get to work. I jumped to the middle of the raft, calling paddle commands, and she listened. The two of us paddled to the closest swimmer. I gave the swimmer my T-grip and pulled him into the raft. I threw my rope to another client floating nearby. Once she was safely aboard, the four of us paddled to the closest eddy, about half a mile further downstream.

One by one, all the clients from both rafts were retrieved. The trip leader checked for injuries and did a head count to make sure everyone was accounted for. Taking a deep breath, guides and crew members collected their wits. The senior guides made eye contact with me, offering unspoken support. They had all been there and could relate. Bearing the weight of responsibility for clients in the water is enough to rattle the most seasoned guide.

Continuing down the river, I talked with my crew about what had happened. Raft guides were trained to never apologize for a flip or swim on the river. I was also careful not to blame my crew for what had happened. After all, I worked for tips! An adversarial approach rarely puts money in the pocket. We were a team, sharing in successes and failures.

I was proud to note that every client followed safety protocol once they hit the water. They kept their feet up and downstream while swimming to the closest raft, instead of trying to stand in the river. By keeping their feet up, my clients avoided the risk of getting a foot trapped in the rocks, leaving them pinned in the fast-moving water. Nobody was injured. We all had smiles on our faces. We congratulated ourselves for being in a better position than the raft in front of us. The rest of the trip was flawless, and everyone went home with a great story to tell friends and family.

At the end of the trip, guests were dropped at their respective hotels, and the guides went back to the boathouse to unload, wash gear, and debrief. Once the guests were gone, my game face came off. I was deflated. I felt like a failure. I felt that I let everyone down.

The senior guides walked me through the sequence of events, offering suggestions for improvement. They provided positive feedback on recovery efforts and on the rest of the trip. The company owner ordered that all rookie guides be relegated to shuttle driving for another week, until the water dropped to a lower level. Though some of the newer guides resented the fact that my mistake cost them time on the water, most of my fellow guides just gave me a load of crap.

I learned a very important lesson that day, one I shared while training new guides the following season. As one of the senior guides explained, "A rookie raft guide's sphere of awareness extends to the borders of his raft. That is all he is able to focus on, and it maxes out his field of view in such a way that he is reactive to anything outside that sphere. As that rookie becomes a second-year guide, he might remain actively aware of his own raft plus the raft in front and behind him. With experience, that same raft guide can be aware and mentally prepared for every raft on the trip. He fully embraces the trip beginning to end as he loads up the trailers in the morning. He is mindful of his actions and can anticipate the actions of his co-workers and clients in real time without having to react to an unexpected circumstance."

My role with the rafting company evolved, and kayaking was becoming second nature. I knew I wanted to be a safety kayaker. I would get more work, which equaled more income, and I would be getting paid to do what I loved—kayak. I needed to qualify as a guide on every section we worked and show that I was a proficient Class V kayaker. My ability then needed to be approved by one of the senior safety kayakers.

Fortunately, I was surrounded by great friends and leaders. Becoming a safety kayaker, I learned to extend my sphere of awareness to include myself, the crew of each raft, and each guide. I needed to have a plan in the event a trip member was in need of assistance. I also needed to be able to step onto a raft if one of the guides was injured or worse. I had to be able to act intuitively, freeing me to direct the actions of others. I had to be mindful of myself and everything within my sphere of awareness, with the intent of executing the task at hand with grace and style.

I continued to work as a safety kayaker and rafting guide while taking side jobs as a sales rep or photographer or working security in bars over the next five years. I spent summers kayaking as much as possible while raft guiding and working in bars. For three months, during the fall seasons, I worked as a safety kayaker and video kayaker on the Gauley River in West Virginia. My kayaking improved enough and my involvement in the industry had me active enough that Dagger Kayaks invited me to join their pro team. In the winters, I worked in the ski shop and tended bar on weekends

Application: Awareness of Yourself

This chapter offered some insight into my life and shared some of the experiences that contributed to the awareness of myself and the world around me. How are you able to relate to these lessons in your own life?

1. What key words describe awareness?
2. What is the difference between awareness and self-awareness?
3. How has your family helped to shape your values?
4. Have you ever made a decision that was contrary to a parent's or superior's wishes for you?
5. What was that decision, and what was the outcome?

MINDFULNESS

A pattern began to emerge. Rather than taking the career path others expected me to take, I gravitated toward opportunities that led to new, unique experiences and allowed the flexibility to master my skills in both snow and water sports. My chosen path, while financially poor, was experience rich. Truth-seeking endeavors in my youth continued into my adulthood. I never stopped asking questions.

I was becoming both self-aware and externally aware of the flow of energy. I made many mistakes. Those mistakes fueled a passion to do better, climb harder, dig deeper, and become more than I was before.

Mindfulness played a central role in my work as a guide and safety kayaker for rafting companies, an emergency medical technician (EMT), and eventually as an instructor in both fields. Though some people associate mindfulness with breathing exercises or yoga retreats, my lessons in mindfulness emerged from daily experiences on and off the water. These lessons taught me to expand my awareness, acting with precision and intentionality.

Adventure

Every day on the river was a perfect day; however, not all river runs were perfect. I started kayaking season early my third year in Colorado. I paddled Barrel Springs and Shoshone on sunny days in February and March during four-hour lunch breaks when working at the ski shop.

By the time spring runoff arrived, kayaking muscles were toned and paddling skills were polished. Successful runs on Gore Canyon and Barrel Springs boosted my confidence, and I wanted to push the envelope a little more.

Creeking, a type of kayaking that involves descending very steep, often narrow, low-volume sections of water, was my next step. I thought Homestake Creek would be a good introduction. Word to the wise: Homestake Creek at 350 CFS was big and pushy. It was somewhat forgiving, yet probably not a "starting point" by any stretch of the imagination. Homestake Creek's short, precipitous descent drops over 120 feet in a quarter mile. Compounded with the volume of water cascading down the narrow slot from spring snowmelt, this short run was a high-speed test of my reflexes and ability to read water on the fly.

Arriving at the put-in, I was jittery and checked to see if I could spit. Check. OK, I was nervous, not frozen. Climbing into my boat, I went through my ritual: check gear, mentally review the safety list, and kiss my bow. I slid into the current and was immediately swept downstream.

My start on the run was anything but graceful. I muscled my way to the main flow, approaching the introductory rapid and struggling to keep from getting pushed into the right bank. Missing my boof, I melted down the first four-foot falls and surfaced upside down in the pool below. I did my roll and looked over to see Bill and Matty grinning ear to ear. Phew. First drop complete.

My nerves were settled. *Take a deep breath, and just take them as they come, one at a time,* I told myself. As I visualized the next few rapids in sequence, I reminded myself, *Focus.*

The next three rapids were pool-drop, meaning, there's a calm pool, then a vertical drop into another calm pool. The second-to-last drop, called Leap of Faith, was the biggest. It is a shoulder-wide entrance protected by a fin-shaped rock that leads into an eight-to-ten-foot waterfall. After Leap of Faith, I would eddy out and set up for the last rapid of the run, called

Piece of Shit. Cluttered with sharp rocks, as well as railroad and mining debris, it is manky[27] and has earned its name.

Compartmentalizing each drop made the run mentally attainable. I was no longer thinking about the entire run. I visualized the next paddle stroke and the next drop, taking them one at a time. I was able to bounce back after missing the first drop by slowing my mind, clearing extraneous thoughts, and maintaining focus. Executing one move at a time created space for awareness and mindfulness.

One year later, when spring runoff arrived, Homestake was running at about half the volume of my introduction. Paul, a friend and fellow paddler, set up on the right bank, just below Leap of Faith, to get photos of us as we paddled down. In a twist of fate, my bow got hung up on the fin rock above the drop, and my boat stopped abruptly midstream. Even at the lower water level, the force of the river's current spun my kayak 180°, leaving me backward two feet above the lip of the falls. In an instant, I adjusted to the boat's new trajectory, taking a huge boof stroke backward off the drop. The boat sailed over the drop, coming to a near-flat landing with my back facing downstream. Exhilarated by the perfectly executed adjustment, I looked over at Paul with my fist in the air and saw him clicking away.

After the warm-up on Homestake Creek, as we worked our way into Gilman Gorge, Paul, Hobie, Vierling, and I cooked up the idea of running a kayak race. It would be a three-part series. We would start the event with a race down Homestake, then move to a race through Gilman Gorge, and finish with a freestyle competition at the bottom of Dowd Chute.

We referred to it as the "non-event" series since there were no permits from the Forest Service to host a formal event on public lands. Our "non-event" was hosted by "nobody." Paul's photo of me coming off Leap of Faith backward was featured on the flyer advertising the race. Flyers were distributed around town and announced on various online boater forums.

---

[27] A very rocky or unappealing section of technical rapids.

Our Homestake Creek non-event was a success. The promoters for the Mountain Games in Vail, a large televised event featuring outdoor mountain sports, adopted the Homestake Creek race as a sanctioned Mountain Games event. The Forest Service began looking for the people responsible for the original event, but it was years before we fessed up to the fact that we were the ones who had started the Homestake Creek race series. By that time, we had a proven track record for safety and conservation, so the Forest Service was no longer concerned.

Many of those early kayaking forays set the stage, cast, and crew for future kayaking adventures. At the time, we were just pushing boundaries and having fun. I used the skills, knowledge, and mindfulness I learned while creeking to navigate other future endeavors.

Precision

Mindfulness required me to expand my sphere of awareness and act with precision. A new profession and new teachers set the stage for teaching these important lessons.

Living in the backcountry for both work and play, I became increasingly aware of potential risks. I decided to invest the time and energy to become an EMT. In addition to the pay increase as a raft guide, EMT training would provide the necessary skills that, in my mind, would play an integral role in safely pursuing my other various outdoor adventures. I studied for the EMT class during slow periods in the ski shop. My fellow co-workers and I often took extended lunch breaks to ski or kayak, and they quizzed me on EMT test material between runs or while driving shuttles.

Interestingly, I had near-perfect grades in my EMT class. In high school, I was an honor roll student because good grades were required to get into college. I was a mediocre student in college because I was taking classes to get a piece of paper, a degree, rather than working toward a specific goal or purpose. Attending classes to become an EMT, I grasped the purpose behind the course material, and I excelled. Medicine held my interest, and I was fully immersed.

One afternoon after ski season was over, I had a few hours to kill before EMT class. Some friends and I decided to kayak Gilman Gorge, a Class IV–V run just south of Minturn, near Vail, Colorado. At the put-in, I said, "Just a reminder, I have to be off the river by five for class."

A friend, Jason, asked, "What class are you taking?"

"It's an EMT class in Edwards. We have the National Registry practical and written exams this week."

"That's awesome. What are you going to do with it?"

"For work with the rafting company. We get an extra ten dollars per trip if we have our EMT cert. Plus, with everything we do in the backcountry, I want to know what to do if something goes wrong."

We geared up, excited to get on the water. It was spring and all the rivers were running fast, putting everyone in a good mood. It was amazing to have technical white water like this in our backyard! About a mile or two downstream, enjoying the beauty of Gilman Gorge, Jason paddled up next to me and asked, "Have you ever thought about working on the ambulance?"

I laughed and said, "Huh? No. I'm just getting my EMT cert for work."

"I'm a paramedic on the ambulance, and we need to hire some EMTs. You would be good at it." Jason and I worked for competing rafting companies. Sometimes, the company he worked with contracted me to safety kayak their trips when short-staffed. He and I had spent countless days and hours on the river for work and fun.

"I don't know if I want to be stuck in a box for work. I'm having fun rafting and kayaking."

"You can still do that. The hours are flexible. We are doing interviews next week. It doesn't hurt to apply. Think about it."

After an invigorating run through Gilman, I booked it to class. Upon arrival, I hung my wet paddling gear off the truck's roof rack before heading inside. I put on a fresh shirt and walked into class with ten minutes to spare. My instructors and classmates, most of whom worked for the fire or ambulance districts, were used to seeing wet gear hanging off my truck and my shoulder-blade-length hair pulled back into a ponytail, dripping water onto the back of my shirt.

Sitting down, one of my classmates asked how the kayak session went. I said it was great and told him about my conversation with Jason.

"Do it," he replied. "I am buying an ambulance service in Jamaica. Get a year of experience under your belt, and I'll fly you down to Jamaica to help run my company."

"Jamaica? Are you kidding me? What don't you do?!" I knew he was a volunteer firefighter, which was the reason he was taking this EMT class. He ran a construction company and had other side hustles as well. He wore more hats than I did.

"I took a trip to Jamaica last year and discovered that emergency services are limited. I'm buying the ambulance company with a friend who lives down there. We want to improve the system so the locals have better access to medical care."

"That sounds awesome. OK. I'll think about it."

I passed my EMT exams, and in the words of our instructor, I was now "licensed to learn more medicine." That statement made a timeless point: the more I learned, the more I found I needed to learn.

Two weeks later, just as I got off the river, I got a phone call from Jason.

"Matt, where are you?"

"I'm at the take-out for the Chute. I just got off the river. What's up?"

"Get down to Eagle right now. We are doing interviews today, and I convinced them to squeeze you in."

Between kayaking and working at the raft company, I had totally forgotten about applying to work on the ambulance. "I haven't even filled out an application yet," I replied.

"Doesn't matter. Get down here. I'll tell them you'll be here in an hour."

With that, I jumped into my truck—shirtless, shoeless, wearing wet board shorts—and drove down to the ambulance station. Fortunately, I was living out of my truck, so my belongings were with me at all times. In the parking lot, I rummaged through my clothes to find a clean pair of pants and a collared shirt. Pulling my hair into a biker braid, I tucked the braid inside my shirt collar and walked into the station for my interview.

Jason met me at the door and told me I was just in time. He prepared me for some of the questions that Tom, the district manager, might ask. Forty-five minutes later, I took a deep breath, climbed back into my truck, and wondered what just happened.

One week later, I was handed a uniform and scheduled to work the following day. I was ready for my first major lesson in mindfulness: one that would require me to slow down, expand my sphere of awareness, and act with precision.

The ambulance station's 9-1-1 alarm reverberated through the building. It was my first call as an EMT. I sprang to my feet and launched myself into the driver's seat faster than Jason could put on his shoes.

Everything felt like it was happening in slow motion. Garage doors were opened, lights and sirens were turned on, and we were finally on our way. We were called to the scene of an MVI (motor vehicle incident) on I-70, the major interstate corridor running through the valley. As we pulled onto the interstate, Jason and I ran through scenarios of what we might find at the scene, anticipating what we would need upon arrival. We pieced together facts from the dispatch call, understanding that 9-1-1 calls often contain incorrect or misleading information. We established roles and attempted to identify what equipment might be needed.

At the scene, we found a single car, upside down in the median of the interstate. State patrol and the sheriff's office were directing traffic as Jason and I pulled up just before the fire department.[28] I opened my door and ran to the back of the ambulance to grab the equipment. Jason slowly got out of the ambulance and told me to stop. I looked at him and said, "What?"

Jason said, "Matt, untuck your shirt, tuck it back in, then walk over to me at the vehicle. The fire guys can grab the backboard."

"Really?"

"Yes. Really. Untuck it. Tuck it back in. Then, walk over to me."

I did as he instructed. As I stood on the side of the interstate, with cars zipping by, I untucked my shirt, tucked it back in, then looked around for Jason. He was already standing by the overturned car, giving direction to the firefighters.

Jason watched me approach. "Good. Are you slowed down now?"

"Yeah. What was that all about?"

"I'll tell you later. For now, help the fire guys backboard our patient and get her loaded into the ambulance. You drive. We are taking her to the hospital in Vail."

We were about half an hour from the hospital. I listened to Jason in the back talking to our patient. After dropping her at the hospital and giving the accident report, we made the thirty-five-minute drive back to the ambulance station. All the while, I was wondering why Jason had been so concerned about how my shirt looked when we arrived at the scene of the accident.

Finally, I could not stand it any longer. "Jason, what was the point of that?"

"Of what?"

"The whole tucking-my-shirt-in thing!"

"You were jacked up on epi.[29] I wanted you to slow down, to be more mindful."

---

[28] The fire and ambulance districts operated as separate agencies, not under one umbrella as they do in many major cities.

[29] Short for epinephrine, also known as adrenaline: a hormone that is secreted by the adrenal glands to provide energy so that the major muscles of the body can respond when triggered into a fight-or-flight response.

"What do you mean?"

"It's your first 9-1-1 call. I get it. I just wanted you to take a step back and slow down. There is a lot to think about and do. It's safer and easier if you can slow down the pace. Be precise in your actions. You don't want to miss details, and you are less likely to get hurt. Less likely to kill a patient, too."

"Oh. I didn't think I was going that fast."

Laughing, Jason said, "Yeah, buddy. You were moving pretty fast. It's OK. It was your first call. What do you think?"

That was the first of many post-call debriefings, where Jason and I discussed what went right, what went wrong, and what lessons could be learned. My analytical mind was hooked, absorbing every detail that would contribute toward making me a better EMT. Precision in thought led to precision in action. This became central to my lessons and discoveries in mindfulness.

I soon found the true meaning behind having a license to learn. As an EMT-Basic, I was limited in the skills I could perform. However, there was no limit to the knowledge I could possess. The more I knew, the more I was able to be aware of my patients' conditions, recognizing and anticipating their needs more efficiently.

Jason took it one step further, informing me that we were practitioners. We practiced medicine. We needed to learn as much as we could, growing our skill with each call. Coupling awareness with a mindful practice provided a better outcome for our patients and a safer environment for us and our co-workers.

During my shifts working on the ambulance, I spent hours of downtime learning more medicine, acquiring new skills, and writing short essays for Jason and the doctors mentoring my growth in medicine. I read wilderness medicine books cover to cover, multiple times. Jason and I studied and reviewed calls. We planned kayak and surf trips, shaped new surfboards, and dreamed of traveling to far-flung parts of the globe, adding fuel to the fire of our pipe dreams.

Building on previous lessons in awareness, I made an interesting self-discovery. It was easy for me to excel at things that held my interest. I was a natural student. I craved knowledge in subjects I found interesting. Whether it was football, philosophy, kayaking, or medicine, my natural state of being was one of mindfulness. I cultivated precision in thought, word, and action in these activities.

I practiced the art of slowing down at work, on the river, and in day-to-day life. The summer passed quickly. I was a sponge, soaking up every bit of knowledge in my new profession.

Living at an ambulance station for twenty-four-hour periods, while exhausting, had its benefits. For one, I was living in my truck to save money, so it was nice to have a bed and shower at the station. Additionally, a full-time schedule consisted of ten twenty-four-hour shifts. Though I was technically a part-time employee, I was working full-time shifts. That still left twenty days off each month for guiding rafting trips and kayaking.

For the previous five years, I had spent the fall off-season in West Virginia, working Gauley Season. The year I started working on the ambulance, I knew it would be my last year working the Gauley. I worked extra shifts leading up to my departure to justify the time off. My co-workers understood how important kayaking and raft guiding was for me, so they accommodated my extra work and request for the time off. The ambulance staff was composed of outdoors people—raft guides, ski patrollers, climbers, kayakers, and fly fishermen. We gravitated toward work that created space for backcountry adventure and worked collectively to allow flexibility for each other to pursue various passions.

Stay the Course

The week before I left for West Virginia, the annual Gore Canyon raft and kayak race was scheduled to take place. Some friends, and fellow guides from West Virginia, came out to join the race. They needed a paddler with knowledge of the canyon to guide a race team. When asked if I would be their guide for the race, I said, "Sure."

We took a practice run the day before the race. Unbeknownst to us, the captain of our team hurt his shoulder during the practice run. Amidst the pre-race festivities the night before the race, he let us know he would not be joining us the next day.

The next morning, waking up to the rising sun and the realization we were one paddler short for the race, we were faced with the prospect of paddling the raft with a crew of five instead of six. I scoured the camp for a willing candidate to replace our injured team member. Among the partiers, racers, and onlookers, I spotted my friend Julie. She was a personal trainer and an athlete, and she was always upbeat and positive. I knew she would be up for an adventure.

"Julie, you're racing with us today. Go get your gear."

"What?! I've never even paddled Gore Canyon before. I certainly can't race it."

"You don't have to do a thing except listen. I'm your guide. Just paddle when I say and stay in sync. You've got rhythm, you're in shape, and you're a badass. You can do this."

"Matt. I can't. It's scary there."

"Julie. You can. You're in good hands. Grab your stuff and meet us at the boat. We're about to drive up."

Julie hesitated for a moment, then decisively said, "OK. I'm coming."

"Yes!!" I responded.

That was easy, I thought to myself. *I better not screw this up.*

After hugs and high fives, I went to tell the rest of the team we were in business.

We spent the three miles of flat water getting our team in sync. Five of us were guides and kayakers, so we took turns bringing Julie up to speed on water safety, paddling techniques, and commands I would be calling out during the race. We reviewed our lines and strategy for each set of rapids. We were ready.

Our biggest threat was Team USA, the current world champions, victors of the previous few years of Gore Canyon races. Their crew was composed of fellow guides, friends, and cohorts. I had occasionally filled in as an alternate on their team. That day, I was not racing for Team USA; I was on a mission to beat them.

Teams were released at one-minute intervals. Timekeepers were placed at both the starting line and finish line and would sync data at the end of the race. We were a, mostly, focused six-person team as we staged at the starting line. Julie was giggling and smiling through her nervous tension, providing much-needed levity. The starting horn sounded. We were off. I called commands to help our team function in unison and made minor adjustment strokes to maintain our line downstream.

We aced Fisherman's and Gore rapids. We were fast. I made a last-minute decision to cut a tight line through Scissors to shave off a few seconds. That minor adjustment put us right over the top of the pour over. We landed square and everyone kept paddling. The soft water behind the pour over stalled us for seconds that felt like minutes. Dammit. I was pissed.

"We didn't flip. We are good," Dave hollered with a grin, giving me a wink. Rather than allowing the setback to deter us, we stayed the course. We dug deep, paddled in unison, and got back into the current. Our team was strong and our lines were tight. We were fast. Our raft cleaned every rapid. We all leaned backward off the raft as we crossed the finish line, exhausted from twenty-plus minutes of paddling with all our strength through Class III, IV, and V white water. Our West Virginia friends told Julie this was nothing compared to the sixty minutes it took for the nine-mile Upper Gauley race. Still, we were whupped from giving it every ounce of energy we had.

The US Team beat us by sixteen seconds. I shouldered the blame for my adjustment at Scissors, even though the rest of the team did not care. We got beat by the world champions with a team that was finalized the day of the race. Mindful of maintaining positive attitudes, we chose to stay the course, finishing the race with our heads held high.

Twenty years later, Julie and I still talked about that day. She gave our team the positive spirit we needed, and we gave her an experience of a lifetime. She said she had been back to Gore since then, but it never held the same excitement or energy as that first race down the canyon.

Jeff, a white-water legend I met at the campground during the race weekend, invited me to stop by his house in Pennsylvania on my way to the Gauley in West Virginia.

"Sure, that would be awesome," I replied.

When I got to Pennsylvania, Jeff taught me how to re-glass my paddle, we swung from the biggest rope swing I had ever seen, and we kayaked laps over the waterfall at Ohiopyle State Park. While staying with Jeff, I saw a picture of a labyrinth on his coffee table with an explanation of its meaning.

The notecard on the table next to the image read, "The labyrinth is viewed as a metaphor for life's journey. It offers lessons as we walk the path. Walking the labyrinth can assist in addressing challenges. Utilizing meditation and prayer, the labyrinth offers peace and serenity. The moment we stop trying to conquer the labyrinth of life and simply inhabit it, we realize it was designed to hold us safe as we explore what feels dangerous. We see that we're exactly where we're meant to be, meandering along a crooked path that is meant to lead not onward, but inward."[30]

I was mesmerized. I could not get the image of the labyrinth out of my head. The message resonated within me. Life is short. I needed a reminder to stay the course, living life to its fullest, no matter what challenge came my way.

---

[30] While the use of the labyrinth as symbolism for life has been noted in Greek, Native American, Christian, and many other civilizations going back millennia, the author of this excerpt is unknown.

When I returned to Colorado after Gauley Season, I went to the tattoo shop and got a labyrinth tattooed on my shoulder. The labyrinth was my reminder to be mindful and stay the course. Little did I know how the labyrinth would soon come to symbolize the infuriating twists and turns life can take while pursuing a goal.

The second thing I did upon my return to Colorado was to let the ski shop know I was going to work on the ambulance full-time. Ten days of work each month provided twenty days to snowboard, ski, and kayak. It was a dream schedule. The ski shop was supportive of my decision, and I agreed to stay on with them part-time for the winter. I also kept working part-time with Paul at SporTube, helping him at the SIA show in Las Vegas, and I worked security at one of the bars on weekends. I was hustling for work so I could maximize my play.

Challenged

The Colorado Rockies received an average snowfall that next winter, providing great conditions for learning to tele-ski, though I pulled my snowboard out for powder days. On days when I was feeling particularly adventurous, I would get a snowmobile to tow me into the backcountry for powder descents on virgin snow.

I had become a proficient enough telemark skier that I could ski almost anything, minus dropping off cliffs or cornices. On a classic Colorado bluebird day that March, I was with a group of five friends, and we were having a blast. My friend Angela came up from Denver to ski with us. We must have done fourteen top-to-bottom runs, through moguls and trees, hitting all of our favorite spots. We were toast. My legs were shaking. It was time for a beer.

Angela asked if I would ski with her to get her car. We needed to take three more runs to get to Angela's car, which was parked on the other side of the mountain. My intuition went on full alert, whispering in my head, *No. Don't do it. Your legs are toast.*

"I don't know, Angela. I can barely stand up," I replied.

"C'mon, Matt, it's just a couple of runs. We will go fast." She had a look in her eyes that I couldn't refuse.

I asked myself, *What's three more runs? We can take it easy on groomers. You can't let Angela go back by herself. You've got to go with her. It's the right thing to do.*

"OK," I said to Angela.

Then, to the rest of our crew, I said, "Guys, I'm going with Angela to get her car. We'll be back in thirty-ish."

"Uh-huh. See ya later," they said, doubtful we would make it back to the bar. They were right, but for the wrong reasons.

Getting off the first lift, we took a blue groomer that led to the second lift. My legs were shaking. I picked up a lot of speed as I took long turns, trying to avoid fatigue. We were flying.

We dropped into a cloud bank and lost all visibility. One minute, I was feeling the corduroy vibrate under my feet, and the next minute, something grabbed my uphill ski. A split second later, I found myself floating through the air.

Tuck and roll, Matt. Tuck and roll, I told myself. I tucked, but never made it to the roll. Landing on my neck, my chin hit my chest just below the nipple line . . . Then, blackness.

When I opened my eyes, Angela was kneeling next to me, saying, "Oh my god. Are you alright? What happened?"

"I dunno. Something grabbed my back ski." *How long was I out?*

"I couldn't see you, then just skied up on you lying here."

"I'm fine. Let's get going."

When I tried to move, it felt like someone was driving a knee between my shoulder blades. It hurt to breathe, and there was a stabbing pain in my back. I couldn't move and was stuck on my elbows and knees. "Arrrrgh!"

"What? What?! What can I do?"

"Shit. It hurts. Nothing." I could not move without feeling the worst pain I had ever experienced. Unable to reach my ski bindings, I asked, "Can you get my skis off?"

She worked as slowly and gently as she could, ignoring my outbursts, cussing, and pain. When my skis were off, she asked, "What now?"

"Put my skis uphill, above us, in an X so other skiers know I'm here. Then I need you to ski down and get ski patrol. I can't move."

"Are you going to be OK?"

"I'll be fine. I just can't move," I replied slowly, tears leaking from the corners of my eyes.

Angela got my skis posted uphill and quickly skied away. I blacked out. When I opened my eyes, I saw a familiar face. Kathy, who worked with me as a raft guide in the summer, skied up in her red ski patrol jacket. "Shit, Matt. When I heard it was you, I got here as fast as I could. Can you move?"

"No. Hey, Kathy," I said with a grimace. "It feels like someone is driving a knee into my back. This sucks."

"I know. I know. Can you get to the litter?"

A few bad jokes and self-deprecating comments later, I said, "I don't know. I feel like such a wimp. Let's try."

Everything hurt. Each movement seemed to take every ounce of energy I had left. Finally, I managed to crawl onto the litter, remaining on my knees and elbows as Kathy sideslipped on her snowboard down the hill, towing the litter behind her.

The rest of the trip down the mountain and how I ended up at the clinic remain a mystery to me. I knew the doctor, as she was our medical director for the ambulance district, and was able to provide information about my medical history, which I recited as if I were the one handing off a patient in the emergency department. I could not remember some of the details from the accident itself, though.

Thanks to my friends, morphine and Valium, I received temporary respite from the pain and was swept away to a happy place. I woke up in the Vail hospital to see Angela, along with the guys who had been skiing with us earlier in the day.

Dr. Corenman, a spine surgeon, diagnosed a compression fracture to T3 and T4 in my spine, just between my shoulder blades. I was lucky. The fracture was millimeters away from damaging the spinal cord.

Dr. Corenman and I began a friendship that lasted decades, yet I never usurped his role as a medical professional, especially when I asked to bend or break protocol. Upon me asking when I could kayak again, Dr. Corenman, the consummate professional, laughed and said, "One thing at a time, Matt."

Due to my barrel-chested stature, a standard chest brace didn't fit. I did not have insurance, nor did I have enough cash to pay for a custom brace. Dr. Corenman and I discussed the options and decided to skip surgery and fancy braces with one major caveat. I would have to be mindful of my body and diligent in following the protocol required to heal. I had to rest, wear a C-collar for at least six weeks, and maintain perfect posture—no slouching.

My hospital stay lasted three days. Every time I opened my eyes, another friend was reminding me that I had a massive support system of people who thought of me as family. In the midst of physical pain and stress at the prospect of mounting medical bills, my friends cracked jokes, raised money to help cover the bills, and offered the support I needed to stay the course. I was blessed and truly fortunate.

I was also an idiot. I should have listened to my intuition. That part bothered me. The last time I had ignored my intuition, I crashed my car. This time, I crashed myself. Why did these setbacks happen?

Lying in the hospital bed, I looked at the labyrinth tattoo on my shoulder, pointing myself to the elusive center. Just when I felt like I was getting close, a setback spun me back out.

I slid my finger to the outer ring of the labyrinth.

"I'm out here now," I muttered out loud, in a room by myself, as I placed my finger on the outermost lane of the labyrinth.

Stay focused. Keep your goals in sight. They will happen. Stay the course, I reminded myself.

As I was being discharged, Eric, Dr. Corenman's physician assistant, and Margaret (Margarita to me), Dr. Corenman's amazing nurse, told me that it was tradition for athletes who had been treated at the clinic to send a signed photo when they were able to return to their sport. They knew I paddled for Team Dagger and wanted a photo for their wall. That meant I had to do everything right. "Don't worry," I assured them, "I'm getting back in my boat, and you'll get your photo!"

The next six weeks were agonizingly slow. I spent a lot of time meditating. I also spent a lot of time high on pain meds, navigating mood swings, and trying desperately to stay positive. As Mather later pointed out, the pain medication kept me deliriously positive. My roommates were encouraging, and an extended network of friends supported me in more ways than they will ever know. Julie was a Pilates instructor. She said that Pilates would help develop core strength and flexibility, which would complement any other physical therapy.

With Dr. Corenman's permission and enthusiastic support from the members of the private athletic club, I commenced Pilates training twice a week. Despite having spent years as a personal trainer and countless hours working out in the weight room, I could barely squeeze my knees together in that class. It was humbling. Through Pilates, I was reminded how strength, stability, and flexibility collectively provided a platform for pinnacle performance.

During my recovery, I had plenty of time for reflection. I noted that setbacks were life's way of teaching me the exact lessons I needed to learn precisely when I needed to learn them. Though accidents seemed to come from out of the blue, hindsight provided context for those events. Bad things seemed to happen when I ignored my inner voice.

I also thought a lot about the word "mindfulness." It was used to describe thoughtfulness, awareness, self-discovery, gratitude, intention, breath work, attention to detail, and purposefulness. Nobody seemed to define mindfulness; they just used it, expecting its meaning to be understood. It felt like a popular buzzword that was thrown around to describe anything having to do with the mind.

Semantics

I felt that the work I was doing as an EMT was important. This practice of medicine became part of my higher calling. I wanted to perform to the very best of my abilities. I did a deep dive into mindfulness and its role in medicine. The more I contemplated mindfulness, the more I was blown away by the number of parallels between kayaking and working as an EMT. This led to a conversation with Jennifer, a friend who kidnapped me off my couch one afternoon in an effort to keep me distracted while my body healed.

"What intrigues me is the way mindfulness has become a central theme in both my kayaking and my medicine. It's related to everything I do and seems to keep coming up," I said.

Jennifer said, "You know, mindfulness is not a new topic."

"Yes, but what *is* it? How do you define it?"

"Mindfulness is breathing and yoga," Jennifer described.

"No. Those are ways to practice mindfulness. At the root, though, how do you define it? I feel like 'mindfulness' is overused."

Jennifer paused for a second and said, "When you're talking about paddle strokes or working in medicine, wouldn't 'intentionality' be a better choice of words?"

"Is 'intentionality' a word? I like it, but is it real?" I asked.

"YES! It's the philosophy behind the intent."

"Cool. I learned a new word. Hmmm. I like it." I became cerebral for just a moment, then continued, "Can we use them interchangeably? Except, I feel they are two completely different aspects."

I took a sip from my drink before continuing.

"Intent. Living with intent. Acting with intention. Being mindful of intentions. Mindfulness has been used and misused by people for decades. Mindfulness isn't yoga, breathing, or meditation. Those are all exercises used to help teach mindfulness. Being mindful of ourselves and our actions, we live, speak, and do with intent."

"OK. So, mindfulness is doing something with intent, or the intentionality behind the action. What about awareness? Isn't that the same thing as mindfulness? Can you use them interchangeably? Maybe awareness is the passive form of mindfulness, and intentionality is the active form of mindfulness."

"To me, I think mindfulness would be the beginning of the process that connects awareness and intentionality." I paused to formulate my thoughts, then continued, "Mindfulness requires introspection. Awareness is an observation of the external. It's the opposite of introspection. Right?"

Digesting this, Jennifer asked, "What about self-awareness? I mean, if I am self-aware, doesn't that mean I'm being mindful of my own strengths and weaknesses? Isn't self-awareness introspective?"

I loved these discussions. Semantics were important for me to establish common ground. The challenge was entertaining. "OK. Let's dive down the hole. Give me an example of a strength and a weakness."

Jennifer replied, "Strength: diplomacy. Weakness: hmmm . . . A lack of focus. I'm easily distracted."

I repeated these two items back to her, and I said, "If I am self-aware, I recognize that diplomacy is a strength. I am aware of my interactions with others and the fact that I am adept at interpersonal communication. I am aware of myself as I interact externally. Does that make sense?"

"Yes, keep going."

"OK. If I am easily distracted, I lack focus. Again, I am aware of myself as I interact externally." I looked over her shoulder and pointed. "Squirrel. Sorry, what were we talking about?"

Jennifer chuckled and said, "OK, I get it. Awareness is knowing what's going on around me, and self-awareness is knowing how I interact with what's going on around me."

"Yes! That's it. So, let's bring it back to where we started. Mindfulness requires introspection. With that introspection, coupled with awareness, I can act with intent, living with intentionality."

"OK. So," Jennifer said, "mindfulness is introspective. Awareness is external. Intentionality is what comes from being mindful. I think I've got it. I like this a lot."

Jennifer took a sip of her beer, then looked at me. "I have always thought of mindfulness as feeling joy or gratitude: feeling at peace. How does that fit into this?"

"The end result of mindfulness would be a precision of thought and action," I replied. "Mindfulness can elicit thoughts and feelings. More specifically, mindfulness yields a precision of thought and action. That focused precision would lead to peace, joy, and gratitude, right?"

As I digested this internally, I thought, *I am precise in my paddle stroke. I am mindful of myself, my use of the paddle, and the current. I'm aware of the current around me and how the water flows and the power of it goes. I have precision in my use of the paddle because I am mindful of myself and how I'm using it.*

Speaking out loud, I said, "I am mindful of people in my life, and the result is that I feel gratitude toward them. That gratitude leads to a sense of joy in our interactions.

"I am mindful of my use of words, using precision in my vocabulary to speak clearly and succinctly. I seek understanding by listening, being mindful of the fact that I have two ears and one mouth. I want to listen more than I speak."

I was on a roll, so I kept going. Jennifer was looking at me intensely, nodding her head and smiling. "Mindfulness requires introspection. If I want joy and gratitude in my life, then they would be the end result of a process that starts with self-discipline, setting aside time and energy for the practice of introspection. I have to discipline my mind to be present in the moment in order to feel gratitude and joy."

"What about yoga, meditation, and breathing exercises? Those are all mindfulness, right?"

"I disagree, mindfulness can be taught or practiced through breathing exercises and through meditation. These techniques train people to be mindful by showing them how to discipline their mind through focusing on one thing, their breathing."

Jennifer then asked, "So we now come full circle. What is mindfulness? We've described ways to get there, we've described ways to practice it. We've described the end result of being mindful . . . How do we define it?"

I answered, "Mindfulness would be the discipline, or precision, of one's thoughts, words, and actions. In order to reach the level of joy and gratitude you wish to reach, you need to be mindful of yourself, reminding yourself, 'I'm going to take a breath. I'm going to feel the warmth of the sun coming through the windows. I can hear the drops of water coming from the faucet in the sink. I hear the birds chirping.' I'm in the moment, fully 100%, and I feel gratitude for everyone and everything around me in my life.

"I am mindful of myself and I am mindful in the moment, and the end result of that is appreciation, joy, and gratitude.

"Does that make sense?"

"Completely. I think you're on to something."

I realized that I had gotten quite animated, talking with my hands, leaning forward in my seat. I took a breath to slow my brain. I also corrected my posture, as my back was getting a little stiff. "I really enjoyed that exercise. Thank you."

Jennifer said, "Me too!"

Grabbing our drinks, we clinked them together. "Cheers!"

After paying the tab, she took me home, and we agreed to paddle when I got cleared by the doctor. I mentally chewed on the unexpected conversation we had. I began to formulate a fundamental philosophical framework that would evolve into teaching methods I would use to train paramedics.

Attitude

Though Pilates, yoga, and meditation helped me physically stay the course, I went through all five stages of grief in the process of accepting the fact that recovery takes time. I tried to incorporate my definition of mindfulness into my self-prescribed physical therapy program, remaining disciplined in my movements, posture, and healing process. No amount of stretching or core exercises would speed the process. More than anything, I wanted Dr. Corenman's blessing to start kayaking again. Finally, after six long weeks, I received the green light to get back in the kayak and get back to work as an EMT.

The day before my month-and-a-half hiatus was up, we had a big party at a local bar, and I took off my C-collar, telling everyone, "I'm back. Let's go paddling!" The next day, Dr. Corenman reminded me that I had taken the C-collar off before he gave me permission. That was the first of two principal's-office-lectures I got from him.

He did give me the green light to take it slow and ease into paddling, beginning phase two of my recovery. It felt liberating to get back on the water when I paddled a flat-water section of the Colorado River the next day.

Kayaking became a form of physical therapy, as I ran through my regimen twice a day. After paddling upstream for forty-five minutes, I would turn around and paddle fifteen minutes downstream, back to my truck. Focusing on body position and strict form, with my back straight and chest up, I imagined a dime stuck to my side and pictured my lats squeezing that dime into my obliques. I used the paddle stroke techniques I learned from Billy to move upstream with as few strokes as possible. Less is more; do less, achieve more. Pressing my foot against the bulkhead, I pulled water with my paddle and found my rhythm.

I took delight in the simplicity and precision of paddling, breaking down each movement to examine its constituents. I gradually began selecting better lines up the eddies and across the current. I became aware of my body's rotation left and right while my hips rocked forward and back.

When each stroke was correct and efficient, taken with intent, not thought, I fell back into the routine of paddling without thinking, meditating on what I had learned about mindfulness as I made my way upstream. I wanted to apply these practices in mindfulness to my everyday life.

Two weeks passed. I was feeling great, gaining strength, and becoming more coordinated on the water. I felt confident. My eight-week checkup with Dr. Corenman was encouraging. My self-designed physical therapy on the water was aiding the recovery process.

My associates at the ambulance district were amazingly supportive during my recovery. During the first six weeks following the accident, I had no income. When I was cleared to paddle flat water at the six-week mark, I was also cleared for light-duty work. By this time, I had accumulated a massive mound of medical bills, so I was eager to be back on the job.

Jason, Tom, Chris, Jamie, and the rest of my co-workers got creative and found ways to keep me busy at the station so I could earn an income without violating the doctor's orders. At one point, Jamie walked outside to find me trying to dig a ditch for the sprinkler system. He grabbed my shovel, scolded me, and sent me inside to study. He then had a few words with Tom as to what the term "light duty" really meant.

Finally, three months after the accident, I received Dr. Corenman's blessing to get back into Class III white water. My light-duty restriction was lifted as well. I told myself that a broken back was just a small bump in the road. A setback. No big deal.

I signed up for every available shift at work and paddled every day I was not at the station. Some friends called to invite me to join them on a kayaking trip to Escalante Creek near the Utah border. Escalante has a narrow window when conditions are right for kayaking. "I'm in" was my answer to anything paddling. Yes, the broken back was just a small bump.

The purpose of that little setback was to remind me to listen to my intuition and appreciate my life on and off the water.

Escalante's Class IV–V water did not disappoint. We spent three days running laps on the raging creek, which churned red with sand from the river's bottom. Rather than white water with whitecaps, we paddled angry red water topped with frothy, unsettling, breaking red waves.

Using a rock as our gauge, we noted that our first day reached the highest water mark of the weekend.

Water levels gradually receded in subsequent days, providing respite for my body. By the end of the weekend, my back was sore and I felt strong. I found myself stretching the trapezius and rhomboid muscle groups regularly to keep them from cramping. The pain was not debilitating. At least the bone was healed. I was happy to be back on the water. However, I welcomed the opportunity to soak in the hot springs on our way back home.

I worked at the ambulance district the next two days, providing much-needed rest for my back, which was sore between the shoulder blades. Between running calls and studying, I was stretching, doing yoga, and resting. I congratulated myself again for surviving a downward spiral. I was back on an upward climb. I got lucky . . . but was it really luck?

A few weeks later, a friend called to say that Oh-Be-Joyful Creek near Crested Butte was running. Like Escalante Creek, there is a narrow window when Oh-Be-Joyful has enough water to kayak. "Absolutely! I'm in," I replied. Always ready, my kayak had taken up permanent residence on the roof of my truck's topper. My kayak gear was stored in the truck bed so I could leave at a moment's notice.

After working a twenty-four-hour shift, I got off work at eight in the morning, jumped in my truck, and made the drive to Crested Butte. I rendezvoused with Ben and a few other paddling friends at the adjacent campground. We loaded boats and gear into my truck, then made our way to the put-in.

The road to the put-in crossed Oh-Be-Joyful Creek. A steady stream of water flowed just above the tires of my lifted Tacoma. Using my tires as a gauge, we knew there was plenty of volume to paddle. At eleven thousand feet in elevation, what was snow a few short hours ago was now liquid cascading down the mountainside. While air temperatures were warm, the water was a refreshing thirty-four to forty degrees.

The put-in for Oh-Be-Joyful is strategically located just above a picturesque waterfall. This quick start to the Class V run generally deters all but the most experienced paddlers. I felt strong. I was not intimidated by the Class V creek; however, I was definitely concerned about landing the falls in a way that would not re-injure my back.

Sitting in my kayak at the put-in, just before sliding into the water, I had the sensation of time slowing down. I became mindful of my breathing, tuning into the sound of water falling against rocks, anticipating the cold splash of melted snow against my face, and feeling the warm sun upon my skin. I smiled to the sky and watched the river disappear at the horizon line as it dropped over a ledge before falling eighteen feet to the pool below.

I remembered my premonition, as I often did prior to moments of potential harm. *This isn't the day I'm going to die*, I reminded myself. *I'm only twenty-six years old. I still have fourteen years left. Send it.* The last three months were a reminder that every moment is precious. I needed to get whatever I could out of this journey.

Attaching my spray skirt to the cockpit of my kayak, I slid into the water and executed the first drop perfectly. After landing that first waterfall, an ear-to-ear smile spread across my face. I was back! The crew looked at me with excitement.

With a grin, Ben commented, "I thought you broke your back."

We all laughed and continued our journey downstream.

The creek's flow was indecisive. It was as if over the course of tens of thousands of years, there had been a battle between the immovable rock and the unstoppable water, leaving a zigzag, winding path behind. We followed the current over a variety of falls and slides, leading up to the main waterfall, where the stream got narrower, made a ninety-degree right-hand turn, a sharp left turn twenty feet later, then dropped twenty-five feet vertically to the pool below.

I oversimplified the lines on Oh-Be-Joyful in discussions, describing them as, "Hey, diddle, diddle, right down the middle."

It was significantly more complicated. I came into the first corner fast. I placed my paddle in a duffek on the right and pivoted, dragging the eddy line on the right to slow down. I then set a duffek on the left, lining up to round the corner in the correct position for the drop. I took one strong right stroke at the lip. Time seemed to stop for a beat as I mentally pictured my landing.

If I was too far right, I would land on the ledge at the base of a vertical rock wall. A line too far to the left would result in a hard-water landing rather than in the soft aerated water at the base of the waterfall. I needed to position myself just to the left side of the tongue, making a strategic stroke on the right.

I was exactly where I needed to be. Launching over the edge of the waterfall, I splashed down at the perfect angle into the pool below. I surfaced right side up, looked at my friends standing on shore, and pumped my fist in the air. I was stoked to be on the water again!

I eddied out on river left, below the waterfall, taking a brief respite until the next paddler arrived. Then, pulling my boat out of the water, I ran up the hill to grab Ben's camera. Ben had disembarked above the waterfall to take pictures of us coming over the drop. He left his camera for me to take photos of him, as he came down last. One after another, the remaining paddlers in our group ran clean lines. After taking a barrage of photos of Ben and the others coming over the waterfall, I ran back down to the eddy where the rest of the group was waiting.

Rather than making our way downstream, I suggested we run a few laps of the main falls before finishing the run to the take-out. Everyone was in full agreement. The sound of skirts snapping off and boats dragging over rocks could be heard echoing off the narrow canyon walls as we hiked up for a second lap. My second line was even better than the first. My back felt good, my landing was soft, and my confidence was building.

No matter how short or tall the waterfall, both speed and angle are critical components for a successful landing. Every drop has its own personality. Approaching the lip of the waterfall on my third lap, I was carrying a ton of speed. *Too much speed,* I thought. I flew off the lip fast and flat. My excess speed and flat angle meant that I would overshoot the soft aerated water at the base of the falls. I knew this meant I would be landing in the green water, which provided a much harder surface. Additionally, the flat angle of the boat would yield a bone-crushing impact.

"SLAP!"

The sound of plastic slapping green water echoed over the sound of the falls. I sat in my boat frozen. Lightning bolts were running down my legs and up my back.

Shit. I got cocky, and now I'm screwed, I thought.

Drifting with the current, I managed to ease my way into the eddy on the left. The guy running safety pulled me onto shore and asked, "Are you OK?"

"Yeah. Give me a second to catch my breath," I answered, grimacing through the pain.

"Man, you came off fast."

"I know," I grunted, trying to mask the pain. "My back feels tight. I need to stretch."

He held my boat steady as I climbed out and stood on shore. I did a few stretches, which did little to ease the shooting pain in my back.

"I think I'm done for the day," I announced reluctantly.

We paddled to the take-out, and friends ran a shuttle to bring my truck back to camp. I tried to relax the spasming muscles. Nothing seemed to help. I took a Valium in hopes that the muscle spasms would subside enough to allow me to paddle the next day.

At camp, everyone was in high spirits after a great day on the water. Ben showed me a photo he took from my second lap of the main falls. I was airborne at the top third of the drop. It was an artsy shot that captured the trees framing the creek and showed the waterfall from a different angle. I was crystal clear in the center of the frame, the trees behind me were slightly out of focus, and my red boat popped. Staring at the picture, I remembered Eric and Margaret's request for a photo for their wall. When I mentioned this to Ben, without a second thought, he said he would get me a copy of the image as soon as we got home.

My back was still tight, and I was sore the next day, so I made the tough decision to run shuttle, set safety, and take photos from shore while the others ran laps. At home, Ben copied his photos to my external drive. I then found the picture I wanted, edited it, and printed an eight-by-ten copy.

A week later, my back was still sore. I was walking fine and had no other major issues, so I ignored the pain and drove to Dr. Corenman's office to deliver the picture to Eric and Margaret.

The office was constantly busy, leaving me amazed at how his staff always took the time to make me feel welcomed. Their skill and efficiency, offering high-level patient care and personal attention to everyone, was a graceful art.

Margaret smiled and gave me a hug when she saw me at her desk. "Hey, Matt! How are you doing?"

"Fine," I replied. "I was just dropping off that photo you and Eric asked for, although I'll admit, I don't feel like I deserve to be on your wall with all of these internationally renowned professional athletes."

Eric walked up in the middle of this conversation and laughed at me. "Matt, you kayak for Dagger, and you're back in your boat again, right?"

"Yes, sir."

"Stop calling me sir." He laughed. Eric was a decade older than me and had been a paramedic before becoming a physician's assistant. He had an easygoing manner and was extremely knowledgeable; we shared a mutual respect for each other.

"Yes, sir," I replied, just to rub it in.

"Let's see what you've got," Eric said, indicating the picture in Margaret's hand. He looked at the photo, then back at me. "When was this? Where was this?"

"Last week, down by Crested Butte."

"Really? This is a great photo. How is your back feeling?"

"Great! It feels good to be on the water again." I hesitated, not sure if I should tell him more. "Actually, I took one more run after this picture was taken. I came in too fast and landed flat. Right away, I felt shooting pain, like lightning bolts shooting up my back and down my legs."

"Hmmm . . . You better take it easy to give it a chance to heal properly. If you still have symptoms in a couple of days, let me know."

"By the way," he continued, "you have to sign this. We can't hang it without a signature."

Eric handed me a Sharpie along with the photo. I wrote, "Nothing hurts in the air. Thanks for getting me 'back' in my boat," followed by my signature.

As I handed the picture back to Eric, Dr. Corenman spotted us and came over.

"Matt! How are you doing?"

"I'm well, Doc."

Eric showed Dr. Corenman the photo. Sounding like an excited kid on his birthday, he said, "Look what Matt brought. Pretty cool, huh? I know just where we can hang it."

Eric made eye contact with me, letting me know that the event of my last run would stay between us . . . for now.

Dr. Corenman looked at the picture, commenting, "Wow. Very nice. Thanks, Matt."

Handing the photo back to Eric, he then looked at me and said, "Matt, come with me."

I glanced at Eric and Margaret inquiringly. They shrugged and smiled. I followed Dr. Corenman to his office. He leaned on the front edge of his desk, arms crossed over his chest, as I sat in a chair in front of him. I suddenly had a feeling of dread, like I was back in seventh grade, sitting in the dean's office.

"Matt, you need to realize how lucky you are. Just a millimeter or two more and you wouldn't be walking right now."

"Yes, sir, I know."

"You need to be careful. If you break your back again, it's very likely you won't walk away. Your cervical spine is already narrowed. Did I overhear you say you may have injured yourself again this weekend?"

"Yes, sir." I was dumbfounded. *How did he hear that?!*

My eyes were bouncing back and forth between his eyes and the ground.

"Keep kayaking. I just don't recommend running any more waterfalls."

"Yes, sir. I will be more aware of the landing and the situations."

"Matt, I don't think you're hearing me," he said with a chuckle.

"No, sir, I hear you. I just don't want to recognize what you're saying."

My sly grin faded and I continued, "I promise, Doc. I will do better and will be more mindful."

"Good. That's all I'm asking. I like you. I just don't want to see you as a patient."

We both laughed and shook hands. He thanked me for the photo and walked me back out to Margaret's desk, where she gave me a hug before I left.

As hard as it was, I took Dr. Corenman's words to heart. A few weeks later, we were doing a late-season creek run. After finishing the top portion of the run, which included drops that were ten feet or less, we approached the bottom half of the run, which started with a forty-foot waterfall. An image of Dr. Corenman popped into my head. I mumbled a few curse words under my breath and told the guys I was going to stay safe and opt out of the lower section.

A few years later, I was presented with yet another opportunity for Dr. Corenman to invade my thoughts, reminding me to be mindful of my choices and potential consequences. A couple dozen factory-sponsored kayakers were assembled during a few days off between circuit events. What do kayakers do during downtime? We kayak. We got wind of a creek that had just been pioneered, and we wanted to paddle it before it was fully discovered.

It was a beautiful, narrow low-volume creek with a very steep gradient of almost six hundred feet per mile. Low volume was something of an understatement. In reality, it was a series of wet slides punctuated by waterfalls that dropped into pools.

Andrew, a friend and Dagger's team manager at the time, looked at me and said, "I know your back is pretty messed up, Matt. If you don't want to run it, don't feel obligated."

I looked at him and said, "Man, it's tough. I want to run it, but you're right: I shouldn't risk it. What if I film y'alls first run, and if it's not bad, I'll run the second lap?"

"That sounds like a plan," Andrew agreed.

I ran the shoreline with a throw bag (rope) for safety and a video camera to document the run for the athlete and company promo videos that would follow. At the end of the run, Andrew and I were chatting, and he said, "It's probably good you didn't run that. My back is pretty beat up."

Part of me was relieved; part of me felt a tinge of regret. I did not portage many rapids, much less watch others run a section I did not run, so it was a hard decision for me to make. I could feel Dr. Corenman watching me with a smile.

Throughout the next decade, I ran many creeks and rivers all over the country, trying to reach balance by selectively making mindful paddling decisions. This attunement to mindfulness served me well in my kayak and even more so in medicine as I grew from an EMT to a paramedic, then applying those practices as an instructor.

Mindfulness in Medicine

It was the end of week one for a classroom full of EMTs who wanted to become paramedics. They had made it through the monotonous exercise of reading through the course overview, they had been introduced to the instructors who would lead various segments of the course, and they had been prepped on expectations for the year-long course. It was time to take the class across the hall to the lab, where they would become familiar with some of the tools they would use as paramedics.

Looking out over the class, I felt the familiar burden of responsibility. This group depended on me and the other instructors to provide the information and teach the skills they would utilize to save lives. Reflecting back on my ski injury and subsequent mindfulness on the water, I made note of the lessons I had learned.

Attitude, decisions, responses, and actions were factors in maintaining mindfulness in the years following my recovery. I wanted to share these lessons in mindfulness. If I could transfer this knowledge to my class, the injury and the tedium of the recovery would almost seem worth it. Attitude drives decisions. Decisions create responses. Responses drive future actions. I broke down these four factors in mindfulness, applying the lessons to the practice of medicine.

Attitude. It all starts with attitude. Through my recovery process, I learned that a positive mindset is something that can be cultivated. Rather than capitulating to fear and depression, I faced the recovery process with the mindset that I would be back in my kayak as quickly as possible.

The same principle applies to medicine. My paramedic students would need to learn to remain calm and collected when managing a medical emergency. They could not allow fear to run the show. This requires mindfulness, an inner gut-check reminder to trust their training. It requires discipline to consistently manage a scene with precision in decisions and interventions.

Decisions. My attitudes drove my decisions. Rather than hanging out on the couch during my recovery, I created a physical therapy routine that strengthened my body and put me on course to accomplish the goal of getting back on the water. I started doing Pilates. I made the decision to get outside my comfort zone in an effort to heal as quickly and completely as possible.

The same commitment to mindfulness impacts decisions made in medicine. There is no room for decisions made in haste, carelessness, inattentiveness, or distraction. The fundamental attitude of a good paramedic is one of mindfulness. Conscientious decision-making is fundamental to success.

Responses. Each decision is generated as a response or a reaction. Pilates classes and my self-designed physical therapy sessions on the river yielded positive results. Dropping off the main falls on Oh-Be-Joyful yielded a negative result. When Dr. Corenman sat me down in his office, I looked at my injury in a new light. Reflecting on this new information, I evaluated future kayaking adventures and weighed my options carefully. How could this drop affect my healing process? Did I need to fine-tune my technique for maximum benefit? Responding required me to take a pause, creating space for evaluation.

A quick reaction is not one carried out with mindfulness. One of my mentors used to tell me, "Take the rock out of your mouth before you speak." My words need to be softer. I need to take a pause to formulate a mindful response. How do I want my words or actions to land? What result do I want? A conversation or an argument? A calm exchange of ideas or a struck match? I need to respond precisely, with intent, not reactively, with unfiltered emotions.

Actions. Acting with intent is a tangible result of mindfulness. There is a big difference between activity and actions. Activity occupies most of a day functioning on autopilot. Activity lacks intention. Action requires me to be present, aware of the task at hand. A mindful action is the end result of intentionality.

I decided that mindfulness is critical as applied to medicine. How could I teach my students to be mindful? What exercises or activities would train them to develop precision in thought, word, and action?

Before our class of paramedic students broke into separate work groups, I pulled the course coordinator and lead instructor, Liz, to the side. "Liz, would you mind if I tried a bit of an experiment this semester?"

"Sure. What do you have in mind?"

"I've been thinking about mindfulness. It applies to everything we are teaching: all the drugs they have to memorize, the skills they have to learn, and the documentation they need to provide. We tell them to have a rhyme to their reason, but we don't show them how."

"Sounds great. What do you have in mind?" Liz replied.

"I want to take it slow. Starting today, whenever they walk from the class to the lab, I am going to have them walk through the door with their right foot first. If they don't, or if they see someone who doesn't, that person will leave and come back into the room. Let's try it for a week, then I will build upon that."

"Ooooh. I like it. Let's definitely do this. It will make them start to pay attention."

As the class stood up, preparing to walk across the hall to the lab, I stopped the class. I let them know that when they stepped through the doorway to the lab, they needed to lead with their right foot. Anyone who failed to lead with their right foot when stepping through the door to the lab would have to exit and reenter correctly, with their right foot first.

The class looked at me like I was nuts. Maybe I was; time would tell.

A third of the class ignored the instruction, thinking it was a joke, and were immediately asked to exit and reenter the lab. When everyone was back in the room, I explained that this was how they would be expected to enter the lab every day for the rest of the year. Chuckles, eye rolls, and mumbling followed and were ignored.

I encouraged them to watch each other, instructors included. If anyone didn't enter the lab with their right foot, that person would need to leave and reenter. No further explanation was given at that time. After a few weeks, the entire class was noticing each other as they entered and departed the classroom and the lab. They were not afraid to enjoy telling instructors to leave, gloating in the opportunity to correct the teachers.

With a class of students now attuned to one another's movements, I began reviewing basic intravenous (IV) therapy skills with students before jumping into the new skill of establishing IV access from the side of the neck. This is also known as "starting an EJ" because we were inserting the catheter in the external jugular vein.

"Lesson one," I instructed, "whenever a needle is out, I want you to announce, 'Sharps!'"

A student yelled, "Sharps!" eliciting a chuckle from everyone in the class.

"Good!" I replied. "Now, everyone, take a turn calling out, 'Sharps!' to notify your co-workers of an exposed needle." One by one, students announced, "Sharps!" in turn, and the word dropped in volume until it was little more than a whisper.

"No, no," I corrected them. "Sharps!" I repeated loudly, with intensity. The next group of students improved. As the exercise continued, the word dropped in volume again.

"Let me describe a couple scenarios," I said patiently. "You are in the back of an ambulance that is bouncing and swaying down the interstate at eighty-five miles per hour or slowly creeping on a bumpy dirt road. There may be a siren blaring. Or you could be in a hospital with nurses and doctors and a lot of commotion all around you. Your patient may or may not have a dangerous, even deadly, disease. You do NOT want someone to bump into you, causing you to stab them, yourself, or your patient. Right?"

I made eye contact and saw heads nodding up and down, so I continued, "During this training, you will be in a classroom with twenty other students and instructors who are engaged in their own activities. You need to let us know that something dangerous—and potentially infectious—is unsecured.

"By yelling 'sharps' in the ambulance, you are alerting the driver to slow down and watch the bumps for the next minute or two. You are alerting doctors, nurses, and other staff in a hospital to give you space. You are alerting the other students and instructors in this classroom to be aware and steer clear. You are reminding yourself and others to be mindful as you hold a potentially dangerous object."

The light bulb went off. Every student understood the gravity of the exercise. For the rest of the semester, and hopefully throughout their careers, each student was mindful in announcing "sharps!" with authority when they had a needle or sharp object in their hand.

Later in the semester, during a daily debriefing, I asked, "Can anyone tell me why we have been walking into the lab with our right foot first?" The students looked around the room, yet nobody raised their hand.

From the back of the room, I heard, "To be a pain!"

Answering for them, once the laughter subsided, I said, "It was to teach you to be mindful of yourself and your surroundings."

I continued, "It has been an exercise to help you become more aware of what you are doing and aware of what other people in the room are doing. Walking into this room with intent and thought is an exercise for being precise in what you do. We apply this precision to administering drugs, intubating patients, moving patients onto the cot, and nearly every skill you are taught in this class.

"Think about this for a minute. You have to memorize over a hundred and twenty drugs, master countless skills, and learn protocols and policies. You also have to know your partner's level of comfort and skill. If that's not enough, you have to write reports that are honest, accurate, and can hold up in court. Being a paramedic entails a lot of responsibility. It can be overwhelming."

I paused, then continued, "Each skill you learn, and every bit of knowledge you absorb, is an arrow in your quiver. Being mindful allows you to have a rhyme to your reason and a method to your madness. Practicing mindfulness in medicine helps you identify which arrow is best suited to hit the mark.

"This is a first step," I continued with a smile, "toward not being overwhelmed while becoming more precise in the medicine you practice."

Seated to my left, Shannon raised her hand, asking, "How do I get more comfortable on scene?"

Shannon was living the van life, having moved to the valley for the sole purpose of becoming a paramedic. She was new to medicine and paid attention to everything.

With a smirk, I responded, "The short answer is to fake it till you make it, but I have a longer answer, if you're interested?"

She nodded her head.

"I am going to borrow from a couple of friends, then merge their sentiments into the long answer, so bear with me, OK?" I looked around the room to confirm interest.

"One of my physician mentors in wilderness medicine told me that 'precision in language is key.' How we speak is a reflection of how we assess our patients, how we write our documentation, and how well we understand our medicine. Be clear and concise. Be precise.

"Another friend from the wilderness medicine world, a nurse, said that in order to be good in the wilderness, 'a person needs to be an observer of themselves rather than, or in addition to, their surroundings.' We need to know our place, we need to know what's expected of us, and we need to know what we can offer. We need to be aware.

"Additionally, if I rush into a scene, in a flurry of excitement, I run the risk of hurting myself or doing harm to my patient. Take a breath."

As I took an exaggerated breath in and slowly exhaled, I thought about my first day on the ambulance, when Jason told me to untuck my shirt and tuck it back in.

"Both of them were speaking of mindfulness. We practiced mindfulness in the classroom by stepping through the door with our right foot first. Be aware of your surroundings, and remain mindful of yourself."

I knew I was stretching their patience, but they were still paying attention, so I finished, "Mindfulness in medicine is how you get more comfortable on the scene. If you have a method to your madness, there is rhyme to your reason. If you are mindful in how you practice medicine, then you will be able to own yourself, your decisions, and your actions by being precise in everything you think, say, or do."

The class was intrigued, so I finished with a final thought: "If you remain aware of your surroundings and are mindful in the process, then you won't have a reason to be panicked or uncomfortable. Mindfulness leads to precision; precision provides efficiency. Did I say fast or rushed or urgent anywhere in that?"

The class shook their heads side to side.

"No, I didn't. If you find yourself not feeling comfortable, think about me being an idiot as you step out of your ambulance or walk into their house with your right foot first." They all laughed as I continued, "If you can be mindful of your stress and identify exactly what is making you anxious, then you can work the problem, address it, and move forward with a plan. Does that make sense?" I looked at Shannon for confirmation as I finished since she had initially asked the question.

She nodded her head and smiled. "Thank you. It does make sense. It just seems overwhelming."

I said, "That's why we are here, now, in this class. To practice, to make mistakes, and to learn. Have a method to your madness. Own yourself and your decisions. Continue to learn. You have six different instructors, and the other five are smarter than I am. Learn something from all of us, and you will come out of this class better than us. I fully expect that I will be adding arrows to my quiver by the end of the year as I learn from you."

Intentionality

My vocations and avocations grew and evolved, presenting exciting new opportunities, often on parallel timelines. Just as years of working on the ambulance and teaching allowed me to instill mindfulness while teaching medicine to new EMTs and paramedics, my passion and commitment for kayaking created opportunities to apply mindfulness to business in the outdoor industry.

I had been a sponsored athlete for a small helmet company for years. One day, the owner asked me if I was interested in owning part of the company. I said, "Sure. Send me the books and financials, and I'll think it over." A month went by. I kept getting stories and promises, but never got the books. I dropped it and forgot all about it.

That winter I was in Las Vegas for the SIA show with Paul and his company SporTube. I came across a booth selling the exact helmets I was wearing for kayaking. The brand was different; however, I *knew* this was my helmet. This was a different company than the one that had offered me a business partnership.

Confused, I stopped at the booth to introduce myself.

A big biker-looking guy behind the counter looked at me curiously. "Do you live in Colorado?"

"I do. Why?"

"I know who you are. Be happy you didn't get into business with . . ."

His voice faded as I stopped listening, wondering, *How does he know who I am? How did he know I was going to buy into the other helmet company?*

My brow furrowed and I asked, "Huh? What are you talking about?"

"He didn't have a company. He sourced all of his manufacturing to us and just put his stickers on our helmets. We had a branding agreement, which he violated, so we stopped making helmets for him."

"So that's why he never got me the numbers I asked for?"

"Probably. I haven't heard from him since," the man behind the counter replied.

"Yeah. Me either. So, what are you going to do now?"

This big guy laughed with his shoulders and his belly, reaching out his hand. "My name is Kim. I own Advanced Carbon Composites."

Kim had been in the carbon-Kevlar helmet business for decades and made a name for himself making chopper-style helmets for bikers. His business blew up when he was hired to wrap a full motorcycle in carbon-Kevlar for one of the Discovery Channel's biker build-off shows. His business expanded from motorcycle helmets to motorcycles to accessories for yachts. He now wanted to get into the outdoor sports market, namely skiing and kayaking, under the name Head Trip Helmets.

We hit it off and met for an hour or so every day during the SIA show. By the time I got home, he had already shipped me six helmets for product testing. Kim asked me to be his sales and brand manager for the outdoor industry, starting with kayaking. "Find the top kayakers. Build a pro team, and do what you can to get our helmets sold. We are going to start a new brand just for the outdoor sports market, and I want you to run it."

Reaching out to friends and associates in the paddling world, I put together a strong team of some of the best kayakers I knew. Kim made custom helmets for each sponsored athlete. I put out a branding survey and offered a free helmet for the top logo design. Along with helping Kim build the brand, I also created long-lasting relationships with paddlers, distributors, dealers, and sales reps around the globe. I worked tirelessly to learn the nuances of the outdoor industry.

I sat through a lot of sales clinics when I worked at the ski shop. One sales rep, TJ, had an approach that was particularly effective. TJ never bashed a competitor's brand. He simply explained how helmets worked. Then he demonstrated the extent to which his company exceeded those standards. In my mind, TJ's approach epitomized mindfulness in sales.

I asked TJ for pointers, and he was eager to oblige. I wanted to adopt the more sophisticated language and terminology used in the ski helmet industry and apply it to the paddle sports helmet industry. Following TJ's formula, I did not bash competitors' brands. I simply educated dealers on how helmets worked and shared information about testing standards. I would then point out what made our helmets unique, without speaking disparagingly about the competition. I talked with other manufacturers to help develop a synergistic message that would meet the end goal of keeping kayakers protected. It was a novel, and well-received, approach.

Though I was still working on the ambulance, my side hustle selling helmets in the outdoor industry was opening new doors. Being associated with a reputable kayak manufacturing brand like Dagger provided credibility that helped open those doors. Before I knew any different, I was drawn into the world of freestyle kayak judging just as the sport was lobbying to become an Olympic event.

An inaugural freestyle kayaking event took place in Reno, Nevada, the year after I began working for Kim with Head Trip. I planned a road trip to visit dealers in the northwestern region of the United States, attend the event in Reno, and paddle.

The freestyle event in Reno was an invitational to which I did not get an invitation. With a field of world champions and freestyle legends, my feelings were far from hurt. Besides, I was happy to hang out with them at the after-parties, talk with some prospective dealers, and go kayaking. Dagger was an event sponsor, so I helped work their tent, answering questions and offering free demos and lessons.

Jim, the producer of the week-long event, approached me one day. "Matt, I'm in a pinch and I heard you're a raft guide."

"Oh, yeah? What can I do?"

"We have a raft race about to start. I have a boat full of media staff, but no guide. Hobie said you can guide them down? It's an easy stretch of river."

The importance of media coverage for this inaugural event was a big deal, and I wanted to help Jim as much as I could. "Yeah, man. Where do you need me to go?"

"You're a lifesaver! Thank you." With that, he took me over to the girl running the raft race. On the way over, I grabbed my guide stick from my truck, a custom wooden paddle made for me by a friend. The put-in was absolutely packed with locals, guides, and anyone who wanted to race. I was introduced to my team, which was composed of four outdoor writers. We sat on the edge of the raft while the organizers handled last-minute logistics.

Introducing myself, I asked, "So, do you guys want to float down the river, compete, or win?"

Without hesitation, all four of them yelled, "We want to win!"

"OK. Then we will need to work together as a team, paddling together as a team, and I need you all to trust me. Can you do that?"

Occupants of surrounding rafts turned in amusement as my crew sounded a chorus of "Yes!" and "Hell, yes!"

I coached them up on basic paddle strokes and went over some safety information. I had never run this stretch of river. I was told it was an easy Class II stretch, so I was not worried. When the race started, our team was fired up.

"We are not going to sprint out of the gate," I told them. "We are going to set a steady pace and keep it through to the end."

Like the Gore Canyon race, this was not a mass start race. Rafts were released from the starting line one at a time, in one-minute intervals. When the horn sounded for us to go, we came off the line in perfect sync. We had a rhythm. I watched the current and picked our lines, paddling stroke-for-stroke with them, adding steering strokes and adjustments as needed. When someone got tired, the rest of us kept paddling.

Passing the raft in front of us gave our team a burst of energy. By the time we passed a second raft, our crew was on fire. We were cracking jokes between huffed breaths, sliding into the finish line after passing a third raft. We worked together to pull the boat out of the water and congratulated each other on a job well done.

An hour later, Jim came to find me in the Dagger tent. "Matt, I hate to do this. We are short judges for the freestyle competition. Can you help?"

I looked at Robin, Dagger's team manager, raising an eyebrow to ask if she was cool with breaking me free.

She smiled, saying, "Sure, Matt. I've got this. Go for it."

I can't remember an interaction with Robin where she didn't have a smile on her face.

With that, Jim took me to the judges' stand where Kristine was running the show. Kristine and I had met several times over the years. When she saw me approaching with Jim, she stood up to give me a huge hug. I had participated in some kayak competitions and was familiar with the scoring system. Kristine gave me the judging perspective, brought me up to speed on the scoring sheets, showed me how to use my scribe, and walked me through the heats.

The competition offered a pretty big cash prize, so we needed to be attentive to the details. Little did I know, judging this event would be the catalyst for future invitations to officiate freestyle kayaking competitions.

Kristine, wife of (and the success behind) Olympian and world champion EJ,[31] was the true backbone of modern freestyle kayaking. She taught me the systems and procedures for scoring freestyle kayaking events. Together, we brainstormed ways to make the process more efficient. Kristine was a huge freestyle kayaking advocate and the intermediary to the national, international, and Olympic governing committees.

After judging the freestyle event in Reno, Jim walked up to me with a huge, Cheshire-cat-like grin. He handed me a trophy shaped like a miniature paddle, announcing that I won first place in the raft race earlier that day. I reveled in the fun of a great weekend, unaware of the fortuitous events that had been set in motion.

---

[31] Eric Jackson is a world-champion freestyle kayaker, kayak designer, Olympic slalom kayaker, founder of Jackson Kayak, and a Professional Bass Tournament angler on the FLW Tour.

From Reno, I traveled to Oregon to kayak with friends, then to Washington for a creek race, then Montana, Wyoming, and back to Colorado. I spent that summer working on the ambulance, raft guiding, and managing helmet sales during the week while working kayaking events on the weekends. In addition to running safety for creek races, I continued judging the freestyle competitions, increasing my knowledge and skill in that role.

Kristine reached out to me at the end of the summer to ask if I could help judge the US Team Trials event in Maryland that fall. I agreed and, after Gauley Season, I went up to the white-water park in Maryland for the competition. Shane Benedict and Kristine ran the event while I filled a supporting role, learning more ins and outs from Shane during the course of the three days.

At the end of the event, Kristine, myself, and several others were talking about how we could make this more formal and set our sport up for the most success. The United States Freestyle Kayak committee was formed, under the umbrella of the American Canoe Association. I was elected the vice-chair, assuming the responsibilities for creating a rules subcommittee and continuing our progress formatting freestyle events.

With Kristine's guidance, I learned to apply mindfulness to the observation of others. I had to watch and observe the precise actions of the tricks being performed, and I had to remain mindful of myself in objectivity—scoring what was completed, not what they wanted to execute. I had to observe, decide, and act with precision, ensuring every athlete was scored by equitable standards.

Our rules subcommittee, Clay, Jeremy, Shane, Steven, and myself, was tasked with more precisely defining each trick, determining point values for competitions, and streamlining the scoring pages and competition format in the USA. It was a daunting task that evolved over the course of two to three years. Kristine was our US representative to the International Olympic Committee (IOC), and she took the new scoring sheet we developed to the European committees. The end goal was to establish freestyle kayaking as an event in the Summer Olympics. We worked with the IOC to standardize our scoring system. We had to organize World Cup events and World Championships events that met the IOC requirements.

Every conscientious stroke of a paddle, each commitment to put my very best into a run, every day I said yes to getting on the water when I could have stayed home led to my work with the US Freestyle Kayak committee.

The Homestake Creek non-event, working as a judge at freestyle events, and many other adventures relating to kayaking, business, and travel were fortunate accidents. Though I categorize them as accidents because they were unforeseen, they were never random. There was a rhyme to the reason and a method to the madness that formed a consistent, predictable pattern. Fortunate accidents were cultivated. The seeds of mindfulness and fertile soil of awareness provided optimal conditions for new adventures to take root and grow.

Application: Mindful of Being Mindful

"Mindfulness" is often used, misused, and overused. How would you define "mindfulness" after reading this chapter?

1. What key words describe mindfulness? Intentionality?
2. What is the difference between awareness, mindfulness, and intentionality? How do they work together?
3. How could you integrate mindfulness into your work and/or personal life?

Identify a time when your absolute concentration on an activity or action was critical to making the appropriate decision.

4. Did that attention to detail come easy, or did you find focusing difficult?
5. What would have made focusing on the details easier?

RESILIENCE

Jasmine was the most beautiful woman who had ever come into my life. About a month after we met, I took her on a road trip to Canada. I was sharing the judging duties for the World Cup of Freestyle Kayaking with Shane, one of the founders of Liquidlogic Kayaks. The series consisted of three events in two countries, with athletes from nearly fifty countries being represented. The first stop was on the Ottawa River, just outside Montreal, Canada. The second and third stops were in the USA—Watertown, New York, and Rock Island State Park, Tennessee.

During the drive to Canada from Colorado, we stopped in Iowa to stretch our legs at a rest stop. When I got back to the truck from the restroom, I could not find Jasmine anywhere. She had been in the truck when I left.

Jasmine was beautiful and sweet; she was also a perpetual puppy that wanted to play with everyone.

I walked around to the opposite side of the rest area and found three truckers chasing her around one of the tractor trailers parked in the parking lot. It looked like an endless game of keep-away. Everyone, Jasmine especially, had huge smiles stretched across their faces.

Jasmine had been abused, then fostered back to health, before I adopted her. When we met, she suckered me in with an innocent look in her eyes, her ears lifted and head tilted. This all-white Staffordshire terrier knew I was hooked.

On the drive home from the shelter, I learned, the hard way, that she liked to chase windshield wipers when it rained. When we got to my house, I looked her in the eyes, understanding she had endured significant abuse, and said that if she wanted to hate every human she ever met, she had my permission; I then begged her to please stop chasing windshield wipers. That was not the last time she chose to ignore me. She loved every human she met and laughed at me as she ignored my pleas to stop chasing windshield wipers.

In the Iowa rest area parking lot, when she saw me approaching and heard me calling her name, she stopped running. With the biggest smile I had ever seen stretched across her block head, she looked at me and momentarily caught her breath. Just as I took one step toward her, she took off around the semitruck and trailer again. The truckers were laughing and I was swearing. After about three more laps, Jasmine looked at me over her shoulder, bolting toward the on-ramp for Interstate 80 East.

Yelling my thanks to the truckers, I ran back to my truck, turned on my CB radio when I got in, and took off up the on-ramp. I could hear on the CB the truckers from the parking lot calling the drivers headed east on Interstate 80 to tell them my dog was about to merge with traffic. At least she was going in the right direction.

Shifting through gears, I sped up to sixty miles per hour as fast as my manual transmission Toyota Tacoma could accelerate. Every eastbound truck had moved to the left lane, just in case I needed more space. I opened the passenger door as I caught up to Jasmine, slowing down to match her pace. I called her name, telling her to jump in. Without breaking her stride, she jumped into the truck and looked at me with a satisfied grin. We were back on the road. I got on the CB to share my thanks, letting them know "all was good," and spent the next thirty minutes swapping dog stories with the truckers. They also shared locations where police had set speed traps, which proved to be very helpful.

That was the first of many adventures with Jasmine. She was one of my best fortunate accidents. Jasmine was mindful—in her own way. Her actions were specifically designed to elicit a desired response. She was a master at getting what she wanted. In short, she lived a dog's life, enjoying an attitude of royalty and her spoils of joy.

According to the foster home where I first met Jasmine, she had suffered a lot of physical abuse in her first six months of life. In addition to the physical abuse of her first home, she spent three months in a foster home that was later closed down after nearly forty animals were found locked in kennels without time for exercise, food, or relief. Jasmine was six months old and had been stuck in a kennel for three months; her hair was burned away from sitting in her own urine, and her body was skin and bones from not being given proper nutrition.

During the thirteen years she lived with me, she taught me the true meaning of resilience. She knew when I was having a bad day and gave me the attention I did not know I needed, bending the rules just enough to remind me that she was in charge. To be abused and still have so much love to share, Jasmine demonstrated resilience beyond human capacity. During times when I felt like I had fallen off a cliff, Jasmine exemplified the forgiveness and grit I needed to regain my footing.

Creativity

I had the opportunity to enjoy a wide range of rich and varied experiences that strayed far from the norm. The breadth of experiences caused some people to try to categorize or file me as noncommittal or lacking focus. It caused other people to view me as countercultural, a social dissident, or paradoxical. In some cases, people were surprised to discover that my opinions and insights were not what they had expected. As people got to know me better, they learned I was, simply, 100% focused, passionate, and engaged in each and every one of my many vocations and avocations.

It was precisely that focus, that intentionality, with which I approached the activities in my life that gave rise to many of the opportunities I experienced. People said I was lucky.

In the words attributed to Roman philosopher Seneca, "Luck is what happens when preparation meets opportunity."[32]

The key was being able to spot the opportunity and act on it. My gun shop was a case in point. I identified the need and filled it.

Starting a new business requires resilience: retail sales are a roller-coaster ride of highs and lows. I faced challenges at every turn, enduring times I wanted to quit, and resisting the urge. In the end, the gun shop taught me valuable skills and honed my communication skills.

The gun shop came about after Hobie and I attended a gun show in Denver because the ambulance district was developing a Tactical Medic program with the Special Operations Unit (SOU, or SWAT, Team). After an interview with the commander of the team, I needed to purchase a new handgun, one that met their required specifications, to use for qualification. I also wanted a new hunting rifle. Hobie and I were commiserating over the fact that we had to drive two hours to buy a firearm. In a spark of inspiration, we realized there was a clear, unmet need for a gun shop in our community.

I had an affinity for firearms and had a basic understanding of the laws. The thought of owning a gun store had never crossed my mind. From the point of conception through to the day I sold the business, I had the opportunity to apply every business lesson previously learned. Awareness, mindfulness, intentionality, business and team development, system design and implementation, medical understanding, protocol and operational guidelines, sales and marketing—each of those skills contributed to the growth of my business

With the start of a new business, I still needed to balance my work on the ambulance with kayaking obligations. The gun business filled a need in the community and helped me generate some extra cash flow. My bills

---

[32] "This saying has often been attributed to Lucius Annaeus Seneca, but there is no proof that he ever used this phrase in any of his works." "Famous Sayings #141 — 'Luck Is when Preparation Meets . . .'" Shmaltz and Menudo. March 17, 2019. https://shmaltzandmenudo.wordpress.com/2019/03/17/famous-sayings-141-luck-is-when-preparation-meets/

were all covered by the ambulance job, my mental state was nourished by kayaking, and my fun and savings would be supplemented by the new business.

I read every local, state, and federal law on the books regarding knife and firearm ownership and sales. I spoke with the Bureau of Alcohol, Tobacco, Firearms, and Explosives multiple times with various questions. I spent a month researching company names and website domains. While I figured out a lot of it on the fly, I did so with as much education and knowledge as possible before any decision was made.

When I finally completed the prework and received confirmation that my licenses were approved, I reached out to a local paper to let them know about the new business venture. My initial desire was to run the gun shop as a side hustle. I offered transfer services and ran background checks for locals who had purchased firearms outside our community. I charged a small fee for the time, and they avoided hours of driving.

The day the newspaper article was published, my first client called to transfer a purchase he had made on the internet. When someone bought a firearm on the internet, that firearm, by law, had to be shipped to an FFL dealer so that a background check could be conducted and the proper paperwork could be completed and filed. If the person did not complete the paperwork correctly, or if they did not pass the background check, they could not take possession of the firearm.

While my first customer was waiting for the background check to process, he asked if I could order some rifles for him. I informed him that I was planning to only do transfers and background checks, as I had a full-time job on the ambulance.

He insisted, saying he wanted to support a local business. He told me what model rifle he wanted. I looked it up. My first retail sale would gross over $10,000, netting me about $1,200. I asked him to give me a week or so to set up some accounts, and I would see what I could do. He passed his background check and paid me for the service. The second the door closed behind him, I was on the phone and sending emails to distributors in an effort to set up the retail side of my business.

The next day, I received another phone call. My second customer wanted to know how I was processing transfers. During our discussion, he asked if I could source the items he wanted, allowing him to spend his money locally instead of spending it online. I told him I was just setting up the retail side, so if he could give me a week, I would get back to him. He emailed me a list of the items he wanted along with his contact information.

While waiting to hear back from the distributors, I worked to remove traces of my kayaking and personal history from online searches, as I wanted a basic level of privacy for this new venture. I scrubbed metadata and search engine parameters to bury online references to me. While I knew that nothing could be erased from the internet, I could still maintain a fairly high degree of electronic anonymity. I wanted to compartmentalize the three areas of my life so that customers and other associates would not be distracted by the multiple hats I was wearing.

Many distributors required a brick-and-mortar storefront and minimum annual sales before opening a new dealer. I managed to find two distributors who would allow me to provide a limited offering. I struggled to fulfill the orders for my two first customers. I even called my hometown gun shop in Florida to get advice. When I spoke with them, they were excited I was in the industry and offered to help however they could. When I called my mother, she reminded me that her father's best friend worked in the gun business. She suggested I give him a call. He, too, was excited and offered recommendations.

Just under a week later, I had a legal pad full of customer requests. I was also discovering that setting up the retail portion of this business was going to be more difficult and much more expensive than I had originally anticipated. On the positive side, I sourced the items for both of my first two customers. Before placing the orders, I reached out to each of them to discuss the price.

I learned an important lesson about pricing and profits. At the time, not much in the firearms industry sold for the manufacturer's retail price. Backyard FFL dealers and online competition drove prices down. The only operations that charged full retail prices were the big-box stores. Customers would shop at the big-box store, then go to a local mom-and-pop shop or a gun show to negotiate a better price. I also learned that there were very small margins in the firearms industry. I was discouraged. If I wanted to get into the retail side of this business, I would need to be resilient. Resilience required hustle and creativity.

Working for helmet manufacturers, I was familiar with pricing based on margin calculations. In the firearms industry, I learned that most dealers based their pricing on markup, which is calculated differently.[33] The end result is a much smaller profit. On the flip side, I had minimal overhead and steady income from other resources, and I was setting this up as a service to the community. I didn't need immediate profits. I had time to figure it out, and I wanted to impress my new clients.

In college, I had a business professor who was critical of a customer-centric business strategy I proposed. In my mind, this professor had an antiquated view for how a business should be managed. I disagreed with his traditional perspective and barely earned a passing grade in his course. I left his class with my head held high, confident in the knowledge that I would one day have the chance to use my innovative business practices in a business of my own.

I tested some of my theories while introducing my helmets to the market in a collaborative, educational way rather than making it a cutthroat enterprise. Now I had an opportunity to test my belief that customers were not objects; they were essential partners in the business.

As I talked with my first two customers, I asked their input on what pricing they felt was fair. I let them know that I wanted them to feel like I

---

[33] Margin is a figure that shows how much of a product's revenue you get to keep, while markup shows how much over cost you have sold it for. Margin: Income = (Price − Cost) / Price x 100. Markup: Price = (Markup x Cost) + Cost.

was taking care of them while covering my expenses and making a profit. This was a first step toward integrating my college business philosophy into my own business. I wanted the customers to take ownership of the business. I wanted them to feel and understand their value. Without having communication with each other, both customers provided the same feedback. They suggested I net a ten percent profit on firearms and charge retail for accessories and ammunition. That is exactly what I did, and they were elated when I told them I had sourced their orders.

The first customer's order came to just over $10,000. He asked, "Do I need to pay up front?"

"Are you good for it?" I asked.

"Yup."

"Ok. Then you can just pay with cash or a check when you come to pick up your guns," I replied.

I had the same conversation with the second customer, then proceeded to place their orders. This was the second philosophical step I wanted to implement: trust. If the client has ownership in a business, they want it to succeed. In order for them to trust me, I needed to show trust in them.

However, I needed to pay the distributors before the orders would ship. By paying for these items, I was out on a limb financially. So, the risk was mine to take, and the trust was theirs to lose.

The second customer came to my house a week later to pick up his order. He was thrilled. As it turned out, we were both Florida boys who had moved to the Colorado mountains decades before; we hit it off quickly.

"Matty, you're my new gun guy. I am going to tell everyone I know to only use you," he said.

Mistakes were costly, and I discovered that every customer I upset spread the word to ten of their friends. Even when I refused to do something illegal, many people were angry that I would not bend the rules. Politicians made laws that did not make any sense, so I did not understand why I was the bad guy for enforcing them. It took a long time for me to not take others' emotional reactions personally. I wanted to please everyone while maintaining a high standard of compliance. I had to be mindful and objective when informing customers about what I could and could not do as a gun dealer. I had to be quick to recover when things went sideways.

I learned a hard lesson after trying to work with the first customer for six months. I was out nearly $10,000. He refused to pay and ignored my phone calls. After six months, I off-loaded the product online to recover my costs. I was bummed out. As much as I wanted to run a business built on trust, there had to be buy-in for that trust to be secured, so I began requiring deposits and prepayment for special orders. Every once in a while, I still made an exception.

I was invited to have dinner and drinks at a local bar with several people I knew from working on the ambulance. The group consisted of sheriff's deputies, dispatchers, and myself. I was due for a relaxed night.

When I arrived, there was one open seat at the table, so I sat down, introducing myself to the woman on my left. She was a beautiful sheriff's deputy. I learned she was the only female on the SOU Entry Team. During our conversation, I told her I had a firearms business in addition to being a paramedic. She said she had been looking everywhere, unsuccessfully, for a new handgun for work. I had acquired some great contacts, so I gave her my card and suggested that she email or text me the details, and I would let her know when I found it.

About a week later, I made one such prepayment exception to surprise this beautiful deputy with her new handgun. We hit it off immediately. Shortly after we met, I flew to Europe to train freestyle kayak judges for the European kayak competition circuit. When I told her where I was going, she exclaimed, "Wow! You get to go to Europe for kayaking? You're lucky!"

Was I grateful? Absolutely! Did I simply luck out? No way. I spent years preparing for that opportunity. I surrounded myself with experts who continually challenged me, encouraging me to fine-tune my skills. I drove countless miles to chase rivers with seasonal flows. When I was injured, the drive to get back on the water was an all-consuming thirst that would only be slaked when I was back on the river.

I truly suffered from a liquid addiction. This suffering, this addiction, coupled with creativity and drive, yielded that invitation. It also helped to be supported by a network of friends and associates who recognized my potential.

Throughout the week I spent in Lyon, France, I was continually exchanging texts and emails with the woman from the sheriff's office for whom I had procured a handgun. Every time I returned to Colorado between trips, we would date more and more seriously and exclusively. Finally, a year later, she began to join me on my trips.

Burnout

I continued to follow a nontraditional path, eschewing the nine-to-five work day. I continued to choose jobs that provided space for kayaking, skiing, and other adventures. The pattern became clearer; there was a method to my madness. I chose flexibility over stability. I chose experience over routine. I became the king of the side hustle. At any given time, I had half a dozen irons in the fire. More than once, I found myself spread too thin. Through it all, working with the ambulance district was my safety net. It provided a steady source of income as I pursued a multitude of side businesses.

I began working with another helmet company, the first to incorporate Bluetooth technology into their helmets. In nine months, I organized a team that generated millions of dollars in pre-orders. We expanded into new channels of distribution, creating branding opportunities that had not been considered. Even though we exceeded the five-year goals in mere months, poor management and processes caused the company to be continually delayed in production. I chose to step away after the company spent an entire year repeatedly making excuses for nonperformance. It was a frustrating experience that led to a shift in gears rather than clinging to a branch that was not yielding fruit. I learned that sometimes it is time to let go, and that is OK.

In my mid-thirties, I was working with a team to get freestyle kayaking adopted as an official Olympic sport, my firearms business had reached my three-year projection in eighteen months, I was involved in a relationship that was progressing toward marriage, I had proven that I could manage and exceed goals with an international team, and I was still working on the ambulance. It was exciting—and entirely overwhelming.

Work with the ambulance district had been a good fit for many years. The fit was becoming stretched, as I was burning out. I lost focus. I felt misunderstood, like nobody cared about the culture I had contributed to building and cared so much about. Though I had trained paramedic students to use mindfulness in medicine, my own interest and passion was waning. I found myself ignoring my intuition and blaming others for my dissatisfaction. I was experiencing lapses in mindfulness and awareness. My heart just was not in it anymore, and I knew it was time for a change.

I had been functioning as an EMT-Intermediate, providing advanced life support (ALS) in the community, and working as a field training instructor for new staff for seven years on the ambulance and had been teaching at the college for nearly as long. I taught the first semester of the college's paramedic class and enrolled as a student in the second semester, while teaching, to obtain an associate of applied science degree in paramedicine.

I had also been accepted for a three-month internship with a fire department, which entailed a cycle of forty-eight-hour shifts with twenty-four hours off. The fire department was two hours away, so my days off were spent commuting and sleeping.

This fueled my burnout at the ambulance district. I asked for paid/personal time off from the ambulance and was denied, leaving me to work full-time while juggling the demands of school, clinicals, and a new internship.

After completing school at the top of my class, finishing my internship, and working full-time as a paramedic, I was exhausted. I later learned that two other members of the ambulance were experiencing burnout at the same time, which led to a general atmosphere of resentment. I spent eight years running a crew as an ALS provider for the ambulance district; however, in this environment of resentment and blame, tenure did not matter.

We were all burned out and I (again) was the nail sticking up that got hammered. I was given a choice: quit or be fired. I announced my resignation the following day.

For the first time in eight years, I did not have a job that provided a reliable source of income. The safety net was gone. I felt vulnerable, unsure of how I would pay the bills.

My girlfriend, who was living with me at the time, supported my separation from the ambulance district. I made a lot of connections developing the firearms business, and I had numerous side hustles, including working as deputy coroner for the coroner's office; I felt confident that these varied endeavors would lead to future business opportunities.

My girlfriend and I made plans to get married, so I discussed my options with her. One of those options was to open a brick-and-mortar retail store for the gun business. I knew the gun shop would require a lot of time and energy. I also knew the long-term benefits would be worth it. I ran through the financial and time commitments required to open the gun shop with my soon-to-be wife. She agreed that the gun shop made sense. I had acquired a wide range of business skills working in the outdoor industry as well as connections working for the ambulance district. I was becoming known as the go-to guy for sourcing firearms, safety, and protective gear.

Immediately after submitting my resignation to the ambulance district, a number of other offers emerged. My commitment to the gun business coupled with my history on the ambulance produced a number of medical and security-related employment opportunities. Though it was stressful to let go of the safety net the ambulance district had provided, I felt a newfound sense of confidence.

New Ventures

In early summer, I was in Vail doing a paddling demo at the lake during the Mountain Games. I got a phone call from a military contractor and training company. After a forty-five-minute phone interview, I was hired as a medic, becoming the only civilian amid a team of Recon Marines providing pre-deployment training exercises for the military.

I was hired because the contractor needed a medic on site to draft the protocols and response procedures for managing sickness or injury during the training exercises. I also helped with transportation and acquisition of firearms and supplies. I could not sit still when deployed on trainings, so I helped with instruction in various lanes of training, prepping scenarios with moulage (special effects makeup) and special effects (which included vehicle bombs, buried explosions, or staged protests). I also worked with the navy medics, known as corpsmen, during their training exercises.

At first, I felt like an outsider because I had not served my country the way these men had, putting my life on the line for our nation's freedoms. After my second three-week tour of work, the guys I was working with pointed out the fact that working on the ambulance was serving my fellow Americans. My service was in-country rather than overseas, and my work on the ambulance was a form of civil service. I was humbled and grateful for the fact that these high-level operators accepted me as one of their own.

It felt good to know I was supporting our military by helping them prepare for their next deployment: hopefully, helping to save their lives with the lessons learned during training.

I wanted to expand my firearms business to include uniforms and body armor for law enforcement, fire, and ambulance agencies in the high country of Colorado. Just like firearms, there were no local resources for uniforms and body armor. The nearest providers were hours away.

Deployed for three weeks every six weeks to work the military jobs, I lived off the contractor earnings while reinvesting the gun shop profits back into the gun shop. This allowed the business to grow more efficiently.

Like any business, the gun business required a lot of work. I had become adept at building businesses from scratch. Having spent over a decade learning manufacturing basics from Paul with SporTube, then StevieG with Mysterioso, as well as launching two start-up helmet companies, I had gained firsthand knowledge of the steps required to craft a successful company. I had also been brought in as a marketing advisor for Airstream and had participated as an athlete with several other outdoor companies.

Launching a new business was exciting. I had the chance to create systems from scratch, build networks, organize logistics, adopt new branding, and prepare for the long term while acting in the moment. It was organized chaos.

This new venture, while local rather than international, was also exciting because I was able to apply the many lessons learned from managing international teams and networks to a small-town business. I was an accountant and an artist. I took a synergistic approach in my perspective as the "owner" of the business. From day one, I adopted the perspective that the only thing I owned was the debt.

I financed the business's birth, and my customers financed its growth. It was a "business family." Without good management on my part, the business would close its doors; without my customers' purchases and insight, the business would not survive. In my eyes, it was a partnership, and we all had to pull our weight. Together, we created a venture that contributed to our community. That collaborative attitude fueled the growth of the business.

This perspective was exemplified in a conversation I had with one of my sales reps.

"Dude, you are killing it up here," Shane said.

"No, I'm not," I replied.

"Yes. You are," he replied. "You're doing better than a lot of my big-city accounts."

"Honestly, it's a huge compliment to be this well received by the community. I think it has something to do with how I've broken down the fourth wall in the business."

"The fourth wall?"

"Sorry. It's a term from when I had my film company. It's when the viewer is brought behind the scenes. They aren't just observing the action, they get a glimpse into the decisions being made. Think *Deadpool*."

"Whatever it is, you're running a good business and it shows."

During a stretch of time when the shop was busy, my friend Ron offered to pitch in.

"THANK YOU for today," I said gratefully at the end of a hectic day.

"Yeah, man," Ron replied. "Just happy for you."

"For us. This isn't mine, it's ours."

"Your time, your money, your brain. It's just yours. I'm just along for the ride to help out when I can," Ron said. "Get some rest, and we will kill it again tomorrow. See you at ten-ish."

Ron was stubborn; I was too. Wanting to make sure he really grasped what I was saying, I fought for the last word: "My project, but the community's shop. Without all of us, it wouldn't exist."

"Alright, I'll let you win with that statement. See you tomorrow," he said, rolling his eyes.

"Not a fight or argument, Ron. Semantics and perception, maybe, but a core philosophy that defines a company is important. Good night, brother. You are correct on all counts!"

"But, Matt, you're the owner."

"No, Ron, I'm not."

"HAHA. Don't go there. You put up all the money, and you have taken all of the risk. The company is yours."

I let him win the "debate" with that statement. The next day, we were busy again.

Through the gun store, I was able to support emergency medical services, law enforcement, and fire departments by providing uniforms, safety products, and firearms. This expansion of the business also supported neighbors in the community by offering first aid and firearms safety classes. Learning to let go twice allowed me the opportunity to build something new.

Communication

To quote Yankee great Yogi Berra, "It ain't over till it's over." Not only do I have an infinite number of do-overs, I have an endless number of paths to take me toward my goal or away from it.

The labyrinth was three-dimensional. Upward spirals led me to the center of the labyrinth. Downward spirals took me away from it. Just when I thought I was hitting my stride, getting closer to my goal at the center of the labyrinth, something spun me down to the outside edge. Those setbacks were usually accompanied by a sense of forewarning. My intuition alerted me to the fact that a cliff was coming up. When I failed to heed its message, I got pulled off course.

As new and interesting professional opportunities continued to surface, I found myself spending more time away from home. When I was married, it was the first time I was truly vulnerable with another person. I fully opened up, not withholding any piece of myself. In my mind, I fully gave 100% of myself to work, 100% to play, and 100% to love. There is no such thing as 300%, so the numbers and the effort did not balance.

My wife became resentful of the twelve-to-sixteen-hour days the gun shop required plus the time I spent developing work with military contractors, instructing safety classes, and creating new marketing strategies. I reminded her that I had shown her the full business plan, which projected both time requirements and financial requirements. I was frustrated that she was holding a grudge, and I noticed her attitude toward me had changed.

Neither of us were communicating effectively. My wife grew more and more distant, as did I.

I began to realize that I had previously ignored my intuition, which took the form of a voice of doubt in my head. On three separate occasions, I questioned my decision to marry this woman. On three separate occasions, my intuition had been trying to save me from falling off a very painful cliff. From a broader standpoint, the fall was necessary to learn communication skills that would serve me throughout the rest of my life. These communication skills would be critical for future work as an elected official.

In a desperate attempt to save the marriage, I reached out to my mother and my mother-in-law for guidance. They both checked in with me daily; however, it was my mother-in-law who challenged me to improve myself. She gave me a film to watch and books to read. In the end, even she agreed that the relationship was beyond repair, and she gave me her blessing when we filed the papers for divorce.

I was lost in a world of doubt. I doubted myself, my values, my self-worth. I doubted my goals and the direction my life was headed. I was in a downward spiral. I created a personal mantra that I meditated on each morning when I woke up. I reminded myself to live with honor, act with integrity, and speak with truth.

George offered a lifeline. George was a counselor and psychologist who offered post-traumatic stress debriefings and employee assistance program support for emergency responders after high-stress calls and incidents. George also provided marriage counseling.

I got to know him during my ten years working on the ambulance. I also had interactions with him while working for the coroner's office as a deputy coroner. When I opened the gun store, George had supported the venture with a few knife purchases.

I had not seen George in a little over a year. When he showed up one afternoon to buy a new knife, I thought nothing of it. The following week, he stopped in and asked if we could get some lunch. He and I began doing lunches every Tuesday. Unbeknownst to me, George knew how much I was going through. He was checking up on me and wanted to offer support.

After my mother-in-law opened my eyes to the truth that my marriage was over, I called George to ask for help.

"If my marriage is ending, I want to be a better man coming out of this divorce. I need to learn where I screwed up and how I can do better. I don't know how to do that. Is that something you can help me with?"

Without hesitation, George said, "Yes."

I spent the next two months going to his office twice a week. It was like a one-sided version of couple's therapy. I learned basic communication skills, which were incredibly valuable in every facet of my life. I was later able to apply those skills to my interactions with friends and customers, and to my work on town council and elsewhere.

George taught me the foundational components of the Gottman Method for communication. Listening for understanding, rather than listening to respond or react, was my first step. Most people formulate a response while listening, so they never truly hear what the other person is intending to communicate. I started to practice listening for understanding, realizing much of my frustration stemmed from feeling misunderstood. George told me to repeat back to people what I thought I heard to ensure I heard and understood what they were saying. This was agonizingly slow at first; however, with practice, it became more fluid and a more natural part of my interactions.

I dove headfirst into George's assignments, doing my best to absorb his teachings. I was not always successful. I kept working to make progress. He taught me to be more emotionally aware of others and mindful of my own emotional state. He reminded me to meditate every morning for ten to twenty minutes to recenter myself before the day began. He taught me empathy and understanding.

It blew me away to realize these basic, fundamental skills were never taught in school or through the process of growing up. In junior high, we had classes on accounting and learned to maintain a checkbook. We took home economics classes to learn to cook and maintain a household. We took classes in typing, writing, mathematics, and civics. We were never taught basic communication skills. I was amazed that our educational system failed to teach this foundational skill set, which impacts every aspect of life.

I began to practice repeating what I heard customers telling me and asking questions for clarification. At first, I had to consciously stop moving, making a focused effort to slow down. I looked people in the eye, repeated what I heard, and asked, "Are you asking *this*?"

Even if I felt it was the most asinine question, rather than snap off a no or a short answer, I would repeat their question back to them for clarification. Sometimes, just repeating the question, customers would hear what they asked and laughingly say, "Never mind. I think I know the answer. Thanks."

Other times, they would correct me, and I would then be able to more accurately answer what they had asked.

Communication became more than a way to bounce back after my marriage failed. It was my reward for being resilient. I learned techniques that helped me communicate more effectively with customers, friends, and leadership cohorts.

Just when it felt like I was making headway, life's labyrinth took another turn.

Grit

Three months after my divorce, while working for the coroner's office, a dead body fell on me. I had received a call to examine the body of a petite woman, weighing around 100 pounds, who had died facedown in front of a fireplace. She appeared to have been seated in a chair in front of the fire prior to her death. When I arrived, her buttocks were resting on the edge of the chair, and her chest was resting on the hearth in front of the fire. It looked as if she had fallen asleep and was resting on the edge of the chair.

I was bent over examining a puncture wound on her heel when someone removed the chair she had been propped on. Rigor mortis subsided, and she dropped backward onto my chest. Though she was a small person, dead weight is dead weight. As I tried to catch her, I felt a familiar lightning bolt of pain shooting up from my feet to my neck, similar to the pain I had felt after going off the Oh-Be-Joyful waterfall.

A couple days later, my back was still tight. At the time, I walked to work every morning and home every night. It was a quick one-mile trek that Jasmine loved. I began walking slower and limping more. I deteriorated to the point where I could not stand up at work. After six weeks of physical therapy, I was screened by Dr. Corenman, the back surgeon who took care of me fifteen years prior. It was a great reunion during which he pointed out my photo hanging on the wall.

After a multitude of images and exams, he told me the primary problem appeared to be in my hip. Dr. Corenman pulled some strings to get me referred to a hip surgeon, hoping that by fixing my hip, we could avoid cutting into my back. The hip surgeon found issues with both hips; however, the problem was more pronounced on my left. He recommended having surgery on the left hip followed by a re-evaluation. If the problem persisted, I would undergo back surgery. If the other hip was still having issues after back surgery, I would possibly need a second hip surgery.

Three surgeries? After enduring the recovery from my previous back injury, I knew how energy sucking the process could be. The prospect of three separate surgeries was preposterous. What if there were complications? What if I got an infection? I could not contemplate the financial implications of three major surgeries. I knew it would require every ounce of grit and determination I could muster. Even then, I did not realize just how massive the climb would become.

Nevertheless, we had a plan. The surgery on my left hip was scheduled for June. Thankfully, the surgery went smoothly and successfully. My exit from the hospital was pure comedy. Several police officers had become friends through EMS and the gun store. When four of them realized I would be discharged while they were on duty, they decided to meet me at my room and escort me to the physical therapy center downstairs.

The four officers and I snuck into a private room. A therapist arrived with my discharge instructions. I was seated on a table, and the officers, in full uniform, were lined up, solemn-faced, against the wall. I was high on Dilaudid, so the scene felt fantastically hilarious. The therapist went through the items on her checklist. Everything seemed funny, and I was struggling to maintain my composure. Then she asked, "Do you know what Kegels are?"

I was bursting at the seams. "No, ma'am. Would you mind showing me?"

Snickers from the corner turned to raucous laughter that was surely heard throughout the floor. When we finally quieted down, she rolled her eyes, saying with a sly grin, "I can't show you, but I bet one of the guys would be happy to help." The room erupted in uncontained immaturity.

After prescribing limited movement and exercise for the first week post-surgery, the therapist opened the door, indicating it was time to leave. Two officers walked out first, followed by me and the therapist, and the remaining two officers took up the rear. You could have heard a pin drop as we walked through the therapy center's exercise room. All activity stopped, and every eye in the room was focused on me.

The therapist whispered to me, "What are you in for?"

I stifled a giggle as I hobbled on my crutches out the front door. Outside the hospital, we burst out laughing.

I spent the next few months doing daily exercises at home, going to physical therapy three times a week, and doing therapy in a swimming pool one day a week. While my body was limited, my brain could not sit still. Lying on the table while the therapist worked on me, I flipped through catalogs and magazines and inquired about the equipment the therapist was using.

I came up with a device that would help patients track their recovery, then worked with an electrical engineer to draw up the design. Eight weeks later, our patent application was submitted. In ten weeks, I had a sales agreement with another company for the rights to this new device, so long as the patent was approved and other contingencies were met. I did not have the money necessary for a private launch, so the partnership would be ideal.

The stimulation of the patent design process kept my mind occupied, distracting me from the constant pain and frustration associated with physical limitation. It was as if I had fallen off a cliff and there were no stairs to the top. The mental engagement provided a psychological foothold, like digging steps into the hillside.

After sixteen weeks, I barely passed the physical test to fully resume normal daily activity. My back was getting worse. My patent application also came back denied. The patent office stated that we were only combining existing technology, that we had not invented anything. We had argued that the combination of technologies constituted a new use and design. Still, the initial design concept was denied.

Rather than give up, we went back to the drawing board. Starting over in the design process required the same grit as continuing to do the work in physical therapy. It was frustrating when progress was slow. It often felt like a waste of time.

One day, I woke up with an epiphany. Grabbing a pen and paper, I immediately started sketching out the new model. I took a picture of the image and emailed it to my engineer. He agreed this new design would work. It was a radical shift and would definitely get the patent approved. The new design would also save hundreds of thousands of dollars in manufacturing costs over the previous design.

I called the company that wanted to buy the rights to the patent and shared my new design concept. They sent a link to a European company's website. This company had a CAD drawing of something similar to my design. Though my product was superior, the difference was not significant enough to compel an investor to finance the operation. The steps I was digging melted away in the rain. I had to accept the fact that four months of patent design work had merely been a distraction.

I also had to face the hard reality that a successful hip surgery did not alleviate the pain from the injury I sustained when the dead body fell on me. I suspected back surgery was looming in the near future.

My staff was growing weary of running the store in my absence. I was not in physical or mental condition to run the store. A half-hearted effort would damage the gun shop's reputation for excellence. If I went back to work before being cleared by the doctors, the insurance company would not cover my medical bills. A hard decision had to be made. I told my staff and friends that I was going to close the doors temporarily to make space for another surgery and ensuing recovery.

Prior to the hip surgery, I asked my vendors to freeze my accounts and grant me four months to pay for any inventory I had purchased on credit. They were all amazed at my candor and agreed.

Four months post-surgery, I was coming up short, and another surgery loomed on the horizon. I asked Dr. Corenman if we could delay my back surgery by two weeks. He agreed and wrote me a letter allowing light-duty work for two weeks so that I could get my affairs in order. Dr. Corenman had one caveat. I had to promise not to lift, move, or do anything requiring physical exertion.

I used those two weeks to prepare for a sale. I was fully transparent in a newsletter sent to my customers where I shared my physical and professional struggles. My customers responded with resounding support. The sale was huge. I was able to pay all vendors in full and even paid my landlord rent through the end of the year.

Two weeks later, my back surgery was successful. Post-surgery, I could stand up straight for the first time in over nine months. I was elated.

However, three months after the back surgery, I was still in pain and still walked with a limp. The back surgery did not fix the underlying problem. It soon became clear I would need surgery on the other hip.

As per doctor's orders, I could not return to work. The work compensation insurance carrier denied the surgery for the other hip. I hired an attorney, who informed me this was common in the insurance industry. The worker's compensation insurance carrier wanted to catch me breaking the doctor's orders so they could avoid paying for additional medical care. Working in the gun shop would be a violation of doctor's orders.

I was stuck in a game of cat and mouse with the insurance company that lasted eighteen months and nearly cost me everything. I had to get creative in order to save the gun shop and continue paying the bills.

Creative is what I did. I hustled behind the scenes to keep the business functioning enough to break even. I began shopping for real estate and planning for a grand reopening once the insurance games were wrapped up. In the meantime, I kept myself distracted with physical therapy, socializing with friends and neighbors, writing, and outlining business ideas.

On the positive side, life provided a multitude of opportunities for do-overs. What goes down must come up. Upward spirals led me back in the direction of my goal. I was not relegated to living a life on the outside fringe of the labyrinth. I had new opportunities to trust my intuition and cultivate mindfulness. This was the essence of resilience. Grit and determination were required to stay the course.

Taking Risks

Looking at the amount of money I was paying every month to rent commercial space for the gun shop, I realized it would be prudent to find a commercial space to buy. When I called Scott, a local friend and realtor, to ask about properties to rent or to buy, he got very animated and said, "Matt. Do you remember that smaller space you looked at a few years ago?"

"Yes," I replied.

"It just got listed for sale." He continued, "It is half the price it was selling for when you looked at it a few years ago!"

"How is that?"

"It's a long story, but the company that owned it went into foreclosure, and another client of mine bought it for pennies. He's thinking about selling it, so there's a window. You should make an offer," Scott suggested.

I hesitated. "Can I think about it?"

Scott was a straight shooter. He was not just a realtor; he was my friend. I knew Scott was being sincere when he said, "Don't take too long because if he doesn't sell it, he may just decide to keep it."

I had never purchased commercial real estate and recognized the need to seek help from people who had more knowledge than me. Through the gun shop, I had become friends with many local ultra-high-net-worth individuals (UHNWIs), several of whom started from nothing and built companies and portfolios that would provide a solid and lasting financial legacy for their families.

One friend, John, was twenty years older than me and owned a company that provided services to governments and corporations all over the world. He started out with a small ski business and leveraged his early successes by investing in a variety of business ventures. I sent John an email asking if he had time for a quick call.

Within five minutes, my cell phone rang. "Hey, Matt."

"That was fast. Thanks!"

"I'm driving back up to the mountains, so the timing works out. What's going on?"

"I want to buy a commercial space for the store."

"Don't do it. You're in the retail business, not the real estate business."

"Really? Even if I can get it below market?"

"Why tie up all that money in real estate when you can invest it in merchandise that will give you faster profit?"

"OK. I can see what you're saying."

"Where are you looking? When are you going to build your range?"

I described the two properties I was considering, then explained, "The range is a no-go right now. I nearly lost everything when I had those surgeries, so I'm starting over from scratch financially. I turned the special use permits back into the town."

"I hate to hear that. I'm meeting with someone this afternoon. We will talk about it. Maybe we can all come up with a plan together."

"Wow. That would be awesome! Let me know what I can do!"

"OK. I gotta run, Matt. Find a nice place to rent, and buy more inventory."

"Yessir. Thanks for calling, John. I really appreciate it."

That gave me a lot to digest. Should I play it safe and focus on the gun business like my friend recommended or take a risk and branch out into uncharted waters? I fully understood John's guidance. However, something was tugging at the edge of my consciousness.

The two properties were very different. One would require creative investment and third-party financing. It would be a step up in size, and I would have enough room to build a range and rent a portion of the space to another business. The other property was less than half the size of my current store; however, I had a chance to buy it for almost 40% less than the appraised price. Plus, my worker's compensation attorney knew the Small Business Association loan officer. With his referral, I could minimize loan initiation fees and bank surcharges. I labored over the decision for a week, running the numbers daily.

When my mom called that Sunday, she could tell I was distracted. "What's the matter, Matthew?"

"Nothing. I just can't decide what to do."

"What do you mean?"

"I need to move the store, and I have a chance to buy a commercial space for a great price, but one of my advisors told me not to do it. I get what he was saying, but something is nagging me. The numbers work, and I can't put this to rest."

"What did your friend say?"

"Basically, he said that I'm not in the real estate business, so I shouldn't spend money on real estate."

"Matthew, your granddaddy said you're never something until you are. You're not in the real estate business until you own your first piece of real estate, and we all have to start somewhere. If your gut is telling you to buy it, then buy it."

"Grandaddy said that?"

"Yes, he did. He was a smart man."

"I'm just torn. I get what John was saying. I just have a feeling. I could pay for it all with cash, or I could compromise between my gut and John's advice. Put a twenty percent deposit down, get a loan, and invest the rest of the cash into inventory. Best of both worlds, right?"

"Would the loan payments be the same as you are paying for rent now?"

"With the mortgage, taxes, insurance, and utilities, it's a breakeven. I'd pay the same as I'm paying now, with a smaller footprint, though."

"Smaller might be easier to maintain, and if you grow out of it, you can rent it out, and it can pay for itself. Matthew, I think you know what you need to do. Buy the property. The rest will work itself out."

The minute we hung up, I called Scott and told him to put in an offer on the commercial space. Then I registered a new company name with the state, obtained an employer identification number, and emailed the loan officer to let her know I was ready to apply for a loan. Everything happened quickly. I was soon in the commercial real estate business as well as the retail business. I took the risk needed to break out of an old cycle.

Overwhelmed

With help from several friends, I built out the new shop and prepared to reopen it as a showroom as opposed to a full-service retail store. During the surgeries and the standoff with insurance, my inventory had been liquidated, along with my savings. I used the little money left over from purchasing the space to acquire just enough inventory to stock the showroom. I could not justify hiring new employees with the scaled-down footprint, so I ran it as a one-man operation.

I began to feel stressed. My girlfriend was moving out, my business was impacted by a new round of gun laws, and I had no strategy for this new playing field. My work with the town council was becoming hectic as well. I then felt trapped.

The pendulum had swung back. Rather than biking, paddling, or exercising, I buried myself in work for fifteen hours a day. I stayed up late reading books and watching movies. I ate crappy food because it was cheap and easy. In a matter of months, the results of poor diet and a lack of exercise resulted in gaining back thirty of the forty pounds I had lost.

Reflecting on my "death-at-forty" premonition, I realized that it felt like a part of me had actually died. I needed to be resilient on a daily basis. The accident with the coroner's office and ensuing surgeries left me depleted and overwhelmed. In addition to dealing with the emotional trauma of a failed marriage, the surgeries prevented me from participating in the athletic pursuits that played a central role in my self-image.

The word "recovery" sounds positive, hopeful, maybe even somewhat peaceful. There are so many other facets of recovery: self-doubt, depression, and pain. Recovering from back-to-back surgeries coupled with financial stress and insurance games, my emotions ran the full spectrum, from celebration of minor achievements to the soul-sucking void of depression.

I felt like I was swinging on a pendulum. The longer the pendulum swung to one side, the more momentum it gained to swing back again. I gained nearly fifty pounds. I was full of self-pity and self-doubt. I was having a hard time getting back into the game, constantly slapping a happy-face sticker on the gas gauge pointing to empty.

I put a positive spin on every setback and sold everyone on how great I was doing.

"I'm good to go," I would say.

In truth, I was emotionally and psychologically stuck in a mire, embroiled in stress-filled hell. After some time, I finally admitted to myself that I needed help. I needed a coach to hold me accountable and motivate me. This was a huge step. Prior to the shift, I told myself, "I used to be a personal trainer and an athlete! I know what I need to do. I don't need help."

Yes. I did need help.

When I had been at a crossroads for the business, a solution had appeared. Now I needed a more personal fortunate accident.

My friend Luke came by my house, delivering what I needed when I needed it most. He told me about Ben Wright, a nutrition and fitness expert who had been working with the police department. Ben was a veteran who had been featured on the Netflix documentary *Icarus*. He agreed to meet me for a coffee; more accurately, Ben and I met so he could interview me.

I gave him my best sales pitch. I told him I knew what had to be done, I just needed some help. He saw right through my bullshit. After all, if I knew what to do, I would have done it. After patiently listening and politely calling me on my bluff, he took me on as a client, assigning me to one of his nutritionists, Katie.

I can be a pain in the rear as a patient. It killed me to admit I needed help. I was depressed, angry, and humiliated. To this day, I am amazed that Ben and Katie still talk to me. They are masters at their respective crafts and were patient and kind as I made slow, steady progress. With their help, I gained the momentum to make my climb back up the hill.

I managed to lose forty-five pounds and four inches off my waist in four months. It felt so good to finally take control of my life. I began to envision a kayak season filled with epic runs. I was back.

My family, friends who were like family, and the kayaking community were all very supportive. Even my clients would call to check in, remaining loyal to the business as I struggled to find my way.

There is a saying, "Misery loves company." C. R. Rogers states it much more eloquently: "What is most personal is most universal."[34] I've found that to be true. Humans in crisis bond together.

I had a good friend who was fighting demons of his own. Guska and I had met a decade prior when he was still in high school. I sponsored him with helmets and took him kayaking after noticing his aptitude for freestyle kayaking and his proclivity for hard work. Guska was one of the local up-and-coming kayakers. He also owned his own business filling vending machines. I used to make fun of him for being a park rat—meaning he would go to waves or holes to play for hours rather than kayaking down a river. After he graduated from high school, I took him to kayaking events, and we had fun paddling the western states. He began calling me his older brother. At some point, people began thinking we actually were brothers.

Though we were each traveling independent paths, we were connected in the journey of recovery. Guska had suffered injuries of his own at work, so we began texting periodically to offer encouragement and support. One late night in the spring, he reached out to me just as I felt like I was hitting an emotional bottom:

> BG: How's it going?
>
> MS: Still feel like a has-been, but I'll get back.
>
> BG: Takes time to get confidence up! Every day is a success in my book.
>
> MS: I am 207 right now. 25# overweight and it is depressing. Literally. I feel stuck and fat.
>
> BG: Dude. You and me both. I'm 232! Just stay positive and keep working hard every day is a gain. It will shred.
>
> MS: What is wrong with us?!
>
> BG: Ah, it's life man! My surgery was almost one year ago. I'm just

---

[34] There's evidence to suggest that this quote comes from his book *On Becoming a Person: A Therapist's View of Psychotherapy*. Houghton Mifflin Harcourt Publishing Company; 1972. However, no official sources or credible evidence could be found.

thankful that I can do the things I enjoy. We were pro athletes at one point in our lives we will get it back. It's a start. I think for me the river is very spiritual...

MS: Yup. Me too. Thanks for that.

BG: Just got to stay at it! I didn't even want to bike today, but I made myself and I feel great now. Hard part for me is everybody around us is a badass. The average is not average. I just have to remind myself to give it time because I'm not average. When I wake up, I remind myself that it is time to train.

Through the recovery process, I drew on earlier lessons in awareness, intuition, and mindfulness. I realized that it was one thing to know what I was supposed to do; it was another thing to do it. That was my lesson of resilience. Awareness and mindfulness were just concepts in my head until I applied them to life's challenges. Resilience was the process of actively applying life lessons. Resilience required grit. It required determination. It required taking risks. In the end, resilience began with a series of decisions that redefined my character.

Diplomacy

When a local congresswoman spoke at a local town hall meeting, I was in attendance, as were several of my customers. They were looking to me to be their voice regarding the congresswoman's perspective on gun laws in our state.

My initial question for her: "You have a lot of pressure and a lot to balance. How do you balance the demands of your constituents, your personal beliefs, and the requirements of the constitution when you need to make a decision in public office?"

She answered honestly, with a lack of precision and poor choice of words, saying, "I vote for my conscience first and my constituents second." She never mentioned the constitution. She went on to voice her strong anti-gun perspective, not knowing I was the owner of the local gun shop. I repeated back what she said and later confirmed with others in the room to make sure I heard her correctly. I was awestruck. Our representative was representing herself first. My eyes began to open.

The next day, I sent out a newsletter informing my customers that this state representative put her own personal initiatives ahead of those of her constituents. More importantly, she was lackadaisical in protecting our constitutional rights related to gun laws.

I was asked by a state and national lobbyist to speak before a state senate subcommittee that was preparing three new gun laws to be presented in Colorado. After reminders that everyone was allocated three minutes to speak, I was the first to present. In the face of senators, news cameras, and the audience, I finished in two minutes and fifty-nine seconds. After the senate subcommittee chair thanked me for my judicious use of time, he opened the floor for questions. I spent the next forty-five minutes answering questions from the subcommittee members about the implications the proposed gun laws posed for local gun stores as well as clarifying requirements outlined in current gun legislation. I could tell that my efforts did not change any minds in regard to legislation; however, this was my very public introduction to diplomacy.

Even though I had presented a very logical and factual case, I was ignored and written off as a gun advocate, not a rational participant. A reporter pulled me aside and asked for an interview after I completed my session of questions and answers.

She began by saying, "So, I am guessing you are a far right pro-gun conservative."

I chuckled when I responded, "No. I'm not."

She looked surprised. "What do you mean? You just gave the best testimony I've heard here, and it was pro-gun."

"No, it was anti-legislation. The laws they are proposing are completely out of sync and will not address the problems they promise. In fact, most of the issues the senate subcommittee claims the legislation addresses are already written into law."

"That makes sense. What do your customers think about you being here?"

"They don't know I'm here, yet. I have a rule in the gun shop. It is a place of business, not a place for political discussion. If someone is visiting my place of business, they are there to spend money on something tangible or on education and training. Once politics enters that doorway, I have found that people either agree or disagree—both of which take money away from the register. The rule is that we don't discuss politics in the store."

"And your customers support that?"

"Not only do they support it, they appreciate it to the point that they correct each other or inform new clients visiting for the first time. It's been fantastic."

"Wow. That's a great practice. So where do you fall on the political spectrum?"

"In the middle. Keep the government out of my pocket and out of my bedroom."

Marijuana had just been legalized in Colorado, so it was a second hot topic in the state. I had recently written a column for the paper highlighting how it would interact with gun laws, as Colorado is a state full of hunters and recreational shooters. With that in mind, I laughingly added, "I want all of my gay friends to own firearms so they can protect their weed."

The reporter started laughing loud enough that the committee chairwoman rapped her gavel several times, asking for silence in the room.

While the reporter was laughing, I was very serious about the topic at hand. I was mindful in my choice of words. I was precise about my true feelings and thoughts regarding very divisive and emotional topics. In my various endeavors in small business and government, I learned the need for choosing my thoughts and my words carefully with the same purpose and intentionality I applied to kayaking and medicine.

At the local level, I had already walked through the process of obtaining special use permits to build an indoor range. Through the permitting process, I became closer friends with the town manager at that time, Jon Stavney. We would meet occasionally for a beer to discuss ideas and policies. People assumed we had vastly different perspectives. They could not understand how Jon and I could have the in-depth discussions we would have, yet walk away shaking hands. We agreed on some things and disagreed on others. This introductory interaction with the state government opened my eyes. Sometimes, resilience requires diplomacy.

One evening, I was standing bar side at the local brewery when Jon walked up next to me and ordered a drink. We picked up on a conversation we had started earlier in the week about local mountain bike trail development, maintenance, funding, and responsibility. Jon was the town manager. He had also been a council member, mayor, and county commissioner. I respected Jon for his political acumen. He was astute when it came to navigating the waters of public opinion.

"Jon, do you know what we need to do?"

"What's that, Matt?"

"We need to clean up the rest area and build a white-water play park."

I pointed out the side door of the brewery toward the dirt truck parking lot that was barely visible through the trees, located on the other side of the river from where we stood. The river bank was covered in overgrowth mixed with dead vegetation. A chain-link fence caught trash blowing in the wind. Semitrucks filled the dirt lot, and dumpsters sat in plain view. It was the first thing visitors saw when they arrived in our small mountain town.

What was not visible was the river. Thirty years prior, the stream was a strange yellow-orange color from mining taking place fifty miles upstream. Over the previous three decades, the river had been cleaned up and had become a mecca for trout fishermen. As a kayaker who had visited a variety of rivers and play parks all over the world, I knew paddlers would appreciate the gradient. It was perfect for paddling. Few people were aware of the potential we had in our own front yard.

"That parking lot is disgusting," Jon began. "I was down there cleaning it up a couple of weeks ago. Throwing away shopping bags and plastic bottles that were blown into the fence and hanging from the trees. It was everything I could do not to vomit from the smell of waste."

"Exactly! It's atrocious," I responded.

"Matt, do you know the river used to swing about a half mile north, but was diverted when they built the interstate? I think the added gradient put a small wave down there."

"Yes. I can't confirm or deny that two people rolled giant boulders into the river to enhance a surf wave below the dam," I said, winking. "Between the reroute of the river and the remnants of the old diversion dam, there is enough gradient for a play park."

"How do you propose we do that?" Jon was genuinely intrigued. He looked at me with a glint in his eye, excited at the prospect of a fresh idea.

"For the last twenty years, we have dreamed of cleaning out the rebar from that broken-down dam and building a surf wave right behind that lot. If the town approved it, we could work on raising the money. It would be a huge asset for the town!"

Jon said, "I can see it. I hate that the first thing people see when they come to town are two dumpsters. Would it get used?"

"Are you kidding me? Jon, I've traveled to these parks all over the place, and they are all packed. Besides, the list of injuries from people falling out in that rapid is legit."

Right about that time, Hobie walked up. I looked at Jon, winked, and whispered, "Speaking of boulders," just as Hobie said, "Hey, guys. What are y'all scheming over here?"

I said, "Hobie, tell Jon that we need a white-water park behind the truck stop."

"Stop. Stop what you're doing right now!" Hobie exclaimed. He knew where I was going with this and took the reins.

Jon laughed and looked at him. "OK, Hobie, give it to me."

"The town needs to forget about everything it is doing and make this happen. That parking lot is disgusting. We could host the Team Trials for kayaking. We could host a legit surfing event—not in kayaks, but with surfboards. We could have a SUP race and competition. Matt helped organize the first ever North American SUP Championships in Glenwood two years ago. Jon, this NEEDS to happen."

Hobie has a tendency to get emotionally engaged when he's excited. A white-water play park was something that was near and dear to his heart. I placed the bait and Hobie set the hook. Jon was fully engaged.

"OK. I like it. I like it a lot. Let me see what I can do," Jon replied.

Within months, Jon presented the idea to the town council, the council gave him permission to look into it, and the process started. After community engagement sessions, town meetings, input from field experts, and development of a master plan, the town council was ready to begin the approval process. The town council wanted to finance the whole project. I wanted the town to approve the project, not spend taxpayer money paying for it. This was a similar discussion to the one Jon and I had when the mountain bike trail system had been developed. I was outspoken in opposing the use of taxpayer dollars to build the mountain bike trails. My opinion did not change just because the white-water park was my pet project.

The initial proposal included the approval of a sales tax increase to finance the park's construction. I attended every town council meeting to voice opposition to the increased sales tax. It would hurt my business and would hinder our ability to raise money privately.

People in the community knew I was involved in the design and approval process, so they stopped by the store to solicit my thoughts on the ballot measure.

When I voiced my opposition to the sales tax increase, most people looked at me with surprise and exclaimed, "I thought you were for the park!"

"I am for the park. I am against raising a tax to pay for it."

The tax measure was approved. To really add to their confusion, once the tax was approved, I then supported the whole project and financing goals.

People then asked me, "How can you support this? I thought you were against the tax?"

"I was against the tax. It passed. Now we should make sure we manage the money wisely. We should be mindful of how we use taxpayer dollars."

Through the process of developing the white-water park, I became more involved with the town council. Several customers came to the store asking me to run in the upcoming election. I laughed it off and told them I had no interest in politics, then thanked them for their confidence.

Steve, a friend and customer, told me, "Matt, it's not about politics. You're a leader. You're smart. You are an asset to our community. You need to be on the council." I told him I would think about it.

Ray, a hunting friend and president of the local Rocky Mountain Elk Foundation chapter tells the story a little differently. Barely containing his laughter, Ray said, "Matt, the only reason you ran for office is because someone told you that you'd never get elected."

The truth is, after eighteen months of lying low, I needed a challenge, something that would be mentally and socially engaging. It felt good to know that people in the community thought I could make a difference. The day before petitions were due, I gathered the required signatures, had the document notarized, and turned it in ninety minutes later. In a few short months, when the ballots were counted, I was duly elected and sworn in as a member of the town's governing board.

My role as a leader in my community continued to evolve and grow. I knew the town's commitment to outdoor recreation would have a significant impact on our community's economy. With a new mountain bike trail system, we would become host to the state championships for high school mountain bike racing, solidifying our town's reputation as a premier Colorado mountain bike destination. I also saw the extent to which a new white-water park could drive tourism in a community.

Hope

In early summer, Adriene came through town for the Mountain Games. She was a paramedic in South Carolina, one of the top multi-sport female athletes in the world, and my chosen little sister. I had known Adriene since she was fourteen. I was not able to attend the games because I had to run my store, so Adriene took time away from her training to come visit me at work. Seeing her walk through the door made my day! I closed the store early and treated her to a sushi dinner.

Professional athletes rely on sponsorships to help pay the bills, supply gear, or, at the very least, defray costs associated with pursuing their sport. Andrew, the Dagger team manager at the time, along with my stand-up paddleboard sponsor and other gear sponsors, reached out to me after my first surgery to let me know they were filling my spot with someone else. I fully understood. I was immersed in running my own business. I still helped out with Colorado events, just in a very limited capacity. I was not as active in the paddling community as I once was, and there were better, more involved paddlers who deserved and needed those resources. I appreciated the time I had on Team D. I was told that I was an ambassador for life, and anytime I needed gear, boats, or boards just to call, and they would send them my way.

That left me with my sole sponsorship: Capital One VISA . . . which I had to pay back with interest each month. Though paying for sushi felt extravagant, the price of dinner was miniscule when compared to the long-term benefit of my meal with Adriene. After all, friendship and hope are priceless.

Over dinner, Adriene shared paddling stories and talked about plans for her wedding in early September. It was inspiring to see the light in her eyes as she brimmed with excitement. Adriene was marrying another old friend of mine from Dagger, Snowy.

Snowy was Dagger's product engineer. He worked in the research and development department, refining Dagger's white-water kayak designs. Snowy and Adriene shared a passion for white-water kayaking. I had enjoyed a lot of time on and off the water with them. I was delighted when I heard they were finally tying the knot.

Adriene ran through the list of fellow paddlers who would be attending the event. She stopped and exclaimed, "Matt, you need to come!"

"I would love to," I replied. "I'm certainly due for a trip back East. I really miss seeing my paddling family." I hesitated, then said, "Money is tight, but for your wedding, I'll make it work. Let's keep it a secret! Don't tell Snowy."

Adriene leaned forward conspiratorially, a childish grin spreading across her face. "Yes!" she exclaimed. "Great idea! But what about Jessica?" Jessica was going to be Adriene's maid of honor. Jessica and her husband, Corey, were long-time friends. I considered Corey my second "little brother."

"Jessica? Yes. Corey? No way," I responded. "I've known Corey since he was a teenager. He can't keep ANYTHING secret from Snowy."

We both laughed and began planning my dramatic entry. It would be great to see Snowy's face when I walked into the room. As we talked, my head was spinning. How was I going to come up with the money to make this trip? Physically, financially, and emotionally, the odds were stacked against me. Still, resilience begins with hope, and the idea of attending Adriene and Snowy's wedding was just the spark I needed to start climbing the next hill.

Couch to Class V

Turning forty-three, I once again reflected on my death-at-forty premonition. It occurred to me that though my life did not end, I had traveled through an emotional and spiritual death. The recovery process seemed like a microcosm, a small representation of life's cyclical journey.

There was a cycle within a cycle. In recovery, I climbed a hill, fell off a cliff, and learned to climb back up it again. Slowly, but surely, the falls were not as dramatic and the climbs were not as strenuous. I was building resilience, and it was time to take a risk. Adriene and Snowy's wedding was the inspiration I needed to make a leap.

The day after my forty-third birthday, I bought my plane ticket. After all, it was my birthday week, right? There was no denying the fact that money was tight. I had the credit card statements to prove it. In the six-week span between my conversation with Adriene and my birthday, I spent hours devising debt consolidation strategies while watching my savings account dwindle. Regardless, the plane ticket to Adriene and Snowy's wedding was purchased. The decision was made. Financial stresses aside, I felt lighter.

The day after buying my plane ticket, I called Adriene. "I'm on my way!" I announced.

"Sweet!" she exclaimed. "I am so excited. Snowy is going to flip when he sees you. Bring your paddling gear 'cause we are doing a hangover run on the Green the day after the wedding."

My heart skipped a beat, and my voice caught as I felt a gnawing longing in my gut. I love the Green, a gorgeous, fun river that I had not run in nearly a decade. It had been seven years since I had kayaked a "real" section of river, like the Green.

"Awww . . . You know I'm dying to join you guys, Adriene. I don't think my body is up for the Green."

Adriene huffed. "Matt, you're OG Team Dagger—you HAVE to run the Green with us!"

There was silence on the phone as I recalled my spring run on Shoshone at fifty-five hundred CFS just a few weeks prior. It was my first day back on the river in nearly two years because of the surgeries. I was all over the place. My back felt unstable and weak.

I could hear Dr. Corenman's voice after the 2001 skiing accident echoing through my head: *Just a millimeter or two more and you wouldn't be walking right now. If you break your back again, it's very likely you won't walk away. Your cervical spine is already narrowed.*

I thought, *Shit, I'm screwed.*

Out loud, I told Adriene, "OK. We have a month. Let's see where I am in a month, and if I'm feeling strong and my back feels stable, then I'm down."

When we hung up, I immediately called Jessica, Adriene's maid of honor. "Hey! It's official. I just bought tickets for the flight."

"Yes!" Jessica replied. "That's amazing! Snowy is going to be so happy to see you."

"But you can't tell Corey," I reminded her.

"Hah. There is no way he'd be able to keep a secret from Snowy," she agreed.

"I'm going to need you to do some reconnaissance for me. I'm not going to ship my boat and paddle. I'm going to need to borrow some of Corey's gear. Would you be able to pull that together?"

"Absolutely. No sweat. This is going to be so fun! I'm so excited!"

The next morning, I pulled myself out of bed and threw myself into a workout routine of sit-ups, push-ups, planks, and pull-ups. If I was going to paddle the Green, I needed to get my core strength back. I needed to cut the carbs and eat clean, healthy food. That night after work, my workout mirrored the one I completed earlier in the day. The next morning, I got up well before work, drove down to Glenwood Canyon, and caught every eddy I could find on Shoshone.

Five days later, I called Adriene and told her that I was feeling good and excited. She and Jessica were on their way back from Adriene's bachelorette party. They put me on speakerphone.

"One month to get my butt into shape," I said. "I'm going to call this month 'Couch to Class Five!'"

The girls laughed. "That's brilliant!" they exclaimed. "Keep up the good work. It will all pay off when we're on the river together."

I did some mental calculations. Thirty days of running Shoshone before work, core exercises at night, and Gore Canyon laps on the weekends might actually put the Green within reach. It would be a stretch, but it was possible. I sent a text to Guska.

MS: Give me a call? #Couch2Class5 is underway and I am sore! LOL

BG: Congrats! I tweaked my back Wed. Been resting and on some meds. Great work. #church

MS: What happened to your back?

BG: Nothing major, just flared up from moving a patient. Back to work tomorrow.

MS: Yeah. Mine is sore as hell from kayaking this week. The core exercises have saved me a ton. Cut the carbs and sugar, and start strengthening your core. Your back will feel more stable.

BG: Mine's been good, just outstretched. Stupid of me. I know better, but it's nothing more than a flair up. Biking has helped me a ton! Lost fifteen pounds last month. Hunting should shed a bit more. Chica and I have been cooking ninety-five percent of the time and it's been good food! Lots of veggies.

MS: Dude – that's awesome!

Mental Toughness

Post-surgery, I realized I had developed a bad habit of referring to myself as a "has-been." Even worse than using that term for myself when talking to other people, it dawned on me that I had adopted "has-been" as a part of my identity. I used to play college football. I used to ski 100 days a year. I used to be a professional kayaker. I used to be a head judge for freestyle kayaking in the USA. I used to be a husband. I used to be and do a lot of things. Rather than reforming my identity in a positive light after my divorce and the accident, I was focusing on the ways I no longer lived up to my old identity.

Even as I took the first small steps toward attending Snowy and Adriene's wedding, I felt the exhilaration of hope. Like a deflated balloon filling with air, I felt a sense of purpose and renewed dedication. Exercise and healthy eating opened a world of possibilities. It also felt great to get back on the water. I looked forward to the days paddling Shoshone and Gore Canyon with friends on weekends. With each workout, I got stronger, which fueled the engine of belief.

After just over a week of training, I paddled Gore Canyon to celebrate Hobie's birthday with him. It was an epic run. I was feeling strong. After only one week of training, I was already doing things I had not done in years. Guska heard I went to Gore and dropped me a text.

BG: Gore was good?

MS: Yup. I'm still looking for my boof. Can't find it. OK. Found it at Tunnel, but I fully melted the sneak and the boof above Gore. Hahaha

BG: Huge day! How was Tunnel?

MS: LOL. Hey diddle-diddle [right down the middle]! Gore on Day 4. Props to me!

BG: That's awesome!!!!!

Concessions

Concessions were sneaky. I committed to a goal: attending Snowy and Adriene's wedding and paddling the Green the day after the wedding. The first week, I was disciplined. My workouts and eating were disciplined and precise. Then in week two, the concessions started.

This pattern was not new to me. Football teams start the year with two weeks of two-a-day practices before the season begins. Week one is easy.

Players and coaches are excited to be back on the field. Motivation is high. Week two is often the toughest week of the season. Bodies sore and limbs exhausted, players cannot wait for practice to end. My second week of Couch2Class5 followed a similar pattern. This time, there was no coach to inspire focus and no team to demand commitment.

After paddling Gore, we celebrated Hobie's birthday with drinks at the bar. The next day, I woke up tired and sore. It felt like I pulled a muscle on the left side of my rib cage. I ate fast food for lunch and immediately regretted it.

Tuesday's town council meeting went late: I did not get home until eleven and could not sleep until one thirty in the morning. I woke up late on Wednesday. I skipped my morning workout and paddling session. Wednesday night's business meeting ended with empty bottles of bourbon and whiskey. Friday night, I skipped my evening workout and went out drinking. The concessions were starting to eat away at my resolve.

My mother encouraged me to subscribe to a daily email newsletter called the DailyOM. By encouraging, I mean that she entered my email address and signed me up. These messages were created by author and recording artist Madisyn Taylor. The DailyOM was one of the few newsletters I did not unsubscribe from, as I found they gave relevant inspiration to my morning meditation.

There were many days, especially as I was going through my darkest hours, where I felt like the DailyOM messages were written just for me. As I began this C2C5 mission, the following email message was delivered at the perfect time:

Your commitment to your responsibilities will likely be unshakeable today, as the persistence you embody can help you overcome a wide variety of potential challenges. If you find yourself coping with difficulties, reaffirming your dedication to success and enlightenment can remind you why you are fighting so diligently to succeed at your chosen goals. However, you respond to problems that arise in your plans today, try to remember that success is an unavoidable element of your destiny. As long as you keep striving to achieve your purpose, you will likely have little trouble overcoming the challenges that stand between you and what you hope to achieve.[35]

That Saturday, I had an uplifting conversation with a new client at the gun shop, Mike, who was a coach and physical therapist. I told him about my injuries and stalled-out rehabilitation program. Mike had some great suggestions for modifying my exercise. He offered encouragement, which rekindled my resolve.

I was reminded that we all share energy; some people steal it, others give it. Sometimes, energy builds through the synergy of a conversation, creating a buzz that benefits both people. The conversation with Mike felt like a gift from the universe. It was like the universe saw me falling into unhealthy patterns that held me back over the past three years. My conversation with Mike, along with my DailyOM message, was a reminder that I could do better. I needed to do better if I was going to accomplish my goal of attending the wedding and paddling the Green.

The previous week of concessions was a wakeup call. I was disappointed in myself. Mindless eating, excessive drinking, and the series of excuses to skip workouts was hauntingly familiar. It was the same demotivating cycle that had inhibited my physical, mental, and spiritual recovery from the divorce and surgeries. I made a commitment that week three would be my breakthrough. I would tame my demons and move decisively toward my goals. Little did I know, the universe had yet another setback in store for me.

[35] Taylor M. "No Chance of Surrender." DailyOM Newsletter. August 9, 2017.

Setbacks

Sometimes, it seemed life threw up a detour sign just to test my resolve, an unexpected turn in the labyrinth taking me away from my goal at the center. These setbacks required me to dig deep, prioritize, and identify my core values.

On Monday, the start of week three of Couch2Class5, it was a perfect summer day. Hobie, Derrick, and I decided to paddle "GORE FUCKING CANYON," as Hobie said when telling me our plan for the day.

I came out of Fisherman's on my left rail in a high brace, planning to exit the brace with a sweep stroke that would propel me out of the drop and into the eddy below. It was a move I had done a thousand times. My elbow was down, my form was perfect. In a single sweep stroke, I would be back on the hull, cruising downstream.

Halfway through the sweep stroke, I heard an audible "snap," and my left arm instantly hung limp, throbbing. I one-arm paddled, with my right paddle blade, into the eddy next to Hobie and Derrick. Seeing my grimace and left arm hanging over the side, Hobie grabbed my boat. "What happened?" he exclaimed.

"I don't know. Halfway through my sweep, my shoulder clicked, and it's killing me."

"Here, let me take off your helmet. Let's get it back in place."

"Shit. We were having a good day . . . OK. Let's get this done."

This was not the first time I had been in an emergency situation with Hobie. Though he emotionally overreacts at times, he is adept in handling wilderness incidents. Hobie and I are both type A personalities, which makes it difficult to navigate logistics at times; we are also brothers and know how to acquiesce to each other's strengths. That day, he was willing to take instruction, and he listened intently as I walked him through the process of resetting my shoulder.

"Give me your arm. Are you ready?" he asked.

"Give 'er," I replied, exhaling, trying to relax my spasming muscles. As I breathed out, Hobie applied downward tension to my bent left arm. With the slight pull, the pain in my shoulder was instantly relieved.

"We are good: it's back," I declared, breathing a sigh of relief.

"Are you sure?" Hobie asked dubiously, still pulling on my shoulder. He had barely exerted any pressure at all.

"Stop. Stop! It's in! Stop! It must've just been partially out. It's in. It's in. No more pain." I had never experienced this pain before, but I had reset dozens of dislocated shoulders, so I was familiar with the anatomy, physiology, and standard patient response.

"OK. Let's get your boat up the hill so you can hike out."

Hobie looked over at Derrick, who was out of his boat and on shore, ready to assist. It was standard practice to hike out if someone got hurt in the wilderness environment. This practice prevented the risk of further injury or incidents.

I knew the rules. A dislocated shoulder equaled a hike out. I also knew I was not going to let anything stand in the way of my goal. Strengthening my paddling muscles was the best way to accomplish that goal.

I let go of Hobie's boat and floated into the flat water, reaching up to check my range of motion. No numbness. No tingling in the fingers. No pain. No tenderness. Just a nagging visceral sensation of hearing "snap" when my shoulder became dislocated.

Hobie yelled, "Matt, what are you doing? Stop. Let's sling it and get you hiking."

Leave it to a paramedic to be his own worst patient. "Naw, man. I got this. No pain, no numbness, good range of motion. We're here. Let's paddle Gore Fucking Canyon!"

With that, I rotated my left arm like a slow windmill from front to back. Just as I swung my arm directly overhead, I felt the humerus slip down and out of the joint. The ensuing pain was worse than anything I had ever experienced. I was suffering more than I had when I broke my back and had surgery on my hip. It was excruciating.

"FUUUUUU—!!!" echoed up and down the canyon.

I grabbed my paddle and one-arm paddled back to the eddy. My left arm hung limp on the deck. Tears of pain, anger, and frustration streamed down my cheeks. Derrick and Hobie looked at me dumbstruck.

Hobie grabbed my arm with the intent to reset it for the second time, but my arm was completely out of joint. The muscles seized.

"Stop!" I exclaimed.

Derrick held my boat steady as Hobie supported my left arm and I slid backward out of my kayak. Grabbing my paddle, I climbed thirty feet to the railroad tracks above the river. Derrick and Hobie secured the kayaks and joined me on the tracks to make a plan. They would help me get my boat to a safe spot for a river crossing since the road was on the other side of the river.

After crossing the river, I would hike up the road to the put-in. Hobie and Derrick would continue downstream, and I would drive Derrick's truck to meet them at the end of the run.

There was just one problem. My shoulder was still killing me. I turned to Hobie. "I know you're going to think I'm crazy, but I think we need to get this shoulder back in place again."

Hobie eyed me doubtfully.

I lay down on the railroad track, putting the steel rail directly under my spine. I took a deep breath and let my arm rotate out to the side. Exhaling, I let my entire body relax. Just as I completed the exhale, the pain completely vanished. My shoulder was back in place. Piece of cake. I cautiously tucked my arm inside my PFD, tightened the PFD around my forearm so it could rest in place without effort, and began the ninety-minute journey back to the parking lot.

Reconnecting with Derrick and Hobie after loading my boat and driving Derrick's truck to the take-out was bittersweet. I was stoked to listen to their play-by-play detailing the rest of their run, and bummed that I had not been part of that action. Derrick pulled out his camera to show me his video footage. Watching my run at Fisherman's, we heard a click and looked at each other.

"What was that?" Derrick asked.

"Rewind that!" Hobie said.

Derrick scrubbed back to my entry and cranked up the volume. Over the sound of crashing white water in a narrow canyon, from thirty yards downstream, we could hear the sound of a twig breaking. The distinct clicking of a "snap" could be heard over the white noise of breaking waves and water crashing onto rocks.

Derrick looked at me, exclaiming, "Was that your shoulder?!"

"Well, if I'm going to go, I may as well go big. Damn," I replied.

"Holy shit, man. Was that really your shoulder?" Derrick asked.

"It's gotta be. That's exactly where it broke. Damn."

Derrick said, "Can I tell you something? You are stubborn as hell."

"Relax and go with it," Hobie admonished. "Don't be stubborn. SUP workouts.[36] We'll get back to Gore next year."

"Thanks guys. It sucks. I was just getting back," I replied glumly.

The next day's X-rays revealed a Bankart lesion. A Bankart lesion that does not heal properly can cause a shoulder to dislocate frequently, creating weakness, instability, and pain. I knew I would need the help of a physical therapist to get my head as well as my body back in the game.

Medical expenses were mounting quickly, and my future was shrouded in uncertainty. Why was this happening to me? How could I run the shop with one arm? How was this going to affect my plans to visit my family and attend Snowy and Adriene's wedding?

I was relieved when the orthopedic doctor said that there was no immediate need for surgery. I was incredibly disheartened to discover how much my injured shoulder impacted my ability to follow through on my commitment to exercise. In addition to impairing my ability to do push-

---

[36] SUP, or stand-up paddleboarding, is a great core workout. Hobie was saying that we would take it slow, rehabilitate my shoulder, and get me back on the water.

ups and pull-ups, my shoulder was irritated with sit-ups, leg lifts, and even standing.

A steady barrage of self-sabotaging thoughts ran rampant. *Should my shoulder be hurting this much? Am I doing something wrong? What if further injury leads to surgery? I can't afford another surgery—financially or psychologically!* These questions and their annoying cousins filled many waking hours and kept me up at night.

When the pain in my shoulder failed to subside, I got a second opinion from another orthopedic surgeon who said surgery was recommended. My worst fear was confirmed. I would be subjecting my body to yet another surgery—my third in three years.

One thing that lifted my spirits was the extent to which friends were willing to offer their time and support. Hobie mowed my yard. Luke scraped stucco in my house to prepare for some new tile, a project I had started just before breaking my shoulder. Gail and others helped me with other chores and meals.

It was difficult to have an injury living in a valley surrounded by athletes. Every day, I was reminded of all the fun I was missing. Most of my friends had suffered sports or activity-related injuries of their own, so they knew how incredibly frustrating the recovery process could be. Many of them offered words of advice and encouragement. Resilience required time, patience, and the belief that healing was possible. In my case, resilience meant re-examining my priorities and making tough decisions based on information received from extensive self-reflection.

Getting better, healing emotionally and physically, was my number one priority. I needed to be mindful of limited financial resources, using my hard-earned money to pay for the medical care required to repair my shoulder. With that new goal in mind, I cancelled my trip to the East Coast.

I sent a very difficult, heartfelt message to Snowy, Adriene, Corey, and Jess. I told Snowy and Corey that I had been planning to surprise them by attending the wedding. I shared my Couch2Class5 training and how excited I was at the prospect of paddling the Green post-wedding. It was a goal that kept me motivated, my light at the end of the tunnel. Then, I shared the details of the injury. As I wrote, the disappointment was deep and heartfelt. Attending the wedding had been my focal point for two months. Now, I needed to shift gears. I concluded by telling them how much I loved them and how they each deserved the happiness they were receiving.

Jess said she cried and smiled and laughed when she got the letter.

Corey said, "You're not a tree, stop being sappy."

Snowy was amazed we were able to keep the surprise and was bummed I could not make it.

Though it was incredibly disappointing to miss the wedding, the decision to make the responsible choice felt good. I would get back on track, pursuing my passions soon.

Balance

Through the recovery process, I learned that knowledge is obtained on different levels. There is head knowledge and heart knowledge. At the head level, I knew that intuition provided the truest measure of health. At the heart level, I was still wrestling with the demons of doubt, fear, and regret. Resilience was a process by which information moved from the head to the heart. The success of my healing journey was directly related to the degree to which I strengthened trust in my intuition.

The next two weeks were a blur of doctor's appointments, pain medication, and unhealthy cravings. Even more than chemical addiction, I felt a deep longing for my liquid addiction. I missed kayaking. The visceral need to get back on the water inspired a whole new kind of craving. I could feel the pull of the water calling to me. It was incredibly frustrating not to be able to answer that call.

At the end of August, my house got a facelift. Stucco walls were replaced with tile. Wood received a fresh coat of paint. Throughout the previous decade, I had made many improvements to the house's interior but had done very little to the exterior. It felt good to drive up to my house with its new colors and fresh, clean appearance.

It occurred to me I was experiencing an inverse metaphor for my house. Though my body was in a temporary state of disrepair, I was the same person inside as I was before the accidents. Whether physically fit or out of shape, I was still *me*. I needed to give myself the time and space to allow my exterior appearance to match my interior growth.

George magically appeared, without invitation, to check up on me, just as he did during my divorce. He encouraged me to start each day with meditation.

"You need to calm your inner mind and stay balanced physically, mentally, and emotionally," George said. "If there isn't a balance of all three, the center is not in the middle."

The prospect of going through physical therapy, for the third time in as many years, was challenging. Turning forty created physical, mental, and spiritual upheaval. As unpleasant as the upheaval was, it provided an opportunity to shuffle the cards and deal a new hand. Balance was possible. I just needed to stay attuned to my intuition.

In early September, I closed the store so I could attend a five-day Wilderness Advanced Life Support (WALS) course in Durango followed by shoulder surgery.

The WALS course was designed to train advanced-level medical providers (paramedics, nurses, PAs, and physicians) to apply their ALS medical training outside the clinical environment. I had taken the class fifteen years prior and used the information regularly. I incorporated it when writing standard operating procedures for employers. I also used it during many emergency situations in the backcountry. By renewing this certification, I would be able to update my knowledge with the latest practices from the man who literally wrote the book on wilderness medicine. I taught wilderness first aid classes, three of which were already on the calendar. This training would help me update my curriculum and stay current in my practice. The revenue from those first three classes would cover the WALS certification expenses.

Personal development helped to offset feelings of physical inadequacy, providing a sense of purpose. It also helped to assuage the disappointment of not attending Snowy and Adriene's wedding. I learned an important lesson in resilience: focusing my time and energy on helping others distracted me from my own problems. At the WALS course, I was surrounded by a group of people who shared my passion to help others. The energy in the group was other-focused, not me-focused. There was power in that shift. The shift jump-started the re-centering process for me.

Three days after the training, I was scheduled for surgery. My insurance had approved the procedure, which greatly eased the mental and emotional pressure of paying medical bills. Rather than carrying the burden of financial stress, I could relax and focus on the process of healing: I am meant to be healthy. I am meant to be whole.

It occurred to me that if I had better insurance and/or more money in the bank, I could have closed the store in early August, and the surgery would be behind me. I might have even been able to attend Snowy and Adriene's wedding. Everything happens for a reason, and the universe's plan is greater than mine could ever be.

The store was busy for two solid weeks in August, providing much-needed capital. If I had closed the store in August, I would not have had the opportunity to serve those customers and recoup capital. As an added bonus, my mom decided to fly out in September to help me during the week following the surgery.

Relying on Others

As the date of my surgery drew nearer, I staved off doubt and fear with lists and organization. Scheduling shuttles, going to PT appointments, and checking items off a long to-do list helped me feel in control. On one level, I knew this was a routine shoulder surgery that did not present a life-or-death situation. On another level, I felt vulnerable and afraid. What if the surgery caused an infection? What if the shoulder had sustained more damage than the surgeon thought? Would my future activity be limited? What if this kept happening? How would I pay the bills if recovery took longer than expected? What if the post-surgery pain and medication caused me to behave irrationally, alienating the people who were trying to support me?

I was humbled and in awe of the people who lent a helping hand with household chores. I felt the need to repay their kindness. The depth of gratitude I felt for their generosity of time and energy made it impossible to repay the debt.

This was especially true as it related to my mother. My mother helped me recover from the two previous surgeries. As much as I was looking forward to seeing her again, I felt guilty for still needing her care. After all, I was forty-three years old. This was the time in life where I should have been taking care of her, not the other way around. Nevertheless, I knew many people my age had already lost their parents, and I was so grateful for my mother's love and company.

My DailyOM message came at exactly the time I needed to hear it yet again:

A deep feeling of gratitude can emerge as we open to the experience of being helped.

Most of us pride ourselves on our self-sufficiency. We like to be responsible for taking care of ourselves and pulling our own weight in the world. This is why it can be so challenging when we find ourselves in a situation in which we have to rely on someone else. This can happen as the result of an illness or an injury, or even in the case of a positive change, such as the arrival of a newborn. At times like these, it is essential that we let go of our feeling that we should be able to do it all by ourselves and accept the help of others. . . .

. . . It takes wisdom and strength to surrender to our own helplessness and to accept that we, just like every other human being, have limitations. The gifts of surrender are numerous. We discover humility, gratitude, and a deepening understanding of the human experience that enables us to be that much more compassionate and surrendered in the world.[37]

When I finally relaxed into the process of accepting help from others, rather than continuing to feel guilty, I was rewarded with a deep sense of peace, harmony, and gratitude.

My mother arrived the night before the surgery. At four thirty in the morning, we departed for our three-hour drive to Gunnison. The sun was rising over the horizon as we reached the summit of Kebler Pass. We stopped to take in the beauty of dawn's early light refracting amidst the autumn gold of aspen leaves. We watched in awe as rainbows cast by dew-filled sunbeams crested the surrounding mountain peaks.

Thankfully, the surgery went well. I exchanged texts with friends I had met at the WALS class the previous week. Old friends and new ones were offering so much support, keeping me inspired, and motivating me to push through the pain. A steady stream of visitors brought meals, offering to help with anything that needed to be done. Some friends just stopped by to wish me well and meet my mom. I was so grateful for the sense of community.

My mom left a week after the surgery. A house that felt so full with her love and compassion now felt empty and lonely. Before leaving, she did the laundry and cleaned the house. Looking around me, I was surrounded by evidence of her love and care. At the same time, I knew it was time to navigate the healing process on my own.

Reopening the store presented a whole new set of challenges. My shoulder was killing me. I had hired a friend's son to help with any heavy lifting that needed to be done. Tasks that I would normally complete in seconds took several minutes. Like walking upstream, against the current, it felt like I was moving in slow motion with great effort.

---

[37] Taylor M. "The Wisdom of Others." DailyOM Newsletter. September 7, 2021.

George stopped by to see how I was holding up during my first day back at work. I was grateful for the wisdom of his perspective. George's visit was exactly what I needed to tackle self-sabotaging thoughts. He reminded me that growth requires challenge. Our physical and mental challenges encourage us to push the boundaries that hold us back. Fear and insecurity push us out of our comfort zone, preventing us from living life on autopilot.

I remained thankful for the steady stream of clients who kept me focused on something other than the pain in my shoulder, preventing me from slipping into self-pity and depression.

My friend Liz sent me a book that she said changed her life. I was stoked to read it. *The Wisdom of Insecurity* by Alan W. Watts. A week after the surgery, we exchanged texts:

> Liz: How's the shoulder today?
>
> MS: Hurts. I didn't have time for my morning ice session, but I'll get through the day and plan to relax all weekend!!
>
> Liz: You got this.
>
> MS: Follow up is Monday. I'm nervous that I may have screwed something up going back to work so soon, but I think all will be good. Hopefully he says I can start PT sooner than later!

A large portion of the mental job on the road to recovery was learning to accept help from others. I tried to remain aware of the kindness and resources all around me, to remain mindful of the fact that I did need help from others.

The Message of Pain

At times like these it felt like Madisyn Taylor had a link to my daily life, delivering exactly the messages I needed to hear:

Both emotional and physical pain are messages that we need to stop and pay attention.

When we feel pain, our first impulse is often to eradicate it with medication. This is an understandable response, but sometimes in our hurry to get rid of pain, we forget that it is the body's way of letting us know that it needs our attention. A headache can inform us that we're hungry or stressed just as a sore throat might be telling us that we need to rest our voice. If we override these messages instead of respond to them, we risk worsening our condition. In addition, we create a feeling of disconnectedness between our minds and our bodies.

Physical pain is not the only kind of pain that lets us know our attention is needed. Emotional pain provides us with valuable information about the state of our psyche, letting us know that we have been affected by something and that we would do well to focus our awareness inward. Just as we tend to a cut on our arm by cleaning and bandaging it, we treat a broken heart by surrounding ourselves with love and support. In both cases, if we listen to our pain we will know what to do to heal ourselves. It's natural to want to resist pain, but once we understand that it is here to give us valuable information, we can relax a bit more, and take a moment to listen before we reach for medication. Sometimes this is enough to noticeably reduce the pain, because its message has been heard. Perhaps we seek to medicate pain because we fear that if we don't, it will never go away. It can be empowering to realize that, at least some of the time, it is just a matter of listening and responding.[38]

At the end of September, I was working in the shop. My shoulder was throbbing, and my back was aching from the weight of the sling. When two new customers walked through the door, I did my best to be upbeat. After brief introductions, I was surprised to discover that one of them was Todd Burpo, the pastor who co-wrote the book *Heaven is for Real*. This

---

[38] Taylor M. "The Message of Pain." DailyOM Newsletter. September 22, 2017.

book, which became a major motion picture, is about his young son's near-death experience.

Todd's story was powerful and deeply inspirational. My own troubles paled in comparison with the struggle of a parent facing the prospect of losing their child. It felt like Todd was there to remind me that we each have a role to play in this life. My lessons were still unfolding, and my story was still being written.

That night, I shared Todd's story with my roommate, who asked, "If you were to write a thesis today, what would your book be about?"

I exclaimed, "In one word, it would be about motivation."

"In what way?" she asked.

I pulled up my sleeve and showed her the image of the labyrinth tattooed on my shoulder. "I've been through three surgeries in three years. The labyrinth is a perfect metaphor for my journey. The center is a goal—one that is always changing and can be multiple things at once. The path I take gives glimpses of that goal, but life puts hurdles in the way or turns the path away from the goal. If I lose sight of my goal, I won't get there. If I stay true to myself and my path, I can accomplish, achieve, or acquire that goal. It may not be what I initially envisioned, but I grow from the experience. In order to do that, I must stay disciplined, challenged, and motivated."

I knew those words were not to be taken lightly. It is hard to stay motivated while recovering from injury. Without motivation, there is no hope of achieving the goal.

Once again, I found that it was one thing to know a truth and another thing to live it. Pain meds and alcohol were double-edged swords. They brought relief from physical discomfort. The tradeoffs were anxiety, de-motivation, and depression. I struggled with feelings of inadequacy. I worried that I would never return to normal. I continually lived in fear that I would make a move that would further damage the shoulder or cause it to heal wrong.

Down and Out

One morning in early October, Jasmine woke me up with her whining. I could tell she was hungry. My shoulder was aching, and I really did not want to get out of bed. Jasmine was persistent. I followed Jasmine to the kitchen and asked my roommates if they fed the dogs. They were both running around the kitchen, late for work. As they rushed out the door, I noticed they left the counters piled with dishes. This was a day I set aside for much-needed rest, pain medication, and ice. It was hard enough to take care of myself. The last thing I needed was to be cleaning up after other people too.

The news was broadcasting footage from a shooting in Las Vegas. Just a couple days earlier, there had been another shooting, killing a friend. The negative energy of this day was stacking up. I felt overwhelmed.

One of my part-time employees was a firearms instructor. A former marine, he exuded confidence and discipline and vibrated with positive energy. Not knowing about my day up until that point, he saw the news and called to suggest that we schedule some first aid classes. I was feeling stressed and unmotivated. I told him that I had tried to offer first aid classes eight years ago, but it had not worked out. The industry was not interested in learning first aid from a gun shop. My bad mood interfered with my ability to seize the positive opportunity right in front of my eyes.

After an hour of cleaning the kitchen and carrying out the garbage, my shoulder was killing me. It was hard to look forward to anything but pain meds.

I stopped to clear my head. Picking up my cell phone, I saw I had eight new email messages. I opened the app, deleted seven messages without reading them, and stopped when I saw the eighth:

Our starting point is not the usual starting point in a discussion of depression. Usually depression is characterized as an illness or as a biological, psychological, social, or spiritual disorder. . . .

. . . With the rise of four powerful industries, the pharmaceutical industry, the psychotherapy industry, the social work industry, and the pastoral industry, it has become increasingly difficult for people to consider that sadness might be a very normal reaction to unpleasant facts and circumstances. Cultural forces have transformed a great deal of normal sadness into the "mental illness" of depression. . . .

. . . According to the psychological depression model, you are the problem: maybe it's your learned helplessness, your unresolved conflicts with your parents, your low self-esteem, or something. According to the social depression model, you are the problem: maybe you've become too isolated, maybe you haven't provided yourself with enough social support, etc. According to the spiritual depression model, you are still the problem: you haven't made the right spiritual connections, given yourself over to God, tapped into your spiritual nature, and so on. These four models identify you as the problem. Life is never the problem. How odd! How odd to think that our sadness might not sometimes be related to our life circumstances or to the facts of existence.[39]

There is power in recognizing that moments of sadness are normal and natural. They are an integral part of the human condition. Sadness is acceptable; I am not abnormal. Paradoxically, accepting my own weakness makes me feel stronger.

Throughout the month of October, I continued to practice my physical therapy exercises and meditation daily. I was eating healthy and even managed to lose ten pounds. It had been weeks since I felt the need to take Percocet.

---

[39] Maisel E. "How to Overcome Depression." DailyOM Newsletter. September 20, 2017.

Send Healing to Yourself

I woke up at six thirty in the morning with tears of pain leaking out of the corners of my eyes. I tried every position to get comfortable. Finally, after an hour, I got out of bed and took my first Percocet in weeks. I went back to bed with an ice pack and rested until getting up for work at ten thirty. The medication created food cravings, and I spent the day filling my body with carbs and sugar. In addition to worrying if the morning's pain was caused by ripped sutures, I felt guilty for scarfing an unmentionable amount of junk food all day.

A couple days later, I woke up in tears again. This time, the tears were due to loneliness. The rampage of unhealthy eating from a couple days ago continued. I could not get motivated to exercise. It was frustrating to feel like I needed so much help. Worse yet, I hated not being available to help other people when they needed it. I had used all of the physical therapy appointments covered by my health insurance and now needed to pay out of pocket. To raise cash, I sold my motorcycle.

Once again, just the right message for my situation arrived.

So often we are busy sending love and healing to others that we forget to send healing to ourself.

If you sincerely believe that there is a part of yourself that exists independently of upset and illness, the love and light you send yourself will help you connect with it. You will see the affirmative impact of this connection almost immediately when you include yourself in the recipients of your healing gifts, as life's frustrations become more tolerable and your bliss becomes ever more palpable.[40]

---

[40] Taylor M. "Send Healing to Yourself." DailyOM Newsletter. October 25, 2017.

Why did my recovery not follow a steady upward trajectory? Why did I keep backsliding? I finally realized that resilience is not about getting back to the place I was before. Resilience is the ability to perceive how life challenges me to be better.

Upward spirals led me back in the direction of my goal. I was not relegated to living a life on the outside fringe of the labyrinth. I had new opportunities to trust my intuition and cultivate mindfulness. This is the essence of resilience.

The true lesson of resilience is trust. Trust requires repetition. It is built layer upon layer. I learned to trust that each challenge would lead to a stronger human being who was more centered and more connected. I gradually learned to trust that the universe had my back.

If good accidents led to an upward spiral and bad accidents led to a downward spiral, resilience was the means by which I could shorten the length of the downward spiral. Resilience prepared me for what lay ahead.

Application: Resilience Is More than a Struggle

Dr. Paul Bartone defines "hardiness" as "a mindset or worldview that characterizes people who are resilient and adaptable in dealing with stress."[41] He describes three characteristics that help people become more resistant to stress, contributing to hardiness. These characteristics are commitment, control, and challenge.

1. Did I exhibit these three qualities over the course of the lessons I learned?

2. How do these three qualities show up in your life? Do you feel like you exhibit hardiness in your workplace? In your relationships?

3. Describe a period when you were at your lowest mentally and physically. When did you decide the situation needed to change?

4. Although probably difficult, what changes did you make, and were there people around you to help you make the changes?

5. Think of an experience that helped contribute to or shape your own resilience. What made it a moment of resilience? What did you learn from that challenge?

6. Is resilience a skill that can be developed?

---

[41] Bartone PT. "Hardiness." https://www.hardiness-resilience.com

EMOTIONAL MATURITY

While sifting through post-divorce emotional wreckage and navigating through the mental stress after three years of surgeries, I read up on leadership, personal growth, and management. I noticed that articles, books, and materials were referencing emotional intelligence with increasing frequency. Emotional intelligence became a master key to the labyrinth. It unlocked doors, revealed shortcuts, and illuminated paths that were previously invisible.

Awareness, mindfulness, and resilience played a role in my ability to have successful, healthy, and positive communication. My effectiveness as a leader depended on my ability to effectively communicate with a wide range of personalities. Facilitating effective communication required emotional intelligence. To grow as a person and as a leader, I needed to become more emotionally mature.

Emotional intelligence can be likened to intellectual intelligence: we are born with God-given skills that can be expanded upon and improved with time and practice. Psychologists use the term "EQ," or emotional quotient, to parallel IQ, or intelligence quotient. Similar to IQ testing, which is a somewhat limited measure of human intelligence, EQ involves complex factors that are difficult to measure.

Intelligence does not always equal maturity. I have known some of the brightest minds in the world, yet they have the maturity of a ten-year-old or no common sense or do not know how to communicate outside their own personal sphere of awareness. Learning to become emotionally mature takes the concept of emotional intelligence and couples it with awareness, mindfulness, and resilience.

I found myself more at ease talking with some people while utilizing and practicing newly learned skills, whereas I could become stressed and triggered during interactions with others. My success as a leader depended on increasing the number and type of people who fell into the former category while minimizing those who fell into the latter. Unfortunately, I was fighting a tendency to become more rigid with age, both in mind and body. I recognized that cultivating emotional flexibility was just as important as physical stretching and exercise.

Bamboo

When playing football in college, I began practicing yoga to help my muscles recover. Yoga helped me remain limber, and I was less sore after heavy workout days.

Spring semester of my sophomore year, I tried to encourage some of my teammates to sign up for a yoga course. Using colorful language, they expressed their opinions of a guy who practiced yoga.

"Seriously?" I replied. "You're going to pass up on the opportunity to stretch out with a group of toned, athletic women?"

Denied by all, I continued to practice yoga in private, on my own. It became my personal time to reset and recharge.

Yoga was key to survival during my first summer in Colorado. I had to wake up before six in the morning to set up for rafting trips every day. After kayaking in the afternoon, I would work in a bar until two in the morning. The next day, I would head back to the river for another early-morning rafting setup. Rather than sleeping four hours, I slept a few hours before waking up for a thirty-minute pre-work yoga session.

Though yoga meant missing pillow time, I rose from my final corpse pose feeling more refreshed. Yoga prevented my mind and body from wearing down. Even when I started dating a gorgeous massage therapist and yoga instructor later that summer, I found I enjoyed practicing yoga alone. Quieting my mind provided time for reflection.

I was surprised to discover that Jason and others in the ambulance district also practiced yoga. After my experience with the football team, it was gratifying to find other men who valued the mental and physical benefits of practicing yoga. We shared tips on strengthening our poses, and alternated between yoga sessions and traditional workouts in the ambulance district's exercise room.

When I broke my back during the skiing accident, yoga saved my life. I was limber enough that my chin could hyperflex down to my nipple line, without causing more damage than was done. The practice of yoga eased the tedium during long days of rest and recovery. Yoga enhanced the benefit of physical therapy sessions, allowing me to recover quicker and ease back into athletic activity.

Throughout most of my life as an athlete, I used yoga as a tool to improve my physical performance. As George's student, my practice of yoga deepened to include more meditation and contemplation, which enhanced my emotional well-being as well. In my commitment to learn lessons from everyday experiences, I began to trust my own intuition and relied on the information I received in meditation.

George encouraged me to meditate daily. Using focus and breath work, I learned to center myself and become mindful. This practice extended to interpersonal communication as well. George taught me to take a break and pause when other people were speaking, becoming aware of their body language as well as their words. This pause provided the opportunity to respond mindfully rather than reacting emotionally. George's techniques laid the foundation for improving my emotional intelligence.

I had a temper as a young adult. I finished more than my share of fights in college and when working in bars. I was rigid in my opinions and did not participate in verbal discourse for expansion of knowledge or growth. I was in it all to win it all. Consequently, people loved me or they loved to hate me. I struggled to balance that aggressive energy. I blamed others for my frustration.

George taught me to stop blaming: to take ownership of my actions. Through meditation, I learned that being mindful means taking responsibility for my role in conflicts and in seeking resolution. I even asked the women I dated to practice George's communication techniques with me, hoping improved communication would yield more successful relationships.

As I transitioned from blaming others, I began to blame myself. I became increasingly frustrated with myself for not communicating well enough or not explaining myself well enough to be understood. Blame turned to guilt as I internalized conflict. Through meditation, I learned that communication, while very important, is only part of the equation. To find peace, I needed to give myself space to grow. In time, I could become more emotionally centered.

There are many definitions of the word and sound "om," as it is used in various religions and yoga practices. In meditation, chanting "om" helps to focus the breath. In Hinduism, the symbol for om is a blending of the self, the soul, and the ultimate reality: the divine.

My interpretation of om was that it encompassed everything. It was a reminder of my humility. It was also a reminder to clear my mind and think of nothing as I lived and breathed in the moment. Om was everything and nothing. It was central to my practice of meditation, allowing me to connect to my intuition.

Bamboo can bend in high winds without breaking. Oak does not flex; rather, it snaps under pressure. Yoga and meditation offered physical, mental, and emotional benefits, which became the cornerstone for my emotional development. Yoga and meditation allowed me to remain physically and emotionally flexible, patient, introspective, and precise—less like oak, more like bamboo.

Intuition

Intuition was perplexing to me. I knew that it was there; however, I did not always listen. It was like this flow of information constantly coming from my higher self, an inner coach talking to me through a headset. Sometimes, I would forget to turn the headset on. Sometimes, I would ignore the coach's directives entirely, brushing them off as nonsensical or irrelevant.

General Mattis discussed intuition as it relates to crisis: "Crisis is something you don't anticipate and don't have control of."[42] Crisis can create a paralyzing fear or a surge of power, fluidity, and energy. My five senses cannot register the source of that energy—I cannot smell, touch, taste, hear, or see it. That does not mean it does not exist. Intuition can help break through fear and doubt, giving an advantage of perspective from prior experience, which is the only way my mind can be clear enough to see a solution.

What is this energy that I feel without the aid of my senses?

"A pang in your gut when you may be doing the wrong thing, or a vibrant zing when your body approves, can guide you reliably at times when logic fails. Sometimes, when logic prevails, we ignore our gut and live to regret it."[43] To become more intuitive, I needed to learn to trust my power center.

I viewed this power center as a river of energy. Like water in a powerful, slow-moving river, the energy around me was a strong, life-giving force. I could not change the course of the river; however, if I tuned into its flow and understood the way it moved, I could make decisions that

---

[42] "General Jim Mattis on 'Call Sign Chaos.'" The Ford Foundation. April 21, 2021. Webinar available at https://fordschool.umich.edu/event/2021/general-jim-mattis-call -sign-chaos?theme=cflp

[43] Taylor M. "Trusting Your Gut." DailyOM Newsletter. April 19, 2021.

maximized the positive force of the river's energy, benefiting both me and those around me. Working in collaboration with that life force energy, I cultivated opportunity and created a life of my choosing.

Observations of external forces enabled me to prepare for what lay ahead. When training white-water raft guides and new EMTs or paramedics, I called it "early setup" or a "broad sphere of awareness." When I was mindful of myself and aware of potential problems and opportunities, I used my intuition to leverage circumstances.

I learned the dangers of ignoring my intuition. As a teenager in high school, I got into a motor vehicle crash because I failed to listen to an inner voice telling me not to volunteer to drive that day. I felt a warning tingle when I brought beer to a party in college. The next day, I was issued a four-game suspension from the football team. Prior to the ski accident that ended in a broken back, I felt a strong sense of misgiving and was hesitant to take one last run to accompany my friend to her car. Finally, there were three separate occasions where I questioned the decision to marry my ex-wife. In each of these instances, I failed to listen to a strong inner voice of intuition and subsequently suffered life-changing consequences.

When I allowed intuition to guide my decisions, I experienced flow and ease. Intuition guided me in finding other like-minded people who shared my passion to take a nontraditional path in life. Teachers, mentors, and collaborators appeared in exactly the right place at exactly the right time. These teachers fueled my quest for excellence and provided opportunities for new adventures.

Heyoka

As I read more about leadership and emotional intelligence, I found that the process of emotional maturity required me to know myself in order to learn about others. I realized that I could not expect others to interact with me in a positive or higher plane if I did not know myself. In an effort to see my own path more clearly, I was drawn to the teachings of philosophers, religious writers, shamans, astrologists, auraologists (not to be confused with urologists!), palm readers, and all manner of psychics.

I was also fascinated with Native American Indian traditions and beliefs. After a philosophical and spiritual discussion with my mother, she asked if I would be open to talking with her friend Karen,[44] whom my mother knew through a mutual friend. I agreed, and a week later, my jaw dropped over new insight.

During our conversation, Karen made a poignant observation. "Matt, have you noticed people seem to misunderstand you, get mad at you, or misinterpret your intentions?"

"Yes! All the time. My whole life."

"Heyoka medicine, or the Sacred Clown, is a medicine person that is revered in the Native American community. Their job is to make fun of you—to mirror back to you your behavior so you can learn from it and grow."

"I can relate to this."

"A white person who carries Heyoka medicine is called a mirror carrier. A lot of your communication with others has to do with the fact that you are a mirror carrier. It means you mirror back to others who they are. Not necessarily who you are, but who they are, so they can see themselves in the mirror and make adjustments. You do this naturally and unconsciously."

She continued, "You have to be careful that you do not become the person that others accuse you of. When someone accuses you of something, you need to take a breath and ask yourself, 'Was I mirroring them, or is that actually who I am?' People are going to bring the worst of themselves out in you so you can mirror it back to them, allowing them to make an adjustment.

"People who carry the Heyoka medicine were on the other side when God walked into the room and asked for a volunteer. Your hand went straight up and you forgot to ask, 'For what?'"

---

[44] Karen McCoy is an author and spiritual astrologer. www.KarenMcCoy.com

"Hahaha. I do that regularly."

Nodding with a knowing smile, she went on, "He gave you a task: 'When people are out of balance and you notice it, I want you to mirror it back to them so they can make the adjustment.'"

"When I get frustrated, I get introspective, trying to determine if it's me or the other person," I replied.

"That's exactly what you need to do."

This description of Heyoka, or mirror carrier, explained many of the communication issues I had in my life. I was a contrarian. I regularly challenged the status quo. People often misunderstand my intentions. It was incredibly comforting to know that Native American tradition celebrates the role of Heyoka, who played an integral role in their culture and community. In an effort to understand how the role of Heyoka played out in my life, I studied Sioux references to Heyoka.

Heyoka's gift was that of perspective. He/she reminded the tribe to look at life from a different perspective by riding backward into battle, shivering when hot and removing clothing when cold. Heyoka carried a mirror to remind tribe members that there is more than one way to view things.

Intentionally annoying, the Heyoka would blurt out during formal ceremonies, reminding tribe members not to take themselves too seriously. Heyoka shifted the community's perspective when struggling or under duress. Nothing is permanent. Everything changes. When food was scarce, Heyoka pretended to be full. When there was plenty to eat, he pretended to be hungry. The Heyoka provided a yin-yang function in the community.

Sacred clowns served an important role in shaping tribal codes. "Unbound by societal constraints, heyókȟa are able to violate cultural taboos freely and thus critique established customs. [45] Paradoxically,

---

[45] Swann B. *Coming to Light: Contemporary Translations of the Native Literatures of North America.* 1st ed. Vintage Books; 1996:433. Cited by: Wikipedia contributors. "Heyoka." Wikipedia. May 3, 2021. https://en.wikipedia.org/wiki/Heyoka#cite_note-5

however, by violating these norms and taboos, they help to define the accepted boundaries, rules, and societal guidelines for ethical and moral behavior. They are the only ones who can ask 'Why?' about sensitive topics; they use satire to question the specialists and carriers of sacred knowledge or those in positions of power and authority."[46]

As a mirror carrier, I was drawn into the uncomfortable role of reflecting a person's bad behavior. I was super selfish with a person who was selfish. I was super egotistical with a person who was egotistical. As a child, I questioned the mourning process after death. As an adult, I walked the razor's edge when it came to socially accepted behavior, sometimes unintentionally causing offense. My actions challenged the people around me, forcing them to examine customs and beliefs they never thought to question.

Like George, Karen told me to focus my energy on communication. This felt incredibly paradoxical since I felt like I was continually being misunderstood. A shaman in Indonesia had offered a similar message twenty-five years earlier; he said that communication was my greatest weakness and also the greatest gift I offered.

I became aware of the fact that I would continually attract people who needed to learn to communicate. I was on the right path. I could not be available to help or teach others if I did not make efforts to master this skill for myself. In an effort to become an effective communicator, I took a deep dive into examining the perceptions and perspectives that were impeding my communication.

Perception and Perspective

My effectiveness as a communicator was hindered by my fears, anxiety, insecurity, and self-doubt. I perceived myself as a has-been athlete. I perceived myself as a burden when I needed to ask other people for help.

---

[46] Wikipedia contributors. "Heyoka." May 3, 2021. Wikipedia. https://en.wikipedia.org/wiki/Heyoka#cite_note-5

I worried about what people thought of me. These limiting beliefs made me hyper-aware of what I perceived as criticism from others. My own self-limitation made me hyper-vigilant when I felt others were making assumptions about me.

The high school I attended had a chapel on the main floor. Every Friday morning, during football season, I would sit in the chapel for about a half an hour by myself. I went there because it was the quietest room in the building, allowing me to clear my mind, visualize the playbook, and walk through the night's game in peace and quiet. Someone said that I was a "good Catholic boy who prayed before every game." That perception was simply untrue.

I bristled at being referred to as a "good Catholic boy." I resented the fact that someone made an assumption about me based on the fact that I was sitting in a chapel. In retrospect, it was a logical assumption, which made me examine my own perspective. What part of me took offense? Where do perceptions come from?

My role as mirror carrier further complicated my attempts for authentic communication. People often referred to me as paradoxical, which I found extremely frustrating until I recognized that my role as a mirror carrier was affecting the way they saw me. The mirror interfered with their ability to see me clearly.

Ralph Messer wrote about the self-serving nature of criticism. "Before criticizing someone else, check your motives. Are you doing it because you are truly concerned about that person? Or are you doing it to build yourself up and make yourself look better?"[47]

In my opinion, criticism shows lack of respect for another person's unique point of view. If I am truly committed to seeing the world from another person's perspective, there is no place for criticism or judgment.

---

[47] Messer R. "Omer Day 12: Daily Reflection, Humility in Discipline." Simchat Torah Beit Midrash. April 8, 2021. https://stbm.org/daily-omer-reflections/?mc_cid =ab058787de&mc_eid=9c951083fb

Communication should be fluid and easy, even when going against the grain.

Not one to follow the herd, my perspective on town council was often akin to wading upstream. Two other council members, Paul and Andy, often saw where I was going and helped communicate that perspective. Fortunately, other council members took a lighthearted approach. They made comments like "I hate to do this publicly, but I agree with Matt/Paul/Andy," or "I thought I had a grasp of this, but now Matt/Paul/Andy have changed my mind."

I was outspoken, and people desperately wanted to make me out to be a far right conservative, largely due to the fact that I owned a gun shop. It never ceased to surprise them when my position on an issue did not reflect their image of me.

A meeting with the town manager, Brandy, was a case in point. She and I were having our quarterly coffee to catch up. I wanted to receive some input from Brandy regarding the upcoming budget work sessions. For clarification, as I processed my thoughts on the presentation, I asked, "We have roughly thirty-eight million dollars in our overall budget, right?"

Agreeing, Brandy added, "Most of that is tied up in enterprise funds that are dedicated and regulated, so that money cannot be spent. Our general fund is what pays for the details and the programs."

Expanding, I said, "So, if we have eight million dollars to utilize for the fixed expenditures, or core responsibilities of the town—police, public works, administration, utilities, and land use codes and management, that only leaves about one point six million for savings and flexible, or discretionary, spending. Is that right?"

"Yup," Brandie confirmed.

"That's not a lot of money, and most people who know me know that I do not like raising taxes to pay for things that 'feel good' and are an overreach or want rather than a need."

Brandy smiled as she looked up from her notes. "We have to balance. It takes a long time to build up our reserve."

"Yes. We need to spell out what is fixed and what is flexible," I replied. "We have a policy for savings, so if we can spell out the other two, then maybe people can see that we don't have the money for every feel-good program they want."

"Town budget is an exercise of resilience. Resilience equals survival. Our town cannot survive without a budget that reflects that relief," Brandy concurred.

"Exactly. It really is, isn't it? Well said," I agreed. "We have to be aware of where our money comes from, and we have to be mindful of how we spend it. Andy is really good at that." Andy was a friend who also served on the town council. He and I met monthly to brainstorm business ideas, discuss town council issues, and share conversation over a drink.

Brandy knew exactly what I was saying. "Andy is laser focused on how we spend the money in our budget. From the outside, some people think he's the one to go to for funding all their programs, but in reality, he is very selective in how and where we spend."

"What does he say? 'Our budget is a reflection of our priorities.' We have to balance our core needs with our strategic plan before approving every request that comes in. He is spot-on."

We moved from the topic of budgeting to discuss other town-related tasks, then talked about family and fun. At the end of the conversation, Brandy said, "Matt, you are a conundrum."

I squinted my eyes, confused, and asked with a sheepish smile, "How am I a conundrum?"

She said, "You are a walking paradox because your perspectives are often contrary to what is expected from you. You just said that people know you do not like raising taxes for feel-good items, yet you helped to orchestrate the river park, which is funded by taxes!"

I scoffed at this accusation, saying, "Brandy! I was fully against the park being paid for by taxes! Once the voters opted to finance it that way, though, I was fully behind the effort and just wanted to see it spent wisely."

"That's exactly what I mean. You pivot," she responded.

Communication is a two-way street. Others can only give what I am capable of receiving. The reverse is true as well. I can only give what others are willing to receive. Perception directly impacts communication. It was my job to change my limiting beliefs, the perceptions that held me back. Changing my perceptions was the only way to create a shift in perspective.

If perception is a collection of inner beliefs, then perspective is the outward projection of those inner beliefs. My unique perspective was the sum total of my experiences and my responses to those experiences. My ego was tightly wound up in these perspectives, as I believed that my unique perspective was more accurate than anyone else's perspective.

With George's guidance, I learned to identify self-limiting beliefs that were affecting my perception of myself and others. I learned to respect the perspective of others whose life experiences were different from my own. By facilitating understanding, my communication improved. By seeking understanding, I found I was better understood. Being a conundrum was not an insult. It simply meant I was making other people think outside the box.

Integrity

Despite the fact that I was taking responsibility for my own perceptions and perspectives, there were still times I felt my intentions were misinterpreted. Rather than allowing my ego to flare up when these misunderstandings occurred, I made an effort to respond with integrity.

Responding with integrity meant staying true to my goal of authentic communication. Integrity was one of the three values I embraced as I navigated the waters of my divorce. That mantra of living with honor, acting with integrity, and speaking with truth helped me to stay centered.

Integrity to me was different from morality. Morality was my moral compass, a directional tool signifying a measure of right and wrong. Integrity was the extent to which I acted in accordance with my moral compass: my desire to do the right thing, even when nobody was watching.

I could only be held accountable for my own words and actions. I could not be responsible for the words and actions of others; however, I remained responsible for my ability to listen, understand, and respond rather than react.

I was aware of the fact that my perception shaped my perspective. Observing the world around me, I formed opinions, or perceptions, based on unique life experiences. Perspective was my point of focus: the way I integrated the lessons I learned and interpreted those experiences.

A friend, and fellow council member, approached me one night after a council meeting, offering, "Matt, you asked, and I offered to help mentor you, so I have some advice."

"OK. I'm all ears." I smiled. "You are smarter and wiser than me."

"First of all, Matt," David was looking me squarely in the eyes, "you are smart. Every time you say otherwise, it diminishes your voice because we all know you are smart. I don't know where you got the idea that you aren't, but let go of that because you are."

I looked away, embarrassed. This was a big compliment. I admired David. I was never good at receiving compliments, and this one meant a lot.

David continued, "I want to share a quote with you that I read to myself every day. You and I are a lot alike, so I think it will help you."

"We really are. Even our DiSC[48] assessments, surprisingly, showed that," I interrupted.

David asked, "Have you ever read Walt Whitman?"

"Yes. I like his work," I replied, curious where this was going.

"Walt Whitman wrote that we should 'be curious, not judgmental.'[49] Ask questions for curiosity, not for judgment."

---

[48] DiSC® is a personal assessment tool to help improve teamwork, communication, and productivity in the workplace. DiSC stands for dominance, influence, steadiness, and conscientiousness. https://www.discprofile.com/what-is-disc/

[49] "While consistently attributed to Whitman, this popular motivational quote has no source. It is occasionally listed as occurring in *Leaves of Grass*, but the closest phrase found in that collection is 'Be not curious about God.'" "Walt Whitman." Wikiquote. March 2, 2021. https://en.wikiquote.org/w/index.php?title=Walt_Whitman&oldid=2934374

"That's good. Listening to that advice tonight would have kept me from publicly changing my mind on that vote," I observed.

David smiled, replying, "Yes, that is definitely one example. I take it to mean that we should stay curious and constantly learn from the perspective of others. Rather than asking questions designed to reinforce your own opinion for a snap judgment, ask questions that will help to broaden your perspective."

If integrity was doing the right thing, even when no one was watching, I needed to hold myself to that same standard. I could not expect others to make an effort to listen to me for understanding without offering the same courtesy to them. I needed to remain open to new information, allowing its validity to change my perspective.

I had proven my ability to pivot, now David was showing me a new path. By slowing down my thought process and listening further, I could make wiser choices without having to pivot. By acknowledging the fact that each person was interacting from their unique point of focus, I was able to interact with others compassionately and respectfully. Each person's perspective was as valid as my own. I understood that their ability to perceive my intentions correctly required integrity in communication. My perspective needed to remain flexible like bamboo, not rigid like oak.

Auras

Some of my more skeptical friends and colleagues are surprised to learn I am open to alternative ideas like premonitions, auras, and expanded consciousness. The extent to which I am willing to shift and change perspectives is the extent to which I am capable of growth. By exposing myself to a broad range of perspectives, I am stocking a rich, bountiful buffet table of ideas to sample, savor, and ultimately grow my understanding.

In my mid-twenties, I took a trip to California. I was walking down the street in Eureka, minding my own business, when a lady stopped me.

"I read auras," she said, "and your aura is amazing! You are a healer. You shine with orange and gold. Animals love you, don't they?"

Taken aback by her abruptness, I dumbly nodded. Animals did love me. I was an EMT at the time, a healer. Part of me was skeptical. She could have said that to just about anyone on the street. To me, it felt personal, like an affirmation that I was in a good place, doing what I needed to be doing.

After recovering from three surgeries, nearly twenty years after that interaction in California, I ran into my friend Emily. She was married to Paul, whom I used to paddle with regularly. She and Paul were leaving the restaurant as I was walking in. We hugged, said our hellos, and, after catching up a bit, Emily hesitated, then said, "Matt, there's something I've never told you."

"What's that, Em?"

She said, "I can see auras, and yours has changed since the last time I saw you. I just wanted to tell you to keep doing whatever it is that you're doing."

"Wow! That's crazy!" I exclaimed. "I didn't know you could see auras. What's different about mine?"

She said, "When we first met, you were super bright with oranges and yellows, almost golden. The last few years (during the divorce and three surgeries), your aura has been pitch-black—absolutely no light coming from you at all. I felt bad for you, but I didn't know what I could do to help. Today, though, today, you are a different person. You are beaming with a silver light. Things must be good for you. You seem to have figured out what you needed to figure out. Anyway, it's great to see you."

As she walked away, I realized that accidents do not happen to me. They happen for me. Accidents contribute to the "who" of who I am. This thing called "life" had become a daisy chain of fortunate accidents.

The space between birth and death is like a freestyle kayaking competition. To the outsider, the wildest ride with the most airtime is the one most likely to earn the trophy. The key is to stay in the hole. Learn to hang on and ride it out, then learn to do so with purpose and style. What may seem chaotic to others was methodical and controlled when I learned to manage the chaos and act with precision.

Damaged Goods

In my initial EMT training, I was introduced to the five stages of grief: denial, anger, bargaining, depression, and acceptance. In my work as an EMT, paramedic, and a deputy coroner, I witnessed people from all walks of life navigating these five stages. During post-traumatic stress debriefings, we would identify what stage we were in and work together so we could all get to the point of acceptance. Acceptance pertained not only to the traumatic incident itself, but to the roles we each played as the incident unfolded.

During my quest for emotional maturity, I made some interesting discoveries. I began to identify how these stages applied to more than just grieving the death of a loved one. They could be applied to the process of developing leadership skills and emotional maturity. In this context, they were the five stages of growth as opposed to the five stages of grief.

Criticism and judgment impede effective communication. I noticed that when I allowed myself to feel attacked, through my own perception, my ego would stimulate a defensive reaction. In some cases, my body's physiological response to criticism was not unlike the neuroendocrine response to shock. The fight-or-flight mechanism caused a hormone dump that activated a systemic response. Critical words were met with a mental arsenal, including denial, anger, bargaining, and depression. Just like the five stages of grief, mindfulness and resilience were required for me to move to the final stage of acceptance.

If someone pointed out a mistake I made, I could respond with denial, anger, bargaining, depression, or acceptance. As I learned to be aware, mindful, and resilient, I became more cognizant of my emotions, recognizing I had the ability to choose my response. I was able to minimize the involuntary chemical and emotional responses, allowing myself to respond rather than react.

If I engaged in a verbal conversation or an argument that seemed to go on for hours, that was a choice. If I asked for space to process the information, that was a choice. More often than not, time and space were required for acceptance. I learned that very little was accomplished by engaging in an argument. Both people became entrenched in their perspectives rather than being open to the shift required to reach common ground.

If both people were patient and committed to the process of growth and understanding, they could recognize and respect the fact that each is coming to the table with a unique perspective, grounded in their individual life experiences that yielded different perspectives.

Working with George, leading up to and during my post-divorce counseling sessions, I discovered that I had a lot to learn in developing communication skills. According to the Gottman Method George introduced to me, the four horsemen that doom relationships are criticism, contempt, defensiveness, and stonewalling. These four horsemen have no place in effective communication; in fact, they impede any chance for bridges to be built or empathy to be shared. When a discussion degrades to the point where it includes any of the four horsemen, the best strategy is to take a pause, step back, and provide space for mindful communication.

In time, I realized that seeking understanding was the remedy for feeling misunderstood.

Denial, anger, bargaining, and depression gave way to acceptance. Sometimes, I would skip denial, go to anger, then go straight to acceptance. By becoming more effective in communication, I moved more efficiently through the process of self-discovery. Lessons were learned more quickly as I became more aware. Life got easier.

I was discussing this with Jennifer, my friend who, so many years prior, helped me get to the root of mindfulness. She had since gotten married, raised two beautiful children, gotten divorced, and moved to the Midwest.

We stayed in touch and remained very good friends. During our conversation, I said, "I am damaged goods and am doing the best I can."

She responded, "How can you say that? It completely takes away from everything we have shared about mindfulness and resilience. If you are resilient, you can't say that you are damaged!"

There she went, again, making me think on a deeper level. She was not going to let me make a statement without thinking it through. I spent the next week thinking about this, drafting my thoughts into an email, which I later sent for her review and feedback.

She was right to some degree; however, if I accepted and recognized that a "bad accident" had occurred, then damage (of some sort) was done. I *was* damaged goods at that point. I had to accept this in order to grow or evolve as a person. I had to accept this in order to allow myself to be open to opportunity. Accepting and recognizing something does not have to mean I identify as that something. An observation of myself is not an identity; however, it can function in a similar capacity.

Acceptance, the last step of the stages of growth, was the first step toward expanding my horizons. Recognizing to myself, or to someone else, that "I am damaged goods" was a sign that I accepted this about myself and I was *open to growth*. I was open to communication. I was open to feedback. I was open to that incident, had received that lesson, and recognized that I was not a perfect being. I would be damaged again. I understood that I would be damaged again, and I was on the alert so I could recognize it accordingly.

Recognizing or stating that I was "damaged goods" did not take away from the concept of becoming more emotionally mature, nor did it minimize my ability to be receptive to fortunate accidents. If anything, recognizing this about myself allowed me to build toward becoming something better. It allowed me to heal. If I spent my time denying that I was damaged, then I was limiting my ability to heal or to grow. Recognizing and accepting this aspect of growth was my way of saying, "I am broken and am willing to receive assistance. I am willing to put in the work to be a better person. I am still learning. I am not perfect. I am in the process of being repaired. I am willing to be better. I want to evolve. I am resilient. I breed fortunate accidents."

If I recognized that I would be damaged again, I was not making the future happen. I was accepting this truth so that I was ready to embrace it when it occurred. Additionally, if I already *was* something, then I would continue to *be* that something. It was not a stopping point. It was a benchmark. I achieved the status of damaged goods—and with the help of friends, mentors, and opportunities, I achieved the status of repaired goods, athlete, success, author, marksman, father, or whatever it might have been. I may become damaged again, repaired again, damaged again, and so forth. The hope is that I learn from each revolution so that I am not on repeat—I should cycle through new levels of growth and maturity.

What if I were an alcoholic? Part of the Alcoholics Anonymous model would be to accept that I have a drinking problem. Just because I may go ten years without a sip of alcohol does not mean I would no longer be an alcoholic. It means that I would have accepted the fact that I am one and that I have gone ten years of accepting that about myself in order to be open to the concept of living without alcohol.

If I have a broken back and am in the recovery process, it hurts every day. If I deny that fact, just pretending everything is fine, I am not being truthful or authentic. By denying physical impairment, I open the door to further damage. I may convince myself to run a fifty-foot waterfall because "I'm fine." Creating space for a current state of impairment *and* accepting that physical reality allows me to gauge precisely what I can and cannot do. Maybe I'll skip the fifty-footer, but the landing on the next twenty-footer looks soft, so I'll run that one.

Healing happens on multiple levels. As my physical healing progressed and I told people, "I'm fine," I was not lying. I was fine because I accepted the fact that healing takes time. I relaxed into the process. On the path to resilience, I was mindful of my limitations while taking the necessary steps to climb the hill once again. I was creating space to heal so that one day I would be able to kayak and pursue the other outdoor activities that brought joy to my life.

I needed to accept my limitations as they pertained to communication as well. Communication continued to be a struggle. I still felt misunderstood. Through the process of maturity, I grew light years ahead of where I was before. I was fine with my skill level in interpersonal communications because I recognized the fact that communication was not a destination, it was a journey. I accepted my shortcomings, knowing I was on the path to improvement.

When a pendulum swings from the far right, the first counterswing goes to the far left. It does this repeatedly, back and forth, losing momentum each cycle, until finally it comes to rest in the middle, centered on its axis. With each revolution, I gain insight into the triggers that move me off-center. Each revolution is one step closer to acceptance and balance.

I had to experience my unfortunate accidents, including my divorce, in order to have the opportunity to grow as an individual. There were lessons there for me to learn. I proved that I was capable of marriage. I also proved that I was capable of learning and growing as a person. In my healing journey, I embraced the divorce. I accepted the events that happened, and I embraced the situation. I took the next step of embracing and enjoying the discovery of the newer version of myself. Next, I needed to embrace the fact that losing myself to my marriage was nobody's doing but my own. I chose to give that part of myself to her, and I chose to apply myself the way I did. This was not a good thing or a bad thing. It was the fact of the thing. I was not a victim. I was an active participant in the way my life unfolded.

How could I avoid being damaged or repeating mistakes in the future? I recognized, I accepted, I embraced, I learned, and I lived with my history as I learned how to apply those experiences moving forward. I lived with awareness, mindfulness, and resilience.

I recognized the fact that there is no missing half that will make me whole. I am complete, just as I am. I looked within myself and embraced each experience in an effort to make the whole bigger, not to fix something that was incomplete or broken. I surrounded myself with people and experiences that contributed to my evolutionary maturity and growth: people who were open to also allowing me to contribute to theirs. Balanced growth. Balanced contribution. Balanced experiences.

The Celestine Prophecy, a book I read decades earlier, touched on this idea of shared, balanced growth. The book's author, James Redfield, refers to it as energy. My takeaway was that some people suck us dry, and we feel tired after being in their company. Some people give us all of their energy, and we become addicted to that boost. When we find that person who understands shared energy, and we equally contribute to the reservoir of energy in the pool, we both are able to charge and recharge sustainably, elevating both of us to higher levels of consciousness.[50]

By creating a reservoir for myself, accepting my past events, taking ownership of my contributions to past events (good and bad), and allowing myself to be open to what may come, I could elevate my own life to a higher level of consciousness.

Just because I recognized a pattern did not mean that I mastered the skill. Even if I mastered the skill, it did not mean that I was not regularly challenged. Recognition and regular challenges did not equal perfection. If I recognized and actively participated in regular challenges, I hoped to become proficient so that the mistakes I made were easily corrected and the pendulum did not swing so far between cycles.

A Buddhist practice is to do without doing. That statement does not say to "do without thinking," and that is a critical component to every daily action and conversation. This was at the heart of my intentionality while kayaking. Taking fewer strokes. Being effective in my movements. Working with the current, allowing my energy expenditure to be more efficient. I had struggled with communication skills in the past. (Why isn't this taught in school?!)

---

[50] Redfield J. *The Celestine Prophesy: An Adventure.* Warner Books; 1993.

My goal was to match intentionality in communication with the same determination with which I practiced intentionality while kayaking. I wanted to communicate effectively without effort—to do without doing.

I created space to accommodate my new reality. I acknowledged my limitations. I was still learning. I was willing to be better. I wanted to evolve. I was mindful and aware. I was resilient. I wanted to become more emotionally mature. I wanted to evolve as a person.

Cycles and Crossroads

When planning the honeymoon trip for after our wedding, my ex-wife suggested places we could go. After each place she mentioned, I would tell her about a friend I had who lived there or an experience from a previous trip I had made. With a touch of annoyance, she asked, "Is there a country you haven't been to or don't know anyone?"

I thought about this, stumped. I shrugged and said, "I don't know. What do you want to do?"

She finally said, "I want to go to an all-inclusive resort and do nothing but sit by the pool, have drinks, and be with you. Have you ever been to Puerto Vallarta, Mexico?"

"Nope, and I don't know anyone there, either. Let's do it."

I was delighted to discover that the date of our honeymoon trip lined up with the tail end of fishing season. I had never been to an all-inclusive resort. In fact, I had never planned a trip where the sole purpose was leisure and relaxation. Would I be able to sit still, or would I go nutty with boredom? I asked my fiancé if we could go fishing for at least one day of the trip. She loved the idea, and we started planning our honeymoon itinerary.

About a week before our wedding, my fiancé and I joined a small group of stand-up paddleboarding pioneers to descend Westwater Canyon. Our plan was to camp at Little D, which was halfway down the canyon, so we roped a friend with a raft into coming along to run support, carrying all of our gear and supplies. One of the guys on the trip asked where we were planning to go on our honeymoon.

"PV," I replied.

"Mexico?"

"Yup. Going to chill by the pool and try to go fishing," I responded.

"I have a really good friend who owns an adventure company. You have to check that out. I'll introduce you guys when we get home. Oh! Another friend of mine owns a charter fishing company. You should go fishing with him too!"

My fiancé looked at me and rolled her eyes. She punched me on the shoulder.

I shrugged my shoulders and tried not to smile. "What?!"

"We can't go anywhere. You know everyone," she pouted.

"In my defense, I don't know anyone in PV—Paul does. I think it's awesome."

I got another roll of the eyes. We booked both a zip lining and a rappelling trip through Paul's friend with the adventure company. We also went fishing with his friend who owned the charter fishing company, and we caught a dozen tuna and another dozen bonito. Porpoises swam by the boat almost close enough to touch. It was a beautiful day and a beautiful trip.

My then wife had some personal demons that we faced one night during our honeymoon. As I struggled to help, listening to what she was saying in her struggle, I realized that life really is cyclical. If I failed to learn a lesson I needed to learn, I would come back to that same lesson over and over in new forms. I could either repeat my mistakes, remaining a victim of my own lack of mindfulness, or I could start a new path and learn a new lesson.

When she and I were on our honeymoon, she revealed cycles that had played out repeatedly in her life. Unbeknownst to me at the time, those same cycles would play out in our marriage. I was powerless to stop them.

I became aware of the cycles repeating themselves in my own life. Failure to pay attention to a sense of foreboding led to downward spirals. Obeying intuition's guidance led me to fortunate accidents. Awareness, mindfulness, and resilience contributed to positive communication. Lack of mindfulness led to misunderstandings and disagreements.

Each crossroads brought me to a point of either repeating a cycle or taking another road. The cycle was familiar. Without awareness, I was in danger of making the same mistakes over and over because my behaviors were rooted in habit. The cycle did not require me to change. Even if it was painful or uncomfortable, it was routine.

The other road felt uncertain because it was unfamiliar. It required me to get out of my comfort zone. Taking a new path at the crossroads required hard work and personal growth. I needed to be brave to take the new path, willing to accept the fact that it could be a waste of time and energy. Taking this new path allowed me to break the old cycles and begin anew.

The crossroads that appeared in the midst of a cycle provided an opportunity to take a risk and try something new. Things that seemed foreign and unknown at first became familiar in time. What began as unstable steps, like an infant learning to walk, became second nature with practice.

I was proud of the fact that I said yes to the many unique and varied opportunities that presented themselves. Many times, I had less skill and knowledge than other likely candidates. Opportunities came my way because I said yes and was ready to acquire new skills and knowledge. This yes-oriented mindset allowed me to succeed and thrive on a multitude of playing fields.

The first major crossroads that tested my growth was deciding to finish college as opposed to helping my high school friends chase a dream. I made the decision to be happy where I was. I chose to finish school. I chose personal growth over instant gratification. That choice changed my life. I became aware of the fact that a change of scenery does not impact life satisfaction.

There are many examples of times when I had two or more options on the table. There is no way of knowing which path would have yielded a better outcome because each opportunity would have yielded its own seeds. In any case, happiness is a choice. The chance to *do* something different does not mean I will *be* something different.

I had an opportunity to go to Japan to film a documentary with National Geographic. Instead, I chose to go on a raft trip down the Grand Canyon with some of my oldest friends. That choice was the end of my video company, yet it opened the door for me to help launch the first helmet company to incorporate waterproof communications technology. Though I quit working for the company due to product delays, the skills I acquired paved the way for starting the retail side of my gun business. The decision to sell the gun business was not planned. Once it happened, it did not go as expected. I had to be flexible and open to a pivot. After my first potential buyer backed out, a series of events led to a second buyer. Each chapter in my life added knowledge and awareness that changed the trajectory of every chapter that followed.

Everything I have done has led me to the here and now. I have become the cumulation of my decisions, experiences, and the people I met along the way. Some people live out their lives pursuing a single career. Others, like me, are nomadic hustlers, integrating a multitude of careers into one life path.

When I share my experiences, people look at me with a dubious expression. Some shake their heads in wonder and ask, "How did you end up doing THAT?" Hell, it amazes me how fortunate I am to have had the experiences I have had. In the end, I was open to the opportunities that were presented to me.

Friendships and Amends

On my first day of work as an EMT, after we restocked the ambulance and after Jason explained to me why I had to untuck and re-tuck my shirt on the side of the interstate, we went to the fire station so Jason could properly introduce me to the crew and the chief.

Jon Jon had been the fire chief for decades. He was legally blind. He also had charismatic intolerance that, like me, begged for people to love him or love to hate him. I learned to know that he was mad if he ever stopped giving me a hard time.

After talking with the crew, most of whom I met earlier on the scene, Jason and I went downstairs to the truck bay, where Jon Jon's office was located. We were standing no less than thirty feet away from his open door. I saw him leaning back in his chair, reading an upside-down magazine. I quietly whispered into Jason's ear, "I wish I could read upside down."

We had two seconds to chuckle to ourselves before we heard, "DAMMIT, SOLOMON! GET YOUR ASS IN HERE. NOW!"

How did he hear that?! How did he know my name?! I looked at Jason, who shrugged while shaking his head, trying to contain his laughter. He smiled—a testament to his amusement at my first impression of Chief—and pointed for me to go first.

"Good morning, Chief," I said as I entered his office.

"So, you're Matt Solomon? The new medic on the ambulance?"

"Yes, sir. Today is day one."

"You think it's funny to make fun of a blind guy?" He was looking right through me. His brow was furrowed in an effort to convey lack of humor; however, the ear-to-ear grin belied his gruff words.

"No, sir. I . . . uh . . . I was impressed that you were reading so easily with an upside-down magazine."

"So, you think just because I'm blind that I'm deaf AND dumb? I can sniff a pile of bullshit a mile away, and I could hear you out there in the bay clear as day. JASON!"

Jason was standing just behind my right shoulder. "Yes, sir, Chief. I'm right here."

"I know you're right there. I can smell your arrogance. Are you going to train this guy to be a prima donna like you think you are?"

"Absolutely, Chief. Matt is going to be good."

Jon Jon was now laughing out loud. "God help us if we end up with two Jasons in the county. We can barely stand the one."

That was the beginning of nineteen years of insults, mutual respect, and love. We had an immediate friendship, which grew into a brotherhood. When we first met, Jon Jon could still see out of the corner of his eye. He memorized streets, distances, voices, and key structural features to help him navigate without the benefit of sight.

Fifteen years after we met, Jon Jon's degenerative ocular disease progressed far enough that he was completely blind, forcing his retirement from the fire services. I spent many of those later years going to his house once or twice a month, reading books to him, studying for courses with him, and taking him to the bar for drinks and dinner. He maintained a position on the board of directors for the ambulance district and was also elected to the fire board a year after his retirement. His life of public service would not be hindered by sightlessness.

One day, years after I left the ambulance, he turned to me and asked, "When are you going to call Chris?"

"I don't know, Chief," I replied.

Chris was the district manager of the ambulance district when I resigned. I was on his hiring committee and had worked closely with him when forming the field training program and updating protocols. Chris was and is a leader and a visionary for emergency medical services. When I was working on the ambulance, he invited me to join an international committee of EMS leaders to brainstorm and design what would become community paramedicine.

When I quit working for the ambulance district, I blamed everyone for my burnout and frustration. This included Chris. It had been nearly ten years since we had last spoken, and I had no real desire to speak with him. Apparently, he felt the same.

Jon Jon interrupted my thoughts. "Matt, I was there when you were the deciding vote to hire him. I saw the two of you work together, and I still talk and work with both of you today. You two are just alike, and you both need to get over yourselves."

"Chief, I don't think he wants to talk to me. If he calls me, I will go meet with him."

"I have a board meeting with the ambulance next week. I'm going to tell him the same thing I told you."

Two weeks later, I was at Jon Jon's house. As I sat down to read to him, he stopped me and said, "Call Chris."

"Sir?"

"I talked to him last week. After listening to him give me the same shit you gave me, I told him that under no circumstance is he to ignore the phone when you call him. The two of you are going to get together and work out your differences."

There was to be no argument.

"Yes, sir, Chief. I will send him a text when I leave here."

I did just that, and within minutes, Chris wrote back asking if we could go get a coffee the next day. I wrote, "Yes," and it was set.

Chris and I sat in the front corner of the coffee shop, out of earshot of the other patrons. We shook hands and set our coffees on our adjacent tables as we sat down, he on the end of a couch and I in a chair opposite and about three feet across from him.

We exchanged hellos and sat for a brief second before I said, "Leave it to Jon Jon to push us into a coffee."

"He is a stubborn old man. Won't stop until he gets his way; and he cares a lot about both of us."

"True. Chris, I don't know where to start. I have held a grudge against you for over ten years."

With that, we talked nonstop for two hours. I shared with him what had been going on in my head and in my life ten years prior. I walked him through how much I had blamed everyone else for my mistakes, choices, and frustrations. I apologized to him and told him I missed his friendship.

Chris was actively listening to everything I shared. To my surprise, he shed a few tears as he flipped the script and began to tell me that he had been burned out at the same time I had been burned out and had been blaming me this whole time. Now it was my turn to sit and listen, holding tight to every word he shared.

By the time Chris was finished sharing his perspective, we were both in tears. We stood up, hugged, both said "I love you," then sat back down and began catching up in proper form, as old friends with no baggage. We made amends. The luggage we had been carrying for a decade vanished, allowing us to walk lighter and feel deeper. We were friends again.

As our time drew to a close, the coffee in our cups long gone, we got up to leave and promised to stay in better touch, thanking each other for the time and the vulnerability. I left the coffee shop and went straight to Jon Jon's house.

"Chief."

"Hey, Matt. What are you doing?"

"I came by to tell you that you're a dick."

That got him laughing, a full belly laugh, with a deep throaty sound. "What did I do this time?"

"Chris and I just had a coffee. You were right. I came by to tell you thanks."

"Matt, you have no idea how much that means to me. I care about you both, and you are both such good people. I am glad you are reconnected."

Jon Jon died less than six months later. Chris and I remain good friends.

Jon Jon taught me the value of friendship. He encouraged me to make amends. For this, I was eternally grateful. Chris and I were able to grow as individuals by being open to hearing each other's perspectives. We allowed our perceptions to shift, which is no small matter. That shift provided insight and allowed us to piece together the puzzle of events that happened ten years prior.

Chris and I chose to stop blaming each other for our own undoing and burnout. After ten years of blame, I was able to accept that my burnout was my own doing. Listening to Chris and his perspective, the burden of blame I had been carrying was lifted, and I accepted my role in my own undoing. I finally worked through the five stages of growth and accepted my role in my burnout.

I remain humbled by and grateful for the friends I made who influenced my life. Every one of them made an impact.

Comfort Zones

Awareness, mindfulness, and resilience yield emotional maturity. Growth opened the door to new jobs and projects, which in turn yielded new opportunities to expand my leadership skills.

Timing, opportunity, trust, and commitment led to my work with Ken Cameron and REAL (Resilience for Executives and Leaders®). I had gained a wealth of knowledge by working in the ambulance district, instructing paramedics, serving on town council, owning a gun shop, and working as a medic for military contractors conducting pre-deployment training exercises. All of these experiences developed the connections and skill set needed to work with executives and business leaders as they learned how to be resilient through stressful situations.

Working with REAL, I could finally see the way my experiences were stepping-stones, perfectly placed in the river, creating a path for future success. Five years after my accident with the coroner's office, my life had come full circle. I had become more adept at listening to a sixth sense that alerted me to potential business ventures. Honing this sixth sense became the foundation for continued growth.

In order to become more emotionally mature, I had to trust in my ability to thrive when stepping outside my comfort zone. I had to take chances. When a new path led away from comfort, into uncharted waters, I had to learn from that experience, becoming more patient, more understanding, more available to receive the next subtle input or chance when it presented itself.

The first day I was an instructor for Ken's company, CAM Mobility, teaching our US military members off-road driving, I had a student from Puerto Rico who had never seen snow before. It was February in Colorado; naturally, it was snowing. We started in Grand Junction for four days of driving and camping on dirt roads in the wilderness around Moab. Leaving the hotel parking lot to begin our week, this student was white knuckled at the wheel. Having never seen snow before, he was very nervous about driving in the snow with a caravan fully loaded for a week of overland travel.

We took it slow as we hit snow-covered dirt a few hours later. Not far into the morning, we could not make it up a short incline on a left turn of the road. Since we were in the middle of the five-vehicle caravan, we backed down the slope out of the way to allow the other two vehicles to pass. My student watched their approach and use of momentum. I could see the frustration and embarrassment on his face. I pointed out strategies the other vehicles were using to attempt the hill climb.

When neither of the other two following vehicles were able to climb the small hill, my student sighed with relief. The packed snow and slick ice, coupled with a small rock protruding right in the track of our rear tire, prevented us from gaining traction, even though the tires were aired down for traction. Momentum was not enough to make the climb. I told my student, "This is the point of the class, so let's get our gear and get back on the trail!"

We found a tree to use as an anchor and winched our way up the hill, one truck at a time. After putting the gear away, we were back on course and moving forward. My student's energy shifted as he became more confident and comfortable driving in the snow. I commented that his knuckles did not look as white. He even had a smile on his face as we navigated the barely visible trails covered in snow.

He said, "It's not as bad as I thought it was now that we've gotten stuck and I learned we can still get out."

This learning moment was not about driving: it was about getting out of our comfort zones. I said, "The beauty of our comfort zone is that it is not fixed. In order to broaden the scope of our comfort, we must discover its boundary. That boundary is different for each person. Once you take a small step out of your comfort zone, you redefine its edges. Through repetition, your comfort zone continually expands. In time, you will be able to accomplish greater tasks with less stress and more confidence. It's an exercise in building resilience."

In his many books and courses, Rob Pincus teaches that defensive shooting is the "balance of speed and precision."[51] I have found that effective communication is also a balance of speed and precision. Listening as opposed to speaking requires me to step outside my comfort zone. That pause creates the space to communicate precisely. In time, precise communication becomes fluid and natural. The pause shortens, creating a balance of speed and precision.

Emotional maturity was one of the most challenging skills I discovered. It required skills from earlier foundational lessons in awareness, mindfulness, and resilience to be applied and balanced with each other within myself. I had to become aware of negative narratives that were holding me back, inhibiting my ability to take ownership for the events in my life. I had to

---

[51] Pincus R. "Diagramming the Balance of Speed and Precision." Personal Defense Network. TN Marketing, LLC. February 2018.
https://www.personaldefensenetwork.com/video/balance-speed-precision-015088/

be mindful of myself and the intentionality of my chosen perspectives. I had to learn to trust myself to have integrity in the process.

Changing these narratives required a willingness to shift perspectives. Learning to apply emotional maturity to my life was some of the hardest work I have ever undertaken. I needed to be resilient in my efforts, as this work would never be truly completed to perfection.

Developing a balance of precision and speed to this shift in perspective was also some of the most rewarding work because cultivating emotional maturity paved the way for new people and opportunities to be present as I grew into better versions of myself.

Application: Emotional Maturity

1. What is emotional intelligence? Is emotional intelligence quantifiable?
2. What is the difference between emotional intelligence and emotional maturity?
3. How does one create a life of balance?

I shared three specific cycles from my life where I learned lessons through consequence. During one cycle, I learned to grow through the consequence of suspension from football. In another cycle, it was through separation from work on the ambulance. In the third cycle, I was taught lessons through both physical and emotional injury.

4. What cycles can you identify in your life?

In this book, I discussed several crossroads in my life. I also identified values that guided my choice of direction.

5. What crossroads have you experienced? What values do you use to make those choices?
6. Do you have relationships at work or home where you need to make amends?
7. Ego can be a major inhibitor in our emotional maturity when dealing with others. Identify a specific incident when your ego was an obstacle to effectively communicating with someone.
8. What did you learn from the experience?
9. Describe how you've dealt with similar situations since the incident. Did you repeat the folly of the ego or realize the feeling and adjust your response?

NOMADIC HUSTLERS

I was fascinated when people shared stories, connecting the dots that led to opportunities in their lives. There were many different formulas. Maybe there was a better formula than mine. By my observation, awareness, mindfulness, resilience, and emotional maturity were key components for building my leadership and success.

My intuition guided me to use awareness, mindfulness, resilience, and emotional maturity at each new crossroads, encouraging me to say yes to new experiences. These four steps reciprocated, reminding me to listen when my intuition tried to veer me away from a cliff.

One afternoon, my friend Mather was telling me how opportunities had arisen in his life. He said, "It's important to have a positive attitude, grit, and drive. I expect positive results when I commit to something. I learned from failures, making different choices the next time around."

I smiled, knowing he was describing my formula.

Mather, having been a friend for decades, has seen me put my foot in my mouth more times than I can count. We traveled across the United States multiple times, worked for rafting companies in West Virginia and Colorado, taught Swift Water Rescue classes, trained new raft guides, and avoided getting caught when we were up to no good.

Mather had listened to me discuss mindfulness, both on the river and in medicine, over the years. As I pointed out the crossovers from his descriptions in the earlier conversation to what I had pieced together in my own formula, Mather looked at me with an ear-to-ear grin and said, "Did

I tell you about the SEALs[52] I was training in Coronado?"

I shook my head. "No."

Like me, Mather had worked with our military personnel. His specialty was rescue—high angle, ropes, and water.[53] As Mather was an animated storyteller, I looked forward to hearing his tale.

"We had the Zodiacs ready to take to the beach for training this one day. I told the guys, 'After you blow up the boats, bring them and the motors over to the beach.' The guys all stopped what they were doing and looked at me. I stopped walking, taking one step back toward them, and turned around to ask if there was a problem.

"One of the guys says, 'Sir, we'd love to blow these boats up, but we believe you would like us to inflate them.'"

Mather paused to catch his breath. He also had to stop laughing so he could finish telling the story. After a minute he looked at me and said, "I hadn't thought about it like that before. Here's these guys who deal with explosives on a regular basis. They literally blow things up for a living. They taught me a lesson in precision that day. I have not asked anyone to blow up my boats since. I do want to use them again."

Mather's wife, Christine, was sitting next to him as he told this story in animated fashion. She said, "He even has me saying 'inflate the raft,' not 'blow it up.'"

I wiped a tear off my cheek from laughing as I watched Mather tell this story with his arms waving in all directions. I said, "Yes! That's exactly it, man. Precision. Precision of thought, having intentionality behind what we say. Being precise in how we say things. Those guys taught you a lesson that day." I was grinning and still laughing.

Mather reminded me, yet again, that being mindful does not mean becoming rigid. Acting with precision and living with purpose does not

---

[52] Not the marine mammal. The US Navy Sea, Air, and Land (SEAL) Teams are the US Navy's primary special operations force and a component of the Naval Special Warfare Command.

[53] www.MatherRescue.com

preclude humor. With humility and grace, we need to learn not to take ourselves, or others, too seriously.

Options

It amazed me how a series of unplanned events could string together to create new opportunities. When it came to deciding what path to take, I found that I gravitated to the most interesting experiences. It was like I had an opportunity radar, always on the lookout for something new, profitable, and exciting. I also chose projects that would contribute to my personal growth.

When someone asked me, "What do you do?" I struggled for a response. At any given time, I was usually working on at least three projects. In the case of military projects or working for high-net-worth individuals, the nature of my work was private, even confidential. When I was at liberty to disclose information about a project, my description usually elicited the response, "How did you end up doing *that?*"

Someone recently asked me what I do for work. I said, as I often do, "I hustle."

"What do you mean, 'hustle'?"

I replied, "I advise companies and help people solve problems. I wear a lot of hats and travel to a lot of places. I guess you could say that I'm a nomadic hustler."

The various hats I wore through the years contributed to the projects I was later offered. My work in medicine, leadership, team building, security, and safety were complementary skills. They offered a synergistic platform that appealed to a broad range of clients and students.

My first week on a new project, I shared some of my past experiences with a fellow worker. He laughed and said, "I'm surprised you took this job. They either forked over a lot of money or you took a pretty big cut."

I chuckled. I had four contracts in front of me when I was considering that job. The other three paid better. I replied, "Yeah, I turned it down a few times before I finally agreed to it."

He asked, "Why did you take it, then? I wouldn't have!"

I paused for a moment. It was a fair question. Why did I take a job that paid less than three other options? "For the experience, and because it felt right," I replied honestly.

Interesting experiences and "just feeling right" continued to be underlying themes in my adult life. I valued experience over money. Do not get me wrong, I had to make money. Living poor as long as I did made me value the chance to cover my monthly expenses plus have a little left over for travel and savings. However, I think the reason I did not have a decades-long career was because I pursued experience over stability. Consequently, I gained a broad depth of knowledge and expertise in a wide variety of subject areas. I had my mother to thank for this. Her words, "You're never something until you are," inspired me to expand my interests and leverage my aptitude for learning.

The best in the world, whether in skiing, chess, poker, kayaking, fishing, et cetera, are obsessed with what they do, pursuing their interest with a single-minded focus. I had that same passion when acquiring a skill. When I played football, I was fully obsessed, fully immersed; I lived and breathed the game. When I was snowboarding and skiing, I was on the mountain every day, all winter long. Then I discovered kayaking. Kayaking was my single point of focus, every day, every week, every month, all year, every year.

When I was not kayaking, I was surfing; if I was not surfing, I was snowboarding. When I was not playing, I was working. If I committed to a project, I fully committed to that project.

At one point, I identified the fact that many of my non-business pursuits centered around water in its liquid or frozen form. I began calling it my "liquid addiction." I think my obsession with water fueled my passion to excel. My need to be on or around water shaped my work life. Pursuit of this liquid addiction led to my career as a nomadic hustler.

Was I a vagabond? No. My life had structure, though it looked a bit chaotic from afar. I think of it as focused chaos. I was living frugally, continually seeking compelling projects that contributed to self-improvement and growth.

When I committed to athletic pursuits, I excelled in each new activity. I was surrounded by the best kayakers in the world, who inspired me to improve both athletically and personally. I paddled with them, I lived with them, I went on the road with them. They were my kayaking family. After physical and emotional injury, I was committed to finding a path that led back to health. My motivation to heal as quickly as possible stemmed from my love for outdoor activities. They were both my reason for healing and the method by which I healed.

I also strived to achieve financial stability and wanted to make a difference in my community. In addition to my time on town council, I assisted as an advisor on the board for a nonprofit organization supporting a medical clinic and pharmacy. I asked a friend, Jonathan, if he had time to lend a hand building a website for the organization. Jonathan and I had worked on a variety of projects over the previous twelve years. He was always intrigued with the various jobs that were presented to me.

After discussing the website project, Jonathan asked, "How are things?"

I told him, "Great. Spent the last two days settling into my new place, and I'm flying out in an hour."

He asked, "Where are you going this time?"

After I told him where I was headed, he said, "Matt, I've known you long enough that I know not to ask what kind of work you are doing this time." I could hear him chuckle through the phone, almost seeing him shake his head as he said, "You are the most random and sporadic person I know, with all of the high-level things you do. It is enviable."

It was that broad spectrum of experience that prompted Liz to invite me to speak to the new class of paramedic students. She asked me to provide insight into some of the many trajectories the students' careers could take. I was happy to have the chance to explain that we were more than just ambulance drivers, a term I despised, or hospital workers.

I explained, "I worked on the local ambulance for nearly ten years. While doing that, I also worked part-time for an oil company at a drill site as a medic with the health and safety director. I then spent about four years working for the coroner's office. I have worked for two different military contractors doing everything from writing protocols and developing curriculum to working as an instructor. I have consulted for several private companies, offering them protocol advice and administrative medical support, including advice for a NORRA (North American Off-Road Racing Association) rally master. I have also been a regular adjunct, teaching EMTs and paramedics here at the college, and have taught wilderness first aid classes."

The students looked dumbfounded. One of the students in front raised his hand. "So, you are kind of a mercenary medic?"

"You could say that, yes. I'm a medic-for-hire, in a way," I replied, chuckling. "The point of this, and why Liz wanted me to share this with you, is that medicine is a practice. We are constantly learning and constantly applying what we will learn this year. We are not limited to ambulance or hospital work. Knowing that, it is up to all of us to practice being the best medics we can be so that, no matter the situation we are in, we can function at the highest level expected of us."

The guy in the front raised his hand.

"Yes," I said.

"That's what I want to do. How do I do what you do?"

"Start by passing this class," I responded with a cheeky smirk. "Then, I recommend you work at least three to five years on the street. Get some experience and develop your skill set. If you remain open and hustle, the opportunities will present themselves."

Most students who enrolled in the paramedic course did so with a single job in mind. They were surprised at the breadth of opportunities their medical training provided.

Paramedic students were also very curious about who their instructors were, what agencies their instructors worked for, and what experience they brought to the table. In training new paramedics, the other instructors and I needed to earn respect by establishing credibility.

Working with the military was an entirely different atmosphere. Our elite military personnel rely heavily on subject matter experts (SMEs) to lead their training. Becoming a SME requires a strong resume, including previous work experience and excellent direct referrals. Instructors do not need to establish credibility or justify their presence during a training event. Their expertise and professionalism are a given due to the rigorous standards the military requires; if a company is not up to par, they will not stay in business.

Standing around the campfire in the desert during one of our off-road driving training weeks, students and instructors took the chance to get to know each other better. We were halfway through the week of training and had completed another long day of driving. One of the students asked the instructors how we had ended up becoming instructors for CAM.

Each of the instructors took turns sharing overland experiences: Land Rover Camel Trophy races; Baja and Mexico 1000 races; one of the guys had his own TV show on the Speed Network; several guys taught civilian off-road or rally driving courses; and then there was me, former athlete, paramedic, and instructor. The students—all top-tier military personnel we respected and admired—looked at us in a new light.

"You guys have done a lot. I see why you all teach for Ken," one of them said.

Charles, with a humility all his own, smiled as he poked the fire with the stick in his hand and said, "Yeah. You could say we're a group of nomadic hustlers."

I share a sentiment held by most contractors and instructors I worked with: I was humbled to offer my contribution to the education and training that potentially saved the lives of the men and women protecting our nation. I am proud of the fact that being of service was one of the options my experiences afforded me.

Unplanned Events

An employer told me once, "I don't care what you put for a job title, [this] is what I need from you."

I responded, "Sir, I'm here for you—your health and safety and whatever else needs to get done."

I considered myself to be a problem solver. When I worked somewhere, I would do whatever needed to be done. I agreed with the sentiment of that employer, feeling that job titles are constraining and irrelevant. This mindset and attitude would soon be tested.

The fall of 2019 was fantastic! I was home for a total of three weeks between July and the end of December. Starting in Central America, I worked my way to Moab, then to Lake Powell, then back to Moab. A scuba diving trip to Cozumel was followed by a trip to Florida to see a friend. After another week of camping/working in Moab, I headed home for a week to see a friend who was in the hospital, then went back to Moab. In the month that followed, I spent two weeks in Costa Rica, a week in Nicaragua, and another week in Costa Rica before flying to Phoenix for the holidays.

When I got to Colorado the last week of December, I put my house up for sale. I enjoyed the itinerant lifestyle and had no need for a three-bedroom house. Downsizing my space and expenditures would provide cash for new adventures. The house needed minor repairs, which were quickly completed. It felt good to have a new plan.

My travel schedule in 2020 looked like it would be a continuation of 2019. John, a newly made friend from the REAL course, had contacted me in November. He knew of a security detail in need of a medic. "Are you available?" he asked.

"I can make it happen," I replied. John introduced me to Tim, a former member of the UK Special Forces and a long-distance athlete who rows across the Atlantic Ocean to raise money for vets with PTSD.[54] Tim spent his time on land providing security services to corporations and UHNWIs. My travel schedule was filling up. I had mobility courses in Moab one week in January, two weeks in February, and another two weeks in March. I was also planning to get back to Central America to surf for two weeks every other month.

In early January, I got a call from Ken. "Something's going on," he said. "The military is cancelling all upcoming training programs. They didn't tell me why. We're in a holding pattern."

I still had a work trip on the books for the end of the month, so I spent most of the extra time moving the contents of my house into storage and confirming that my med kit contained everything needed for the upcoming job.

I was home when my friend Jon Jon died in January. I was grateful for the opportunity to help his son plan the memorial service and settle Jon Jon's affairs. He had been a good friend and had taught me the value of accepting responsibility and making amends. Perspective was and is everything.

When I got back from a job in Vegas, I felt like I had a cold. It presented like the flu, but it was not consistent with flu-like symptoms. I did not typically get sick. This was different. I was in bed for three days, freezing cold, sweating so badly that I had to change the drenched sheets daily. Most concerning were the expiratory wheezes and a month-long dry cough that sounded like I smoked two packs a day.

---

[54] www.TameTheKraken.org

I called two doctors and asked if they had heard of anything like this. Both doctors were vague, mentioning a rumor of a weird bug presenting like the flu that was not the flu.

One of my doctor friends recommended a Z-Pak and some steroids. We did not think the Z-Pak would help, but it certainly wouldn't hurt. The steroids were for the respiratory symptoms I was experiencing. I was working for a high-profile individual and had to notify the asset that I was sick so he could take precautionary measures. Fortunately, he did not get sick.

A month later, we learned that all external military training was cancelled due to an impending global pandemic. By the end of March, the pandemic was officially announced, followed by a nationwide lockdown. I "quaran-teamed" with three friends, renting a house in Texas for six weeks.

I exclaimed, "If we have to isolate, we may as well isolate in warm weather with a fishing rod in hand!"

Regardless of one's opinion of the symmetrical solution applied to an asymmetrical problem,[55] it is worth noting the opportunity presented to us all in regards to personal growth. We were confronted with a global challenge that affected each of us on a personal level. Were we aware of our circumstance, mindful of ourselves, and willing to embrace evolution of mind, spirit, and body? Or did we capitulate to fear, blame, and resentment?

How many married couples barely interacted before lockdown protocols were put in place? How many couples grew apart, rather than together, during the pandemic? An offer on my house fell through because of marital issues ending in divorce.

Without distraction, it seemed that people had to face their demons and were having trouble navigating their way through the five stages of growth.

---

[55] Rapaport C, Ashkenazi I. "Managing COVID-19: Applying an Asymmetric Solution to an Asymmetric Problem." Journal of Emergency Medical Services. September 18, 2020. https://www.jems.com/commentary/managing-covid-19-applying-an-asymmetric-solution-to-an-asymmetric-problem/

The pandemic gave everyone an opportunity to become better individuals for themselves, their families, and their neighbors. Some took advantage of this opportunity. Others did not. We all made mistakes. The choice at hand was to blame others for the mistakes we may have made or accept responsibility for our errors, moving forward in a peaceful, loving manner.

Awareness and mindfulness build resilience. Introspection, acceptance of our own reflection, and a willingness to improve yield maturity and growth. The marriages that thrived and blossomed during the pandemic seemed to be the ones that embraced growth. It made me sad to see the number of marriages that collapsed—and the number of emotional and mental health issues that surfaced during the globalized economic shutdown.

By June, the world was still shut down. I heard and read about increasing suicide rates. This bummed me out. I made a point in our town council meetings to highlight my opinion that we should be attuned to the emotional health needs of our community as much as we were attuned to the economic needs of our community.

We had an opportunity to make the best of a bad situation. I was "lucky" enough to be surrounded by like-minded people. We changed our companies' missions; we were flexible and open to learning new things. Rather than casting blame, we found solutions and did our best to do our best. We were resilient.

My life was in an upward spiral. Sure, I was stressed about financial challenges and the fact that my house was not selling. This was normal for me. I reworked my budget and made a backup plan to my backup plan. I remained positive.

Tim, the man I worked for in Vegas, called to ask for my help drafting a bid for a company who wanted to implement post-Covid medical and security protocols for a TV production company. If Tim's company won the bid, he would have a four-month project with the first live television program to air since the start of the pandemic. When Covid created a situation where Tim's previous employer had to make cuts in order to stay afloat, he invented his own opportunity.

Again, sticking to my lifelong script, I said yes to Tim's request for help.

A week later, Tim called. "Hey, Matt! They accepted our proposal. We won the bid! Are you free to spend four months in LA? We start in July."

"I would love to! But I booked a sailing trip in the Bahamas last year, and the trip was bumped to July due to Covid. If I back out now, I'll lose my deposit. I'll touch base when I get back to see if you still need help, if that's cool by you?"

"I'll keep you posted; there may be something." He then asked when I would be back from the trip and said he would be in touch.

I got back from the Bahamas, and my house sold two days later. After another two days, I bought a new townhouse. At midnight my first night in the townhouse, Tim called and asked if I could be in LA the next day.

"Tim, I just got home from the Bahamas and just bought a new place. I need two weeks to move in, then I'm game to go."

"I'll call you tomorrow."

The next day, Tim called early. "They want you there yesterday. Would four days be enough?"

"Sure. What's the job?" Though I had helped Tim draft the proposal pitching his new company to the LA production firm, I did not know exactly what my role would be.

"You will be writing the Covid-19 protocols for the post-production team and advising the executives of this TV show. You're a fixer: just do you, and they will be happy."

I hung up the phone, bought a ticket to LA, then spent a few days getting moved in.

During my time in Los Angeles, opportunities started coming in. I received calls for projects in Colorado, Idaho, Virginia, Connecticut, and Bimini. Everything from medical support to security details to Covid protocol development. Can you guess how I chose my next gig? The experience.

The person outlining the job description said they needed a medic with experience writing Covid protocols who also had an understanding of executive security and protection. The job paid less than any of the other gigs I had on the table, so finances would not be the driving force behind this decision. On the flip side, it perfectly integrated the skills I had acquired over the previous twenty-five years, providing service to an impressive individual. In short, it offered an interesting experience. Experience made the decision again.

I spent my pandemic year selling a house, fishing with friends, kayaking, training, polishing my skills, helping a friend launch a new company, and sailing in the Bahamas. I improved myself. My perspective allowed me to stay positive and make the best of an unplanned incident.

How It Came Together

While traveling to one of my jobs, I was chatting with a woman seated next to me on the plane. She asked what I did for work. I told her I was a paramedic on a security detail.

"I thought paramedics only worked on ambulances," she commented.

I replied, "I am kind of a mercenary medic. I work in a lot of different fields, but right now I'm working for an individual."

She asked, "How did you end up coming all this way for work? Don't you get tired of being away from home?"

Given the variety of projects I've done, usually involving travel, I get that question a lot. If I'm tired or don't feel like talking, I reply, "I wear a lot of hats and hustle as much as I can," which generates a laugh without me having to answer the question. I had time. So, I replied, "No, I'm used to it. I used to be gone six months a year, so it's nice to be home two weeks a month."

She asked, "What were you doing that required you to travel that much?"

"Before this? When I was gone so much? I used to be an athlete and a sales rep in the outdoor industry, which involved a lot of travel."

"Hang on. A professional athlete? What sport? Really? I thought you said you were a personal medic! What ELSE do you do?! What is a personal medic, or did you say a mercenary medic, anyway? How did you end up doing *this*?"

This rapid-fire sequence of questions was not new. I was used to having to explain the series of odd circumstances that led to a highly unique career path. I chuckled and patiently answered her questions one at a time, starting with my background paddling for Team Dagger, then moving on to working in the outdoor industry, then practicing as a paramedic.

Being a sponsored white-water paddler was fun. It was also a challenge. I paddled with some of the best athletes in the world, I traveled, I published photos and videos, and I met lots of great people; however, it didn't pay the bills.

I did not share the fact that I was also on town council and had recently done consulting work for a Hollywood production company. I didn't tell her how I had made a lifelong friend during a surfing trip to Mexico and had worked with him selling his company's rash guards and board shorts. I left out the fact that I had wanted to buy a helmet company that wasn't even a real company, but ended up working in sales and brand management for the real helmet manufacturer. Or that I had helped structure the global launch of another start-up helmet company with leading-edge tech. It had been me and a marketing manager on the ground, assembling a team of athletes, distributors, and reps who outsold production in mere months. I left out offers from other major manufacturers and the initial design work I drafted for Airstream. Those details would have been too much to share, as it seemed like she was already having a hard time understanding how it all fit into the persona of me as a medic. I wouldn't fit into any box she was struggling to create in her mind.

Instead, I continued, "I worked on the ambulance six months a year in the winter. Working as a medic in the winter allowed for paddling and outdoor-industry-related travels in the summer, and I picked up other hustles on the side.

"As for your next question, yes, I am somewhat of a personal medic. When I was sharing details of my medical career with a group of students, we coined the term 'mercenary medic' as a way to describe that I was working as a medic-for-hire at the time. Oil companies, military contractors, private sector businesses, and so forth. The term kind of stuck."

"That's a lot," she said.

"I don't know. I've never been good at doing one thing at a time," I concluded. "I've always had two to three hustles going. Gotta pay the bills, right?"

She paused and looked at me quizzically, saying, "Yes, me too. My life seems so boring now. I still don't get how all of this happened."

I paused as I pondered her sentiment, then replied with a knowing grin, "It was a series of fortunate accidents."

Application: Nomadic Hustling

It seems that I spent my life searching for meaning or a truth.

1. Can you describe your own search for meaning in your life?
2. When I turned forty, were the injuries I sustained fortunate accidents? Why or why not?
3. Which people and/or events in your life could be considered fortunate accidents?
4. How can the concepts described in this book help you as a leader (manager/employee/mentor/friend)?

[C. R.] Rogers called an individual who achieves self-actualization a fully functioning person. According to Rogers, fully functioning people exhibit seven traits: openness to experience, living in the moment, trust in one's feelings and instincts, self-direction and the ability to make independent choices, creativity and malleability, reliability, feeling fulfilled and satisfied by life.

Fully functioning people are congruent and have received unconditional positive regard. In many ways, fully functioning is an ideal that can't be completely achieved, but those who come close are always growing and changing as they strive to self-actualize.[56]

5. How do the steps presented for fortunate accidents overlap with C. R. Rogers's theory shared above?
6. What can you do to self-actualize?
7. How can these ideals be incorporated into your life at home? At work? At play?

---

[56] Vinney C. "Carl Rogers: Founder of the Humanistic Approach to Psychology." ThoughtCo. Updated May 20, 2019. https://www.thoughtco.com/carl-rogers-4588296

The most beautiful people we have known are those who have known defeat, known suffering, known struggle, known loss, and have found their way out of the depths. These persons have an appreciation, sensitivity, and an understanding of life that fills them with compassion, gentleness, and a deep loving concern. Beautiful people do not just happen.

—Elisabeth Kübler-Ross

ACKNOWLEDGEMENTS

"It takes a village to raise a child" is an Igbo and Yoruba proverb that exists in many different African languages. It reflects the emphasis African cultures place on family and community and may have its origins in a biblical worldview.

My most fortunate accident is the village that contributed to my growth and evolution. They nurtured, supported, challenged, and held space for me to become the man I am continuing to become. For the many people whose paths have crossed my own, I will be eternally grateful. There are not enough words or enough paper to list you all.

People I had not seen or spoken to in years appeared, prompting me to recall a lesson I learned during past interactions. Tao Berman, former Guinness World Record holder and white-water friend, agreed to an interview so I could digest his take on mindfulness. Jason Moore and I reminisced, sparking inspiration to share networks and develop new business opportunities. The OGP—Old Guys Paddling—group became a remarkable support group, as did a text circle of friends from college.

I could not have written a book such as this, or have the experiences to share in the development of these idea(l)s, without the input and insight from the many people who shared a path with me at some point.

To those mentioned through printed stories, you were invaluable in the learning of these lessons. To those not quoted or cited, there is no less value placed on our friendship, nor does that diminish what you have offered.

Dr. Nick Nicholson showed great patience and humor as he provided the insight I needed to get over the hump. His faith in my ability was both humbling and inspiring. The time he took to help me navigate my own self-induced obstacles cannot be repaid or replaced. He is the person who inspired, mentored, and guided me through this process—from the beginning through to the end.

Christy Rounds helped me connect the dots, providing the connective tissue holding the bones and meat of this book together. Her partnership and collaboration really made this a balanced effort—both in written word and personal growth.

John Lane supported me as both a former student and as a friend.

Randy Wyrick answered the tug of his cable tow, introducing both myself and the book in language that can only be his own.

Bartas Urba and Todd Hastey assisted with the initial draft feedback and edits from beginning to end.

Dylan Saunders's fantastic, inspirational, visual language tells the story.

Jonathan Owen's easy-going nature makes a business relationship feel like a family business.

Callie Walker paid attention to detail through final proofreading brilliance.

When Mrs. Nancy Kissinger saw me typing away and asked what I was working on, she was supportive, inquisitive, and offered needed insight, warning me of unforeseen hurdles. Dr. Henry Kissinger, unbeknownst to him, gave me insight and an education in writing that I will not soon forget. I cannot neglect Samantha, the four-legged princess who shared (expected) unconditional love throughout the day.

Dr. George McNeil once told me, "We are only the stories that are in the moment. I only exist in this moment in time and in the perception that you have of me in this moment." He taught me how to be mindful of and in my communication. His Buddhist techniques instilled patience, allowing me to grow at my own speed, with the safety net of a friend. Thanks, Doc.

Elizabeth (Owen) Ross allowed me to implement and experiment with some of these practices when teaching paramedic classes. Without her support and guidance, I would not have been able to mold an initial concept into a curriculum. Little did I realize, the teacher would become the student as I put my own principles into action in my daily life.

My mother, one of the strongest women I know, taught me so much more than the lessons embodied in the chapters of this book. Always supportive, her encouragement offers me the advice and guidance I need, whenever I ask, and most times unsolicited. I love you, Mama.

I am humbled and honored to have the opportunity to share this journey through the labyrinth of past events, exploring the ups and downs in the chaotic roller coaster of life. I truly hope we all find a way to look in the mirror, face our demons, and apply these lessons in our journeys toward emotional maturity, growth, and leadership.

There really is no one person who can teach mindfulness or resilience. We all work together mentoring one another, grooming opportunities, and remaining open to the lessons we need at any given moment. Input may come in the form of advice to read a book or even something as simple as a phrase or a word that we need to hear at that moment.

If we remain mindful of ourselves, aware of our environment and our surroundings, and open to growth and opportunity, we can be receptive to all of the external inputs and people placed in our life, when and how they are there, to help us help ourselves.

Collaboratively, we can groom fortunate accidents.

ABOUT THE AUTHOR

Matt Solomon is a civic-minded entrepreneur with a broad spectrum of experiences. He is an accomplished waterman, paramedic, educator, businessman, and former member of his local town council. Matt has traveled across the country and around the world in pursuit of experiences, fun, and employment. Each of these experiences contributed to adventure and success, yielding a uniquely balanced and well-rounded perspective. As an educator and a leader, Matt challenges himself, his students, and his associates to strive for mutual success and maximum benefit.

In his words: "Be safe, have fun."

This is his first book.